Medicines and Society

Medicines and Society

Patients, Professionals and the Dominance of Pharmaceuticals

Nicky Britten

palgrave
macmillan

First published in 2008 by
PALGRAVE MACMILLAN
Houndmills, Basingstoke, Hampshire RG21 6XS and
175 Fifth Avenue, New York, N.Y. 10010
Companies and representatives throughout the world.

PALGRAVE MACMILLAN is the global academic imprint of the Palgrave
Macmillan division of St. Martin's Press, LLC and of Palgrave Macmillan Ltd.
Macmillan® is a registered trademark in the United States, United Kingdom
and other countries. Palgrave is a registered trademark in the European
Union and other countries.

ISBN-13: 978–0–230–20510–9 hardback
ISBN-10: 0–230–20510–0 hardback
ISBN-13: 978–1–4039–3541–0 paperback
ISBN-10: 1–4039–3541–6 paperback

This book is printed on paper suitable for recycling and made from fully
managed and sustained forest sources. Logging, pulping and manufacturing
processes are expected to conform to the environmental regulations of
the country of origin.

A catalogue record for this book is available from the British Library.

A catalog record for this book is available from the Library of Congress.

10 9 8 7 6 5 4 3 2 1
17 16 15 14 13 12 11 10 09 08

Printed in China

for Daniel

Contents

Contents

Part III   System Perspectives

Part IV   The Interface between System and Lifeworld

Part V   Conclusion

List of Tables
and Boxes

Tables

Boxes

Acknowledgements

My first debt of thanks is to the late Jo Campling, my commissioning editor and a dear friend. She helped me write the proposal for this book and gave me much useful advice.

I would like to thank the British Academy who awarded me a Senior Research Fellowship in 2000. I began work on the proposal during the period of my fellowship. I am also grateful to the Rockefeller Foundation who awarded me a residency at their Study and Conference Center in Bellagio, Italy in 2006. Without the residency, I would still be writing the first draft of this book. My fellow residents were a tremendous source of both encouragement and constructive criticism, and I am grateful to them all for broadening my perspective and helping me to see my material through their eyes. I have been fortunate in having the active support of my colleagues at Peninsula Medical School, particularly John Bligh and Stuart Logan. When I worked at Guy's King's and St Thomas' Hospitals Medical School, Roger Jones was the most supportive head of department who valued my work and by doing so encouraged me to carry on.

A number of colleagues and friends have generously contributed their time and expertise and have helped me to improve the manuscript. I am deeply grateful to all of them. Andrew Herxheimer has acted as an informal mentor from the start of my interest in medicines. He opened the door to his fascinating world when I first approached him over twenty years ago and has been a source of inspiration and expertise ever since. I owe my interest in the whole topic to Drummond Forbes, then a District Pharmaceutical Officer at Bristol Royal Infirmary. He was the first professional to take my experience of an adverse drug reaction seriously and, in doing so, alerted me to the vital role played by pharmacists. Betty Chewning is a kindred spirit and I owe many insights to her, particularly the ideas underlying Table 7.1. Graham Scambler was generous enough to give a series of social theory seminars to a small group of colleagues, and I was fortunate to be one of them. Charlotte Paterson read through the first draft of the manuscript and made useful and insightful suggestions. Zoe Kenyon's enthusiasm for my work has encouraged me to think that it may be helpful to prescribers. Fiona Stevenson's enthusiasm and hard work made a tremendous contribution to our various joint research projects from which I have drawn in writing this book. I also learned a great deal from the cohorts of general practitioners who chose to do the MSc in General Practice at the United Medical and Dental Schools of Guy's and St Thomas' Hospitals (as it was known then). From their small group discussions I began to understand the realities of everyday general practice. I have also benefited from advice given to me by Ebba Holme Hansen, Natasha Posner and Margaret Hewetson. I am grateful to Susan Margetts for help in preparing the final manuscript. I am responsible for any mistakes.

I would like to thank my family for their support and encouragement, especially Annie, Clive, Hilary and Valentine. Last but not least, I would like to thank Daniel for his constant emotional and practical support.

I would like to acknowledge permission to reproduce copyright material from several publishers as follows: Table 1.1 by permission of IMS Health (IMS MIDAS ®, MAT December 2006); Table 2.1 from figure 3 in *Oxford Textbook of Primary Medical Care Vol 1*, p. 119, edited by Jones, Britten, Culpepper, Gass, Grol and Silagy (2003) with permission of Oxford University Press; Box 2.1: 'Penny Brohn Centre' from www.pennybrohn-cancercare.org; Chapters 2 and 3, text from N. Britten, 'Understanding medicine taking in context' in *Prescribing: Seeking Concordance in Practice*, by J. Dowell, B. Williams and D. Snadden, Radcliffe Publishing Ltd, 2007; Box 3.1 reprinted from 'Resisting medicines: a synthesis of qualitative studies of medicine taking', p. 139, in *Social Science & Medicine* vol. 61, by P. Pound, N. Britten, M. Morgan, L. Yardley, C. Pope, G. Daker-White and R. Campbell, copyright 2005 with permission from Elsevier; Box 4.1 reprinted from figure 1 in 'Medications as social phenomena' in *Health: An Interdisciplinary Journal for the Social Study of Health, Illness and Medicine* (2001) vol. 5, p. 447, by D. Cohen, M. McCubbin, J. Collin and G. Perodeau, with permission from SAGE publications; Box 4.2, Parliamentary copyright material from the House of Commons Health Committee 2005, is reproduced with the permission of the Controller of Her Majesty's Stationery Office on behalf of Parliament; Box 4.3 is reprinted from *International Journal of Risk and Safety in Medicine*, vol. 15, p. 165, copyright 2002 with permission from IOS press; Table 5.1 is reprinted from *The BMA New Guide to Medicines and Drugs* (2004), edited by Dr M. Peters, p. 286, with the permission of Penguin Books Ltd; Box 6.1 from figure 1, p. 243, in *Oxford Textbook of Primary Medical Care Vol 1*, edited by Jones, Britten, Culpepper, Gass, Grol and Silagy (2003), with the permission of Oxford University Press; Box 6.2 from 'Who pays for the pizza? Redefining the relationships between doctors and drug companies. 1: Entanglement', p. 1190, in *British Medical Journal* 2003, by R. Moynihan, with permission from BMJ Publishing Group Ltd; Table 7.2 reprinted from 'Perceptions and practice of concordance in nurses' prescribing consultations: Findings from a national questionnaire survey and case studies of practice in England', p. 10, in *International Journal of Nursing*

Studies vol. 44, by S. Latter, J. Maben, M. Myall and A. Young, copyright 2007 with permission from Elsevier; Table 7.3 reprinted from 'Health promotion in primary care: Physician-patient communication and decision making about prescription medications', p. 14, in *Social Science & Medicine* vol. 41, by G. Makoul, P. Arnston and T. Schofield, copyright 1995, with permission from Elsevier; Box 7.1 reprinted from 'The expression of aversion to medicines in general practice consultations', p. 9, in *Social Science & Medicine* vol. 59, by N. Britten, F. Stevenson, J. Gafaranga, C. Barry and C. Bradley, copyright 2004, with permission from Elsevier; Box 7.2 reprinted from figure 3 of 'Using reflexivity to optimize teamwork in qualitative research' in *Qualitative Health Research* (1999) vol. 9, p. 39, by C. A. Barry, N. Britten, N. Barber, C. Bradley and F. Stevenson, with permission from SAGE publications; Box 8.1 from 'Introducing IDDT' in www.iddtinternational.org.uk by permission of Insulin Dependent Diabetes Trust; Box 8.2, 'Ten rules for safer drug use', from www.worstpills.org by permission of Public Citizen's Health Research Group; Box 8.3 from 'Recommended general principles' in *Working with the Pharmaceutical Industry*, 1998, Long-term Medical Conditions Alliance; Box 8.4, information about QRD Advisory Network, from www.qrd.alzheimers.org.uk.

Every effort has been made to trace rights holders, but if any have been inadvertently overlooked the publishers would be pleased to make the necessary arrangements at the first opportunity.

Part I

Introduction

Introduction: Medicines in Time and Space

Few human experiences are so universal and have such potent symbolic overtones as the ordinary acts of prescribing and ingesting medicines. Their meaning far transcends the pharmacological properties of the substances ingested. This symbolism is among the most ancient and deeply placed in human nature. Even today, its roots are an inextricable tangle of the mystical and magical with the scientific and the rational. (Pellegrino 1976, p. 624)

Introduction

Contemporary health care in the industrialized nations is heavily dependent on the use of pharmaceutical medicines. Almost everyone has used prescription medicines at some time in their life; most health care practitioners need to be at least aware of the medicines their patients are using, even if they themselves are not responsible for prescribing. The volume of prescribing is staggering. In England alone, over 700 million prescription items are dispensed every year in the community. This amounts to an average of over 14 prescription items per head of population and a cost to the National Health Service of £8 billion, while in the United States Americans spend $200 billion a year on prescription drugs. Translated into global sales of pharmaceuticals, the North American market, the largest of any region, is worth $300 billion a year (see Table 1.1). The pharmaceutical industry is amongst the most profitable in the world. The drug market can be subdivided into three submarkets: over-the-counter (OTC) products, the hospital submarket and the prescription submarket. Within Europe, the OTC market has a market share of about 6–10 per cent; the hospital market represents 10–15 per cent of the total with the lion's share of 75–84 per cent belonging to the prescription submarket, which is mostly primary care (Ess et al. 2003).

3

Medicines and Society

Table 1.1   Global pharmaceutical sales by region

World Audited Market	2006 Sales (US$Bn)	Global Sales (%)
North America	289.9	47.7
Europe	181.8	29.9
Japan	56.7	9.3
Asia, Africa and Australia	52.0	8.6
Latin America	27.5	4.5
Total IMS Audited *	607.9	100

* Excludes unaudited markets. Sales cover direct and indirect pharmaceutical channel purchases in U.S. dollars from pharmaceutical wholesalers and manufacturers. The figures above include prescription and certain over-the-counter data and represent manufacturer prices. Totals may not add due to rounding.

Source: IMS MIDAS ®, MAT December 2006.

Pharmaceuticals do much more than generate vast profits. They play a key role in the cure, management and prevention of disease and have saved millions of lives. Infectious diseases such as smallpox which used to decimate populations are no longer feared. Increasing numbers of people with chronic diseases such as asthma have come to rely on medicines for their quality of life. The use of antihypertensive medication prevents many strokes and heart attacks. However, prescription medicines have also been responsible for a shocking number of deaths and are a leading cause of mortality. There are wide differences in the use of pharmaceuticals between countries with apparently similar populations, which suggests that there are social and cultural factors at work. For example, countries such as France and Germany have much higher rates of consumption of prescription medicines than the Netherlands or the United Kingdom.

There are clearly tensions between the needs of health care and commercial interests. The interests of industry are best served by products for which there is a lifelong need, while both patients and health care practitioners hope that diseases can be cured without the need for further treatment. There are further tensions between the interests of nation states, insurance companies, health maintenance organizations, professionals and patients. There are tensions between benefits and harms, and between saving lives and causing death. Health professionals responsible for prescribing or overseeing the use of pharmaceuticals have to balance the various requirements of evidence-based practice, appropriate prescribing, hospital or other formularies, prescribing budgets, balancing of benefits and harms, providing information to patients and the problem of 'non compliance'. While some of these issues are technical ones, many are matters of health policy, interprofessional relationships, vested interests and so on.

The starting point for this book is that pharmaceuticals are social phenomena as well as pharmacological agents, and that patients and the public are insufficiently involved at virtually all stages of the life cycle of prescribed medicines. In this introductory chapter, I will set the scene by looking at the use of medicines long before the pharmaceutical industry was born as well as historical differences in the roles of different health care professionals. I will sketch out some of the international differences in the use of pharmaceuticals. Finally, I will set out a theoretical framework for the rest of the book by introducing and explaining the concepts of system and lifeworld.

Historical Use of Medicines

Long before the advent of modern science, and over many centuries, ordinary people used a wide range of remedies to manage their own health and illness. Although many traditional treatments are now regarded as useless or even harmful, others formed the precursors of modern drugs. Contemporary ethnopharmacologists in search of ideas for new drugs are seeking out the secrets of traditional remedies. In ancient times, herbs were used either to strengthen the sick person or to drive out malevolent spirits. The theories of analogy and signatures informed the choice of remedy in traditional medicine, such as the properties of colour and smell in relation to bodily experiences. As Pellegrino (1976) noted, symbolic properties of medicines have not disappeared from contemporary society. Porter (1997) gives the examples of red substances being used to treat disorders of the blood, and yellow plants such as the saffron crocus to alleviate jaundice. Some of the treatments of antiquity remained in the *materia medica* for thousands of years.

In addition to medicinal substances, the use of psychoactive plants to achieve hallucinogenic and other altered states of consciousness can also be traced back hundreds if not thousands of years. On the basis of the similarity between entoptic phenomena (recurring visual patterns generated by psychoactive substances) and abstract markings on prehistoric cave paintings, Rudgley (1993) suggests that human use of psychoactive substances may go back as far as the Stone Age. Paleobotanical evidence confirms the use of the opium poppy in Neolithic times. Shamans combined the roles of healer, sorcerer, seer, educator and priest; the tools of their trade relied heavily on rituals and magic as well as amulets and talismans. Siberian shamans used the psychoactive fly-agaric mushrooms, and these and other types of hallucinogenic mushroom were used by groups as diverse as the Aztecs in Mexico and the Kuma in the Western Highlands of New Guinea. Other psychoactive substances used in traditional societies include yaje in the Amazon, peyote in Mexico, mandrake in Europe, cola nuts in West Africa and betel leaves in Asia (Rudgley 1993).

As Porter (1997) has shown in his comprehensive history of medicine, the ancient civilizations of Babylon, Egypt and Greece all made extensive use of a wide variety of drugs derived from plant and mineral sources. Islamic medicine made a major contribution to pharmacology, while Chinese medicine employed herbs and other drugs as well as the more distinctive features of acupuncture and moxibustion.

In sixteenth-century Europe, it was Paracelsus who provided the strongest challenge to Greek theories of medicine, and whose theories of the sovereignty of nature led to the development of alchemical methods (Porter 1997). He attributed spiritual properties to the three primary substances of salt, sulphur and mercury. His doctrine of signatures included plants and minerals used to treat symptoms to which they bore resemblance or with which they had associations. Paracelsus rejected academic learning, preferring to learn from ordinary people and folk medicine, in a manner which offended orthodox physicians then just as much as it would do now. His work stimulated the development and use of chemical remedies, although not all advocates endorsed his mystical theories. Pharmacopoeias published in the late sixteenth and early seventeenth centuries included chemical remedies such as compounds of mercury and antimony.

Despite the development of chemical methods, treatments remained traditional. In seventeenth-century England these included recipes made up of plant and animal substances such as mallow roots and frog spawn which were boiled up and applied externally. Not all these treatments are now perceived as misguided; for example, cinchona bark, which is a source of quinine, was used to treat fevers such as malaria. In the eighteenth century, blood letting remained popular as did chemical remedies such as calomel (mercurous chloride), but some physicians at least were aware of the dangers of these treatments. The traditional approaches based on the Galenic concept of the six 'non naturals' (food and drink, environment, sleep, exercise, evacuations and state of mind) remained popular with wealthy patients and could be adapted to their individual needs. Travel, sea bathing and visiting spas were all popular therapies. Even so, medication was becoming the dominant form of therapy, as it was easier for physicians to charge their patients for medicines and pills than for visits or advice alone. Loudon (1986) estimated that medicines amounted to not less than 80 per cent of the cost of the large majority of general practitioners' bills throughout the period 1750–1850. Manufacturing druggists were producing new pharmaceutical products in large quantities, giving physicians thousands of medicines to choose from. Most of these were herbs, which were prescribed in a variety of forms, on the basis of individualized prescriptions. These non-standardized treatments required the physician's judgement and experimentation with different doses. Animal products were gradually replaced by minerals and metallic drugs in successive editions of the London *Pharmacopoeia*, and in the words of Porter 'the lumber room of preparations inherited from antiquity was being sorted out at last' (Porter 1997, p. 269). Despite this, a contemporary surgeon claimed that 'even the London and Edinburgh pharmacopoeias were loaded with a miserable farrago of useless trash' (Loudon 1986, p. 64).

The eighteenth century also saw the discovery of some medicinal substances still in use today. Stone successfully used willow bark, whose active ingredient salicin has an effect similar to aspirin, to treat rheumatic fever. Withering used foxglove to treat patients with dropsy and heart disease. More dramatically, Jenner established the efficacy of the smallpox vaccination, and this discovery was immediately taken up in England and in Europe. Napoleon had his army vaccinated and was an enthusiastic supporter of Jenner.

In addition to treatments prescribed by physicians, ordinary people used a wide variety of traditional and magical cures for their health problems. The doctrine of signatures continued to inform the choice of treatments such as the plant eyebright for eye problems. The eighteenth century has also been called the golden age of quackery due to the large number of patent medicines available and the extravagant claims made for them. Thus, many of the treatments available over the counter or from a physician were frankly dangerous, either due to poisoning, addiction or interactions with other treatments being used at the same time.

In this context, in England and other parts of Europe, some doctors published manuals of self-treatment which recommended home remedies based on foodstuffs such as honey or liquorice. These could also be supplemented with ready-made remedies bought in shops. These texts were very popular, and some ran into many editions and foreign languages. Writers like Buchan and Wesley were critical of their colleagues' promiscuous use of treatments. At the same time the German physician Hahnemann, who was similarly critical of the use of dangerous drugs used in high doses, developed the system of homeopathy, which used tiny doses of pure substances (Porter 1997).

Development of laboratory medicine in the nineteenth century, particularly in Germany, led to the scientific discipline of pharmacology. Early work investigated the properties of poisons in the subdiscipline of toxicology and refined the active ingredients in medicinal plants. For example, two French pharmacists isolated morphine from raw opium in 1803–04, which was named by a German pharmacist. Once these chemicals had been isolated, it was possible to control their strength, purity and dose and to use them in a systematic fashion. As a result, pharmacists and physicians now had a powerful range of alkaloid treatments at their disposal including digitoxin, ephedrine, cocaine, quinine, atropine and reserpine.

The latter part of the nineteenth century saw the advent of bacteriology, which led to new theories of disease and new possibilities for treatment. Pasteur's work established the existence of microorganisms in the atmosphere, their role in putrefaction and disease, and their sensitivity to heat. He made the case for the germ theory of infection to the French Academy of Medicine and went on to test his ideas on chicken cholera and anthrax. He tested his rabies vaccine in dogs before trying it out with great success on a young boy who had been bitten by a rabid dog. In Germany, Koch identified the bacilli responsible for tuberculosis and cholera. A vaccine was found for diphtheria which successfully immunized large numbers of children; in contrast, the purported remedy for tuberculosis, tuberculin, turned out to be useless.

Large scale drug manufacturing began in the nineteenth century, and many of the later pharmaceutical giants such as Merck and Eli Lilly started production at this time. Manufacturing was greatly helped by developments such as sugar coated pills, the gelatine capsule and the tablet-compression machine. Industry and academia, in the form of university pharmacology departments, collaborated from the beginning. Not everyone approved of such collaboration and, for example, the newly established American Society for Pharmacology and Experimental Therapeutics excluded employees of drug companies (Porter 1997).

In Germany, Paul Ehrlich was responsible for coining the phrase 'magic bullet'. His work focused on the search for chemical cures and began with experiments on dyes. Ehrlich studied microorganisms such as bacteria which could produce antibodies; these antibodies were nature's magic bullets, so called, because they targeted their intended organism and nothing else. The challenge for medicine was to identify chemical substances with the same properties; this was the role of chemotherapy. Ehrlich's work led to the discovery of Salvarsan for treating syphilis; the treatment was effective but also toxic and painful. It did not fulfil the dream of the magic bullet. Subsequently, Domagk successfully used Prontosil, a dye, to treat streptococcal infection. Its action was bacteriostatic meaning that rather than killing bacteria it prevented them from multiplying thus allowing the body's immune system to do the job. This work led to the identification of sulphanilamide, the first of the sulpha drugs. They were effective in the treatment of a range of infections including gonorrhoea and meningitis and were widely prescribed.

However, the modern pharmaceutical era began with Fleming's discovery of penicillin in 1928, and its subsequent development over ten years later.

Even antibiotics have their link with folklore, as mould was widely used for treating wounds or cuts. By the time Florey and Heatley had shown that penicillin was effective, the Second World War had started, and British pharmaceutical companies were concentrating on the war effort. Florey and Heatley thus worked initially with American pharmaceutical companies who manufactured penicillin in industrial quantities. Penicillin was used with great success towards the end of the war in treating wounded soldiers. Other antibiotics followed soon after, and from the 1950s onwards, large numbers of new drugs were discovered, manufactured and prescribed.

Scientific discovery and industrial manufacturing have produced medicines far removed from the traditional treatments of earlier times, although some of these medicines had their origins in folk remedies. Some traditional remedies are still used in the form of self-care as we shall see in the next chapter. Professional control of pharmaceutical treatments has restricted people's access to medicines; in most developed countries, only qualified and registered practitioners are allowed to prescribe medicines. To understand contemporary use of medicines, it is necessary to understand the role of professionals in prescribing and dispensing.

The Role of Professionals

The earliest healers included shamans, herbalists, wise women, medicine men and traditional healers of different kinds. Although there were doctors as long ago as ancient Greece, they coexisted with other kinds of healers. In ancient societies, healers could also have spiritual, magical and educational roles. In ancient Mesopotamia and Egypt, there were three kinds of healers: seers specializing in divination; priests conducting exorcisms and incantations; and physicians who used drugs as well as carrying out bandaging and surgery. In ancient Roman cities, healers were more heterogeneous and included wise women, body-builders, root gatherers and hucksters and, of course, women midwives and nurses (Porter 1997).

The Renaissance saw the establishment of the London-based institutions which were the precursors of the current separate Colleges for surgeons, physicians and general practitioners. Medical practitioners in the eighteenth century were a diverse group without licensing or a standardized training. Their qualifications could be university degrees, membership of the Company of Surgeons, certificates of attendance at London hospital lecture courses or apprenticeships. In addition to the regular practitioners, there were unqualified irregulars, 'empirics' or quacks. However, Loudon (1986) makes the point that it was sometimes difficult to distinguish between these two groups if a practitioner's qualifications were unknown or if someone moved from one kind of practice to another.

Some practitioners started out as grocers and then practised as surgeons or apothecaries; there were also examples of well-qualified doctors practising as quacks. Underlying the divisions between the different kinds of medical practitioners themselves, and the divisions between regular and irregular practitioners, was the relationship between the practitioner and their treatment. Practitioners with the lowest status were those most closely associated with drugs and medicines: the quacks as well as the druggists, chemists and apothecaries. The physicians enjoyed the highest status and considered themselves too superior to dispense the medicines they prescribed. Women were professionally excluded partly because they were also excluded from universities.

Irregular practitioners included quacks, midwives and the druggists and chemists. Quacks were people who sold patent medicines and were often itinerant and extremely energetic in advertising their wares. They were portrayed as ignorant and unscrupulous, taking advantage of gullible customers who believed their extravagant claims. Most midwives were women. They usually had no formal qualifications but carried out the majority of normal deliveries. Less is known about other kinds of women healers and herbalists. In earlier centuries, thousands of women healers had been tortured and executed during the European 'witch craze'. Loudon (1986) points out that irregular practitioners were both a source of competition to the regulars and also scapegoats when the regulars were threatened.

Regular practitioners fell into three groups: physicians, surgeons and apothecaries. Physicians dealt with internal diseases, had university degrees, and those in London were required to be members of the London College of Physicians. Physicians carried out no manual treatments and prescribed medicines but did not dispense them. Their superior status derived from their university education which gave them the right to oversee the work of the surgeons and apothecaries. Surgeons dealt with external disorders including wounds and skin problems and anything requiring manual treatment. Apothecaries were based in their shops and dispensed the prescriptions written by physicians. The role of the apothecary was not supposed to include the giving of advice or diagnosis of the person's complaint as this was the responsibility of physicians. Apothecaries could be prosecuted for encroaching on the work of physicians and were also liable to have their premises inspected by physicians wishing to ensure the purity of the drugs dispensed. Despite this, many apothecaries did provide advice and began to visit patients in their homes. A landmark court case and subsequent appeal in 1704 (the Rose case) confirmed the right of apothecaries to practise physic, but it prevented them from charging their clients for anything other than the medicines provided. Although this judgement allowed the apothecaries to become doctors, it perpetuated their low status by emphasizing their dependence on the sale of medicines rather than their knowledge and advice. Despite these distinctions, in eighteenth-century England, it was possible to practise in all branches of medicine, and some doctors did so.

The Rose judgement gave apothecaries the incentive to over prescribe and to dispense medicines in such a way as to maximize profits. This usually meant that frequent doses of small amounts of medicines were dispensed sometimes on a near daily basis. As a result, many apothecaries became rich. At the same time, there was a stigma attached to commercial activity which lowered the status of the apothecaries, who could be caricatured as mere shopkeepers. It was the fact that their main treatments, medicines, were commodities which could be bought and sold, and that they were involved in such buying and selling, that damaged the apothecaries' standing. The tension between healing and profit making remains problematic for community-based pharmacists to this day.

Loudon (1986) has described the period of medical reform in the first half of the nineteenth century as a transition from a disparate group of practitioners loosely characterized by this tripartite formation to a structured and unitary profession. He identifies the trigger for reform as the rise of the dispensing druggist. Just as, a century earlier, the rise of the apothecaries had threatened the practice of the physicians, the rise of the druggists threatened the apothecaries' livelihoods. Druggists opened shops all over the place, and because their customers came to them, they could service a larger number of customers than the surgeon apothecaries could do while home visiting. Apothecaries, such as William Broderip in Bristol, lost their fortunes when undercut by dispensing druggists. The apothecaries responded by attempting to organize themselves into medico-political societies. The short-lived General Pharmaceutical Association of Great Britain, established in 1794, attempted to discredit the druggists by portraying them as quacks: uneducated people providing dangerous adulterated substances and encroaching on doctors' territory.

The Apothecaries Act of 1815 set out a mechanism for the examining and licensing of general practitioners. It required a minimum of five years apprenticeship to an apothecary and the production of testimonials of education. Those people practising without a license could subsequently be fined, unless, under a grandfather clause, they had been in full practice as apothecaries at the time of the Act. Two aspects of the Act were hated by the apothecaries: the fact that they were required to compound and dispense the prescriptions of physicians and the power of the Society to search their premises and destroy any faulty or contaminated drugs.

The aspects of medicine thought to be degrading by the physicians and surgeons were pharmacy and to a lesser extent midwifery. Remedies could take the form of mixtures, draughts, boluses, pills or lotions. Even at that time, there were those who doubted the efficacy of these treatments. In a competitive environment, the general practitioner's success depended on his ability to persuade patients to accept and pay for large quantities of medicines.

The Medical Act of 1858 established a register of approved medical practitioners, specified entry qualifications and created the General Medical Council (GMC). It took another 20 years before women were allowed to qualify in the United Kingdom, although women were able to qualify in the United States much earlier than this. The GMC has powers to discipline malpractice and to regulate medical education. It was dominated by the medical colleges, and the question of whether it places the interests of patients before the interests of doctors remains pertinent to this day. The Act marginalized quacks and irregulars without making unlicensed practice illegal. It remains the organizing principle behind contemporary medical practice in the United Kingdom.

The current division of the medical labour force is such that all practising doctors have the right to prescribe, although in numerical terms the bulk of prescriptions are written by general practitioners. Except for rural areas, general practitioners do not dispense their own prescriptions but rely on pharmacists to do this. The different responsibilities of pharmacists, nurses and doctors for the prescribing, dispensing and management of medicines arise from these historical relationships. Recent changes in the United Kingdom have extended prescribing rights to nurses and pharmacists thus eroding historic boundaries between medical and other health care practitioners. The availability of OTC medicines is increasing as supermarkets and other outlets now sell a limited range of analgesics and other medicines.

The International Context

In developed countries, most people can only obtain prescription medicines by consulting a qualified and licensed health professional. Different professional groups have different rights in relation to prescribing and dispensing; only dispensing doctors in rural areas have the right to do both. Different systems of health care throughout the world provide and regulate the supply of medicines in different ways. The use of medicines varies enormously even within Europe, and this variation reflects cultural and sociological factors. For example, the total spending on pharmaceuticals per capita, measured in US dollars per person in 2001, varied from 537 in France to 223 in Denmark (Kooiker and van der Wijst 2004). These differences also reflect differences in health care systems which determine people's access to medicines. The situation in developing countries is beyond the scope of this book but has been covered elsewhere (see, for example, van der Geest and Whyte 1988).

Van der Zee et al. (2004) have distinguished three broad types of health care system: the state or Beveridge model; the social security or Bismarck system; and the predominantly private funding system. In the state system, health care is funded out of general taxation and is provided free at the point of access. The philosophy underlying the state system is one of equal access to health care for all citizens regardless of ability to pay, and the funding of health care is in effect a redistribution of income from richer to poorer. In state systems, drugs are either provided free of charge or patients pay flat rate prescription charges which do not reflect the price of medicines. This is the system of health care in the United Kingdom, southern Europe, Scandinavia and Australia. In countries with state systems, there may be a coexisting private sector as, for example, in the United Kingdom and Australia. In the social security model, state regulation harmonizes the provision of health care by a range of insurance companies and mutual societies. Health care is funded by premiums paid by employees and, unlike general taxation, these funds are ring fenced. The intervention of the state ensures that coverage is extended to all employees and to people who are self-employed. This system arose from historical situations in which groups of citizens or workers formed mutual societies and other kinds of arrangements for protecting themselves against loss of income due to sickness or disability. In this system, patients usually make co-payments which may or may not reflect the price of medicines. This is the system of health care in Germany, where it was originally established, and Austria, the Netherlands, France, Belgium and Luxembourg. In the predominantly private model, the state plays a minimal role and health care is provided by private organizations either on profit or non-profit basis. This is the American model, and the state provides health care only for people on low incomes and the elderly. This system reflects a free market and individualistic philosophy. In the United States, approximately 15 per cent of the population is either uninsured or insufficiently protected against health care costs and loss of income due to sickness or disability. In a private system, patients have to pay for their own medicines if uninsured; different health care providers have different systems for meeting the costs of medicines. Within the European Union, there is a range of payment systems with different levels of co-payment, eligibility for exemption and methods of refunding or compensating patients depending on income and disease state. Unsurprisingly, demand for prescription medicines is reduced when patients have to make direct financial contributions. Noyce et al. (2000) examined prescription charges for the same or similar clinical conditions in eight EU countries and found that the diversity of payment systems resulted in patterns of consumption at odds with clinical need.

A further fundamental distinction of health care systems is between those based on primary care and those which are hospital based. In primary care based systems, general practitioners usually act as gatekeepers to secondary care; patients can normally only access hospitals (secondary care) if they are referred by their general practitioner. Patients are usually registered with a general practitioner and have the opportunity to form a long-term relationship with either a single doctor or at least a single health centre. This restricts patient choice while also containing costs. In hospital-based systems, patients are free to consult whichever doctor they think most appropriate for their problem. They can 'shop around' and consult several doctors in order to obtain second opinions, although the extent to which they can do so may be constrained in a state or social security system.

The supply and consumption of medicines is affected by another aspect of health care systems: the supply of doctors. In some countries, the supply of doctors has been deliberately limited by governments, while in others there is an oversupply of doctors. On the one hand, this leads to situations in which individual doctors have large numbers of patients who are registered with them and relatively little time for each one, and on the other, in which individual doctors have to please their patients for fear that they will otherwise choose to consult another doctor. In terms of prescribing, one might expect that doctors would be much more likely to over prescribe in the latter situation irrespective of whether the medicines were really needed or not.

For the purposes of comparison, we may then contrast systems which are state run and primary care based (such as the United Kingdom); social security systems which are primary care based (such as the Netherlands and Denmark); social security systems which are hospital based (such as Germany and France); and private systems which are hospital based (such as the United States). There would seem to be no examples of state systems which are hospital based, presumably because hospital-based systems are more expensive, and no examples of private systems which are primary care based. However, in the context of the United States, health maintenance organizations and other health care providers serve to restrict patients' choices as part of managed care systems.

Theoretical Approach

As already stated, the starting point of this book is the claim that pharmaceuticals are social phenomena as well as pharmacological agents. This is because the availability and use of medicines is determined by many social actors such as national governments, regulatory agencies, industry, health maintenance organizations, professional associations, financial markets, patient groups, individual practitioners and patients, to name a few. At a societal level, the pharmaceutical industry is a major part of the global economy and pharmacological treatments are the mainstay of Western medical practice. The rising cost of health care all over the world is driven, in part, by the cost and expanding use of pharmaceuticals. For health care professionals, evidence-based practice aims to improve rational prescribing and to eradicate inappropriate prescribing. There is a long-standing problem of 'non adherence' referring to the fact that many patients do not take their medicines as prescribed.

The aim of the book is to explore the tensions between lay and professional perspectives about prescribed medicines, with the intention of identifying the 'democratic deficit' at various stages, and the consequences of this deficit. A further aim is to examine the social processes involved in the production and consumption of medicines. Most of the current discussion about medicines is too narrowly focused, both at the individual and policy levels, and often excludes the perspectives of patients, carers and the public. I hope to demonstrate the need for broader engagement about the appropriate use of medicines. To do this, the discussion needs to be set in a sociological context.

The work of Giddens (1990) provides a starting point for considering the interplay between health care systems and industries operating at the macro level and relationships between individuals at the micro level. His proposition is that we are living in a state of high modernity, and he discusses the concept of globalization in which local and global settings affect each other. Social relations are based on both physical presence (for example, when patients and practitioners meet) and its absence (for example, when governments legislate in the interests of public health). In globalized systems, politics and economics are to a great extent independent of each other, and multinational companies are beyond the control of nation states. Giddens refers to the process of disembedding in which social relations are lifted out of local contexts and restructured across indefinite spans of time and space. He proposes two general types of disembedding mechanisms: symbolic tokens such as money and expert systems by which much of our lives are organized such as electricity and air travel. Medicine is another such expert system. All such disembedding mechanisms depend on trust and provide guarantees of expectations across distanciated time and space. Trust becomes relevant in situations of absence and when there is a lack of full information. It requires faith in the correctness of principles of which non-experts are usually ignorant. Giddens argues that risk and trust intertwine as trust normally serves to reduce or minimize dangers associated with particular kinds of activities. Security is defined as a situation in which a specific set of dangers is counteracted or minimized. The experience of security usually rests on a balance of trust and acceptable risk or on ignorance of the dangers involved. However, Wynne (1996) has criticized Giddens' view of public trust as being simplistic; he argues that when lay people are dependent on experts, they have to behave as if they trust them, because to do otherwise is socially and psychologically unviable.

In contrast to disembedding mechanisms, reembedding is the reappropriation or recasting of disembedded social relations so as to pin them down to local conditions of time and place. This involves what Giddens calls facework commitments and faceless commitments. The former are trust relations sustained by or expressed in social connections involving copresence, for example, patient–practitioner consultations. The latter concern the development of faith in symbolic tokens or expert systems such as those involved in the licensing of prescription drugs. Giddens' theses in this respect are that all disembedding mechanisms interact with reembedded contexts of action, which may act to support or undermine them, and that faceless commitments are similarly linked in an ambiguous way with those demanding facework. This provides us with a way of understanding the links between the work of experts in establishing the efficacy and safety of drugs and the face-to-face interactions between patients, pharmacists, physicians, nurses and others in the context of prescribing. One type of link is provided by access points which are the points of connection between representatives of expert systems and lay individuals. These can be points of vulnerability for expert systems but also opportunities for the fostering of trust. Giddens argues that experts usually presume that lay people will be more reassured if they are unaware of the extent to which uncertainty and luck inform expert performances. Experts may take risks on behalf of their clients without revealing that they are doing so; they may, however, be unaware themselves of the full extent of the risks they are taking.

Giddens also draws attention to the ambivalent attitudes of the lay public to science and technical knowledge. To the extent that lay people are ignorant of science, they are required to trust the experts. Yet, this ignorance also provides grounds for scepticism or caution. Giddens argues that ambivalence lies at the heart of all trust relations; we should not be surprised that it is evident in relation to medical practice. The paradox of modernity is that while the Enlightenment provided a vision of progress and rationality based on science, the basis of science is the provisional nature of knowledge and lack of certainty.

The work of Beck (1992) provides further insights into the relationship between lay and expert knowledge. He coined the concept of the 'risk society' in distinction to class society. The latter is about the production and distribution of goods and services while the former is about the distribution of 'bads' or risks. Safety not equality becomes the goal in risk society; to be spared from poisoning is to succeed. In risk societies, individuals experience social dependency on inaccessible institutions over which they can have little influence. Within scientific discourse, a deficit model operates in which the public is often characterized as ignorant and in need of education. For Beck, this model is problematic:

> The non-acceptance of scientific definition of risks is not something to be reproached as 'irrationality' in the population; but quite to the contrary, it indicates that the cultural premises of acceptability contained in scientific and technical statements *are wrong*. The technical risk experts *are mistaken* in the empirical accuracy of their implicit value premises, specifically in their assumptions of what appears acceptable to the population ... the scientists ... serve as judges of the 'irrationality' of the population, whose ideas they ought to ascertain and make the foundation of their work. (Beck 1992 p. 58, italics in original)

Beck draws attention to the discrepancy between lay and expert perspectives on risk and makes the same point as Wynne (1996) that the lack of conflict or protest does not necessarily indicate acceptance of risk. Rather it may result from resignation and a sense that people have no power to change the situation they find themselves in. If they want to try and make sense of their situation, they may, as 'thinking individuals', have to find their way through a confusing assortment of contradictory scientific literature with no guide. Within scientific communities, a sceptical attitude is encouraged and scientists are trained to criticize one another's work. This contrasts with the often authoritarian enforcement of scientific results on the public, although it must be said that the news media tend to present simplified messages, and many patients desire unambiguous answers to their questions or requests for advice. Beck argues that the high standards of scientific proof can lead to the accumulation of unrecognized risks for which there is no acknowledged cause. In fact, science conducts experiments on people by putting substances into populations and waiting to see what happens. This is the case with prescribed medicines, usually tested on small numbers of people, as well as on the environmental substances Beck was writing about. In relation to medicine, the prescribing of drugs is used to deal with the consequences of secondary industrialization (diabetes and heart disease, for instance) instead of removing the causes in primary industrialization (the food industry, decreased mobility due to the manufacture of cars and so on). Referring back to the components of the system, business (the economy) is not responsible for the side effects it causes, while politics is responsible for something it has little control over.

Wynne (1996) has criticized both Giddens and Beck for overlooking the 'grass-roots' or lay public dimension and for neglecting the cultural and hermeneutic character of modern knowledge. His own position is that 'a general reason for possible divergence between expert and public knowledges about risks is that expert knowledge embodies social assumptions and models framing its objectivist language, and that lay people have legitimate claim to debate those assumptions' (Wynne 1996, p. 59). He argues that lay and expert knowledge is far more interdependent than is conventionally recognized.

Habermas' concepts of lifeworld and system will provide the main theoretical framework for considering the relationship between lay and expert perspectives in this book. This is because they provide a means for linking macro and micro levels of society while also enabling a detailed analysis of lay perspectives. For Habermas, societies consist of two basic spheres of sociality, lifeworld and system (Finlayson 2005). The lifeworld is the everyday world shared with others and provides culturally transmitted ways of interpreting experiences as well as the language to describe them. The lifeworld includes cultural reproduction such as continuity of tradition, coherence and rationality of knowledge; social integration such as stabilization of group identities and solidarity; and socialization such as transmission of generalized competences for action and harmonization of individual biographies with collective forms of life (Outhwaite 1994). In contrast, the system provides a mechanism for material rather than cultural or symbolic reproduction. It consists of two subsystems, money and power, which together form the 'steering media' of the capitalist economy and of the state administration and related institutions such as the civil service and political parties.

These concepts provide a framework for considering the extent to which there is any consideration of lifeworld perspectives at different stages in the life cycle of medicines and, if not, the consequences of the lack of such consideration. The production, licensing and use of pharmaceutical medicines can be viewed as purely technical processes, and much of the discourse surrounding them is couched in scientific language. This serves to exclude the public and patients. However, all stages of the production and consumption of medicines are also dependent on interpretive processes and value judgements which are not amenable to scientific analysis and which need to be legitimated in the lifeworld.

In Habermas' characterization, the system consists of the economy and the state, with their respective goals of profit and regulation. The system is based on scientific rationality and objective measurements. In the context of medicine use, system imperatives include governmental health policies, the licensing and regulation of medicines, fiscal considerations and the influence of pharmaceutical industry. The lifeworld consists of public and private aspects, including public opinion, norms and values, as well as individual experiences and behaviours. It contains knowledge of the everyday as well as the interpretive work of preceding generations and is concerned with cultural reproduction, social integration and socialization. Members of a community normally share a lifeworld which is the medium within which culture and social integration are sustained and reproduced. The lifeworld is the context in which traditional remedies discussed at the beginning of this chapter were used and in which most contemporary medicine use is discussed, evaluated and acted upon.

One value of this characterization of society is that it draws attention to the goals of strategic action and system imperatives. Generally, for health care, the lifeworld/system distinction points out the tension between the experiences, needs and concerns of lay people, patients and carers on one hand and, on the other, the need to make a profit in a capitalist society (the pharmaceutical companies) and the role in enacting government policies (health professionals). For example, in the United Kingdom, the Department of Health has the role of overseeing the profits of the pharmaceutical companies as well as the role of promoting and providing for the nation's health. Individual doctors, nurses and pharmacists have to reconcile their role in sympathizing with and advocating for their patients with the role of meeting government or managed care targets and protecting the health of communities. Individuals who become ill not only find themselves as members of the familiar lifeworld but also members of an unfamiliar health care system with different rules and modes of behaviour.

Linked to the ideas of lifeworld and system are those of communicative and strategic action. Communicative action is oriented to understanding while strategic action is action oriented to success (success being defined by the goals of the people or organizations involved). The lifeworld is reproduced through communicative action and the system is reproduced through strategic action. The latter may be open or concealed: direct requests are an example of open strategic action while concealed strategic action involves deception. Difficulties arise when actions oriented to understanding become confused with actions oriented to success. Concealed strategic action may involve conscious or unconscious deception on the part of the speaker. Conscious deception is a form of manipulation while Habermas describes unconscious deception as 'systematically distorted communication'. The difference between communicative action and manipulation is discussed further in Chapter 7. Colonization of the lifeworld by the system occurs when system imperatives come to dominate and distort the lifeworld and result in certain pathologies. The pathologies discussed in this book include a lack of attention to patients' own perspectives, an overemphasis on pharmaceutical treatments coupled with a neglect of other ways of managing health and illness, a tendency to emphasize the benefits of pharmaceutical treatments rather than their harms, a converse tendency to pay more attention to the harms of complementary and alternative treatments than to their benefits and treating strategic issues such as licensing or prescribing decisions as if they were purely technical.

Scope and Structure of the Book

This book is about the range of treatments used by patients and professionals to manage illness in contemporary industrialized societies. It will mainly refer to medicines used in the English speaking world and in Europe, as the social contexts of medicine used in parts of Asia, Africa and South America are rather different. The book focuses on prescribed and OTC medicines, rather than recreational or illegal drugs, as well as complementary and alternative treatments. For some people, the words 'medicine' and 'drug' are used interchangeably while for others the two words refer to very different kinds of consumption. The UK 1968 Medicines Act defines a medicinal substance, or medicine, as one which alters physiological processes and which is used for the treatment of illness, for anaesthesia, for contraception, for maintaining health or as a test for diagnosing illness. Collier and Dwight (1997) point out that a drug is any active substance that modifies a physiological process, while a medicine refers to a drug that has been licensed. In everyday life, the word drug is commonly associated with addiction and dependence. Thus the process of licensing is crucial to the creation and use of medicines. From a social point of view, one could say that drugs are used for purposes that are not professionally sanctioned while medicines are only intended for professionally sanctioned purposes. This does not rule out the possibility that medicines may be abused, only that such use is not professionally sanctioned. There are other grey areas here: some medicines are prescribed by doctors for 'off license' use, sometimes legitimately (for children, for example) and sometimes not. The fact that drugs and medicines are distinguished by the terms of the license, or the social context in which they are used, and not by their chemical composition is illustrated by the opiates and a few other drugs (see Box 1.1). Similarly there are initiatives to license cannabis, another predominantly recreational drug, for the treatment of patients with multiple sclerosis and other conditions. The distinction between medicines and other substances such as foodstuffs (for example, vitamin pills and supplements such as cod liver oil) is not always clear. Thus the overlap between the terms 'medicine' and 'drug' exists in both popular and professional contexts. This ambivalence is also visible in people's attitudes to medicines as we will see in Chapter 3.

The book is divided into five main parts: introduction, lifeworld perspectives, system perspectives, the interface between lifeworld and system, and conclusion. The main argument is that system colonization of the lifeworld results in a series of pathologies at various stages in the life cycle of medicine use. Although medicines are produced and regulated by expert systems, these systems depend on legitimization in the lifeworld which is where medicines are consumed. Health professionals are, by the nature of their work, part of the health care system; system imperatives dominate over the needs of the lifeworld. Part I sets the historical and theoretical background for the rest of the book. Starting with lifeworld perspectives in Part II, patients use a range of self-care and complementary treatments in managing their own health and illness whether or not professionals are aware of it (Chapter 2). They have their own rationalities in relation to prescription medicines and carry out their own evaluations (Chapter 3). From the perspective of systems in Part III, those set up for licensing and regulating medicines do not reflect consumers' interests well, but when patients contribute, this can lead to improvements (Chapter 4). Much information about medicines tends to emphasize benefits rather than harms and reflects the professional goal of increasing adherence (Chapter 5). The characterization of prescribing as a technical issue obscures the various conflicting interests and differing values (Chapter 6). In considering the interface between lifeworld and system in Part IV, much doctor–patient communication about prescribing ignores patients' lifeworld concerns (Chapter 7). Patient groups are a mechanism which enable lifeworld experiences to be shared, and can help to further lifeworld goals provided they keep their independence (Chapter 8). Chapter 9 aims to find ways of establishing a better balance between the lifeworld and the system and makes several proposals for clinical practice and research. Each chapter, except the last, ends with an illustrative example. By engaging those interested in the various health care professions whose work includes the prescribing, dispensing and management of prescribed and other treatments, I hope that this book will contribute to a broader public debate between professionals, patients and citizens about the use of medicines in contemporary society.

Box 1.1   Example: opium to heroin

Opium is a drug produced from the unripe seed capsules of the opium poppy *Papaver somniferum* and has been used for thousands of years. It was included in the *materia medica* of Greek, Roman and Arabic systems of medicine.

The London pharmacopoeia of 1788 included liquid opium for the first time. Opium was freely available from pharmacists and by the mid-nineteenth century there was a distinct culture of opiate use. Opium-based preparations such as laudanum, paregoric, and chlorodyne were widely available from grocers' or druggists' shops. Products aimed specifically at children and babies included *Mrs Winslow's Soothing Syrup* and *Atkinson's Infants' Preservative*. Such self-medication was used to treat a wide range of problems with opium being widely used not only as an analgesic and sedative but also for treating fever, diarrhoea and alcoholic hangovers. Apart from its addictive properties, other reasons for the popularity of opium were people's lack of access to medical care, the fragmented nature of medical treatment and hostility towards it. Regular opium users were known as opium eaters, without fear of disapproval, and opiate use was celebrated by Romantic writers such as de Quincey and Coleridge. The Pharmacy Act of 1868 introduced the first restrictions to the widespread availability of opium by limiting the sale of the drug to professional pharmacists. Access was restricted due to concerns about working class use of opium as a stimulant. But it was not until the 1916 Defence of the Realm Act regulation 40B and the 1920 Dangerous Drugs Act were passed that opium use came to be controlled by the medical profession.

Morphine was the first alkaloid to be isolated from opium in the early nineteenth century and is still prescribed for pain relief in contexts such as palliative care. The semi-synthetic substance, heroin, was produced from morphine in the late nineteenth century and, known as diamorphine, it is also used in hospitals as a licensed pain reliever. In the form of heroin it is widely abused. Fully synthetic opiates such as methadone and pethidine are used for medically approved purposes such as treating heroin addiction and pain relief in childbirth.

Thus opium is a plant-based drug which has been widely used for thousands of years for both self-medication and professional use. Its semi-synthetic derivatives and synthetic counterparts continue to occupy a niche role in contemporary health care as well as constituting a major cause of illegal drug use and addiction. Political disputes in opium growing areas of the world such as Afghanistan threaten the contemporary supply of products for both medicinal and illegal use.

Source: Berridge 1999.

Part II
Lifeworld Perspectives

of prescribed medicines, the question arises about how people make choices or comparisons between different kinds of treatment and different ways of responding to distress.

It is often forgotten that the first choice of treatment is no treatment. Some people will automatically reach for analgesics in response to headaches or other sources of pain, while others will prefer to stop what they are doing, lie down or even continue as before. A significant minority of people endorse the view that most diseases cure themselves without one having to go to the doctor (Britten et al. 2002). Menopausal women may prefer to experience symptoms than to take hormone replacement therapy (Hunter et al. 1997). A study in the United Kingdom found that nearly half of adults surveyed had done nothing in response to minor ailments experienced in the previous two weeks (British Market Research Bureau 1997 cited in Blenkinsopp and Bond 2003). Non-pharmaceutical responses to illness include changes in diet, exercise, working habits and social activities. For example, someone with a skin rash may think that it is caused by something they ate and alter their diet, someone troubled by headaches may drink more water, someone with rising blood pressure may try to take more exercise, and someone experiencing insomnia may try to work shorter hours. Although professionals may think that people turn to them far too readily, it is easy to underestimate the extent of self-care especially if few ask about self-care practices. One study based in England showed that, for example, only one in 37 headaches experienced were reported to the family doctor (Banks et al. 1975).

Traditional remedies and healing practices may have developed over many centuries, as discussed in Chapter 1. They are less common in developed countries now than they were in the past, although there is some evidence of a rise in the use of these remedies in Aboriginal and First Nations people in Canada (Novins et al. 2004). I will use the term traditional remedies to refer to systems of healing that have their own rationale and may predate Western medicine. Traditional remedies are used by cultures and communities in which the treatments originated. These treatments may come under the heading of CAM if they are also used by people living in other cultures and communities for whom such treatments are not traditional. Contemporary traditional or home remedies include the use of herbal remedies for hypertension amongst Afro-Caribbean groups in the United Kingdom (Morgan and Watkins 1988), nettles for knee pain and copper bracelets for arthritis. Brown and Segal (1996) found that people diagnosed with hypertension in the United States were using a range of home remedies including vinegar, garlic, aloe vera juice and multiple vitamins. These ingredients were used in different ways either singly or in combination. For example, some people drank vinegar on its own or mixed with water, while others put it on their foreheads with cloths. Garlic cloves were eaten or mixed with water, used as a cooking ingredient, or taken as a tablet or capsule. A study of two generations of Scottish women carried out in the late 1970s found that the older generation, who were born in the early 1920s, were more likely than the younger generation to talk about home remedies (Blaxter and Paterson 1982). Home remedies such as steam inhalation are used to treat respiratory problems including colds, coughs and sore throats. A survey in the North West of England in the 1990s found that over a quarter of people who reported one or more days of restricted activity because of their health, illness or injury had taken home remedies (Hassell et al. 1998).

Home remedies appear to be viewed as safer than and in many cases preferable to prescribed drugs. A study of hypothetical choices in the United States which compared preferences for a high-risk drug, a low-risk drug and a home remedy for the treatment of sore throat, hypertension, arthritis or gastroenteritis showed that 72 per cent of respondents chose the home remedy. These remedies were salt water gargle for sore throat, low salt diet for hypertension, a heating pad for arthritis and a clear liquid diet for gastroenteritis. Those choosing the home remedies had concerns about the potential side effects of the drug remedies (Povar et al. 1984). While the results of a hypothetical study do not necessarily tell us about actual behaviour, they suggest that professionals could usefully explore the use of home remedies with their patients.

Overall, however, little is known about the use of home and traditional remedies as they have not been the subject of much research. It is very likely that these traditional remedies are regarded as 'natural', and that when people refer to natural remedies, it is these kinds of home and traditional remedies that they mean.

The popular sector also includes self-medication with OTC pharmaceuticals and vitamins. Some OTC preparations may be based on traditional remedies such as honey and lemon with the inclusion of some analgesic. Others are milder versions of prescription drugs or may be drugs that were formerly prescription only. One of the reasons for the deregulation of prescription medicines is to encourage people to take responsibility for their own health care as well as transferring costs from the health-service budget to individual patients. A survey in the United Kingdom showed that, in response to minor ailments in the previous two weeks, over a quarter of adults had used an OTC medicine while 14 per cent had used a prescription medicine already in the house (British Market Research Bureau 1997 cited in Blenkinsopp and Bond 2003). The common types of problems for which people treat themselves include headaches, athlete's foot, dandruff, heartburn, migraine, vaginal candidiasis and period pains. Some of these problems may be long term and hence also be treated with prescribed drugs leading to a risk of both being used at the same time and consequent interactions or overdose. The evidence suggests that doctors do not ask patients about the use of OTC treatments, and that patients do not tell them (Stevenson et al. 2003). On the whole people tend to regard OTC treatments as safer than prescribed medicines believing that if they were not safe they would not be so widely available. They may be unaware of the dangers of interactions between OTC and prescribed medicines or that ingredients may be the same. Someone taking an OTC and a prescribed analgesic may not realise that both often include acetaminophen (parac-etamol). Self-medication thus involves the use of commercially produced treatments, some of which are manufactured versions of home remedies or are substances such as vitamins which can be obtained from food.

Although doctors may not ask patients about OTC treatments, phar-macists are in a good position to do so. The difficulty for pharmacists arises from the tension between health care and profit making referred to in Chapter 1. Their clients may be more inclined to see them as suppliers of consumer goods rather than people with expert technical knowledge; in addition, consumers may not know the relevance of expert knowledge in relation to OTCs. While governments may want to encourage people to seek the advice of pharmacists about minor ailments in order to reduce the demand for GP consultations, many lay people may not think that pharmacists are the appropriate professionals for this role. Cunningham-Burley and Maclean (1987) found that mothers of young children used pharmacists in a variety of ways: some wanted advice about the 'differen-tial diagnosis', some consulted the pharmacist as an alternative to the doctor while others used the pharmacist as a stepping stone to the doctor. Pharmacists often enabled mothers to do something for their children without going to the doctor. In a household diary survey in the United Kingdom, Hassell and colleagues (1998) found that most respondents self-managed their illnesses rather than seeking a consultation with a health care practitioner. Only 5.5 per cent of the sample had sought the advice of a community pharmacist. In a review of communication about medicines, Cox et al. (2004) found that pharmacists tended not to offer counselling about prescription or OTC medications. Most clients said they would prefer to ask for advice about OTC products, and a small minority seemed to resent counselling about prescription and OTC med-icines. Most people did not expect to be questioned when buying an OTC medication, although the majority considered it to be important for pharmacy staff to ask clients questions about the condition they were buying the medicine for, other medications they were using and whom the medicine was for. People who reported that they were asked more questions by their pharmacist were more likely to feel that their pharma-cist could help manage their treatment and prevent problems. The review also showed that people discussed their OTC medicines more frequently with pharmacists than with doctors. Thus, the extent to which pharmacists can use their professional knowledge when clients are buying OTC products varies.

The notion of self-management of long-term conditions is becoming part of the professional discourse as a way of responding to the growing burden of chronic disease and the limited capacity of formal health care systems to deal with it. A number of self-management interventions have been tested using randomized trials (Newman et al. 2004). The content of such interventions is highly variable ranging from alterations in diet and exercise to cognitive behavioural therapy. Such interventions tend to be led by health professionals and often aim to change individuals' behaviour. This concept of self-management, as defined and even taught by health professionals, is not the same as spontaneously arising self-care within the lifeworld.

Within the popular sector, people use a wide range of self-care practices which form the backdrop against which any suggested pharmaceutical treatment will be judged. Strong views in favour of home remedies or against drugs will influence decisions about use as will economic considerations. For those people exempt from prescription charges, it may be cheaper to obtain a free prescription than pay for an OTC medication. People's views about appropriate forms of health care may include family or traditional folklore based on collective experiences, and any diagnosis or prescription that contradicts these beliefs will not be easily accepted.

The Informal Sector

The informal sector includes forms of health care delivered by health care professionals who are not part of the formal health care system. This includes a huge range of practitioners ranging from purveyors of 'fringe' treatments to well-established therapies such as acupuncture and medical herbalism. The former includes those who in earlier times would have been branded 'quacks'. Although the use of complementary medicines is widespread, it is not considered as part of the formal health care system. Most CAM therapies represent different rationalities from those informing biomedicine.

While prescribed medicines are generally taken by those with diagnosed diseases, or with known risk factors for disease, complementary and alternative medicines are taken by people who are both 'sick' and 'well'. Complementary and alternative medicine is growing in popularity throughout the developed world. It constitutes the second of Kleinman's sectors of health care: the informal sector, which is also part of the lifeworld. Complementary and alternative medicine treatments include those that have arisen in response or parallel to Western medicine (such as homeopathy) as well as traditional forms of healing which have been adopted in other cultures, for example when Californians or Londoners of Anglo-Saxon descent use acupuncture. The term Complementary and Alternative Medicine is now established as a generic term to embrace both of these types of healing system as used in the developed world. They may be defined as those forms of healing that are not usually taught in medical schools or are not part of the politically dominant health care system.

Charlotte Paterson (2002) defines complementary, or alternative, medicine as comprising three dimensions: knowledge base, legitimacy and therapeutics. Thus complementary medicine depends on knowledge bases distinct from that of biomedicine/ orthodox medicine, does not share the special legitimation that the state has conferred upon biomedicine/orthodox medicine, and does not base its therapeutics on modern pharmaceuticals and surgery. Thomas (2003) has classified the various types of CAM therapy under five headings: ethnic medical systems such as traditional Chinese medicine; non-allopathic systems such as homeopathy; manual therapies such as osteopathy; mind–body therapies such as Reiki; and nature cure therapies such as naturopathy. There are other taxonomies; for example the five-fold comprehensive categorization used by the US National Center for Complementary and Alternative Medicine at the National Institutes of Health. This categorization encompasses four domains as well as whole medical systems which cover more than one domain. The domains are as follows: mind–body medicine including techniques such as meditation and prayer; biologically based practices, mainly substances found in nature such as herbs and special diets; manipulative and body-based practices including chiropractic, osteopathy and massage; and energy medicine such as biofield therapies including Reiki and bio-electromagnetic therapies. The whole medical systems include those arising within Western cultures such as homeopathy and naturopathy and those arising from non-Western cultures such as traditional Chinese medicine and Ayurveda.

Thus, the range of therapies included under the umbrella term CAM is highly variable. While there is not yet any consensus about the content and classification of CAM therapies, I shall follow Paterson (2002) in using the term CAM to refer to those therapies which require consultation with a practitioner thus excluding self-care and self-treatment with OTC products.

Estimates of the numbers of people consulting CAM practitioners depend on the definitions used but suggest that they are heavily used in Australia, the United States, Canada and the United Kingdom (Thomas 2003). Studies conducted in the United Kingdom and United States of America suggest that between a quarter and a half of people in these countries have consulted a complementary practitioner at some time in their lives. Estimates for visits in the previous year vary from 13 to 20 per cent in the last year, which rises to 30 to 40 per cent if over the counter CAM products are included. Results of the 2002 National Health Interview Survey in the United States found that 36 per cent of adults were using some form of CAM, but this figure includes the use of OTC products (Barnes et al. 2004). A population survey carried out in South Australia found that 20 per cent of respondents had visited at least one alternative practitioner in the previous year (MacLennan et al. 1996). In the United Kingdom, some complementary therapy is available within the National Health Service free of charge, but provision is dependent on the prevailing policy and funding climate (Paterson 2007). In some countries, CAM represents a form of private health care, and access to care depends on the ability to pay. In the United States, where drug prices are high and many people are not insured, CAM may represent a cheaper form of health care for some people. The National Health Interview Survey found that 13 per cent of Americans said they used CAM because conventional medical treatments were too expensive.

Users of CAM therapies tend to be younger and better educated than non-users. Women and members of non-manual social classes also tend to use CAM more often than men and members of manual social classes. The National Health Interview Survey also found that people who had been hospitalized in the previous year and former smokers were more likely to be using CAM than other people (Barnes et al. 2004). However, users of CAM are very far from being a homogenous group, and the socioeconomic status of users varies between therapies. Most people consulting CAM practitioners in Canada, Australia, the United Kingdom and United States wanted help with musculoskeletal problems but a wide range of other problems are presented less frequently (Thomas 2003). Some of these problems were of long standing, and surveys suggest a mean of 8–9 years duration. A significant minority of people consulting CAM therapies have no specific health problem at the time and do so to maintain or enhance wellness. People consulting chiropractors are less likely to have chronic problems, as are children. A systematic review of people with cancer found that women and younger people were more likely to use CAM as were those with higher incomes and more education (Verhoef et al. 2005).

Most research into CAM suggests that it is more often used as complementary to orthodox medicine than as an alternative. People consult CAM therapists with a range of chronic problems, choose different therapies for different problems and may continue their treatment as a preventative measure. Most of these people will have consulted their orthodox doctors about their problem and may still be receiving such treatment. Some will be attending other CAM therapists and many will be continuing self-help measures. If the use of CAM treatments is as much a supplement to orthodox treatment as it is a substitute for it, then both CAM and orthodox practitioners need to understand one another's approaches. Complementary and alternative medicine therapists are often asked by their clients to explain the nature of their biomedical diagnoses and treatments, and to help them make treatment choices.

Characteristics of CAM

Bakx (1991) used the term 'folk medicine' to emphasize the two elements of culture and choice claiming that it has been transformed but not eradicated by the modernist project. He attributed the appeal of folk medicine to the cultural gap between biomedical practitioners and their patients. He argued that the current expansion of folk medical practices in Western societies was a direct result of the inability of biomedicine to come to terms with the alienation that it had itself induced amongst consumers of its own services. Folk medicine offers services that biomedicine cannot or does not wish to offer including the management of some chronic incurable illnesses. Bakx argued that biomedicine is in danger of losing its hegemony due to its cultural distance from consumers, its failure to live up to its own propaganda and patients' negative experiences. While Bakx may have overstated the degree of alienation, given that many people use both orthodox and complementary medicine simultaneously, he is right to point to the cultural aspects of the appeal of folk medicine.

Despite the range of therapies included in the various definitions of CAM, there are some common features. Fulder (2005) sets out six such features:

- The notion that self-healing is paramount
- Working with, not against, symptoms
- Individuality
- Integration of human facets
- No fixed beginning or ending
- Conformity to universal principles, such as Chi in Chinese medicine.

The notion of integration of human facets is also known as 'holism', a defining characteristic of CAM therapies. In the holistic view, mind, body, emotion and spirit are seen as interdependent, and this interdependence may also extend to environment, society and individual. The practice of holism means that CAM practitioners enquire about all manner of daily habits, personal biographies and individual preferences that are hardly ever discussed in consultations with biomedical practitioners. Paterson's review of the concept of holism included other features (Paterson 2002):

- A positive view of health as well-being
- Individual responsibility for health
- The importance of health education
- Control of the social environmental determinants of health
- Natural therapeutic techniques
- More equal therapeutic relationships.

For some, the concept of holism is characterized by saying that holistic therapies treat the person and not the disease. Although there is little research examining the actual interactions between CAM practitioners and their clients, claims made by practitioners are corroborated by their clients, some of whom believe that CAM has the ability to enhance the immune system (Boon et al. 1999) and that they choose to consult CAM practitioners because they perceive them to be better listeners and to provide more emotional support than conventional practitioners (Boon et al. 2000).

The emphasis on individual responsibility for health has been criticized by Coward (1989) who argues that it can lead to victim blaming. To be held responsible for one's own health may be a liberating experience for those wishing to escape the passivity of the traditional patient role in biomedicine, but it can also lead to the feeling that you 'created' your own illness (a popular New Age concept) and that therapeutic failures are one's own fault. McClean (2005) studied a spiritual healing clinic in the United Kingdom to explore the extent to which the healers focused on individualistic approaches to health and illness. He found that the healers' focus on the individual was not so much part of victim blaming as a need to redress the depersonalization experienced by the patients of biomedicine. In fact there is a thin line between responsibility and blame, and it could be argued that anyone wanting to regain some sense of control over their own condition runs the risk of being blamed if things go wrong. The difference between the two, in relation to health and health care, is that whatever the causes of illness (and they are likely to be multifactorial involving individual, social, environmental and genetic causes), the notion of 'responsibility' refers to having active engagement in its management. Thus to take responsibility for managing one's own health problem, and to believe that it is possible to influence its prognosis, does not necessarily involve the belief that it was caused entirely by one's own actions. The notion of personal responsibility in CAM does not always distinguish between these two aspects of causation and management.

Another important aspect of this debate is the difference between having sole responsibility for managing one's own health and sharing this responsibility with a practitioner. This is the difference between what has been called the consumer model of patient–practitioner relationships and the mutuality model (Roter and Hall 1992). While the notion of taking responsibility for health may seem like a consumerist model, the ideology of CAM also refers to equal relationships between client and practitioner. The combination of these two aspects of CAM, individual responsibility and equal therapeutic relationships, produces a scenario in which it is claimed that the client feels both empowered and supported.

The characterization of CAM therapies is fluid and wide ranging; what all these aspects have in common is a stated or unstated contrast with bio-medicine. Some biomedical practitioners refute these distinctions and claim to be practising holistically themselves. But whatever the ideologies, it is clear that the content of CAM and biomedical consultations differ in their attention to the patient's lifeworld. From the perspective of the patient/client, the concept of holism opens the door to their lifeworld experiences, which are no longer irrelevant or ignored (see Chapter 7) but central to the consultation. The example at the end of the chapter illustrates the approach taken by the Penny Brohn Centre in the United Kingdom, formerly the Bristol Cancer Help Centre.

Reasons for Use

Some people use CAM therapies to maintain their health and as a preventive strategy and may seek treatment even though they have no current health problems. In this way CAM therapies, including bodywork therapies such as massage and osteopathy, can help people take responsibility for their health. Complementary and alternative medicine may be seen as one aspect of the project of body maintenance for those pursuing healthy lifestyles. Within contemporary culture, the pursuit of health flows over into other aspects of life. Thus eating is not merely a question of enjoyment or the satisfaction of hunger but becomes the site of 'healthy' and 'unhealthy' choices. Walking or cycling are not ends in themselves but are part of a 'healthy' lifestyle. However, similar practices are also found in traditional forms of healing such as traditional Chinese medicine. The pursuit of healthy lifestyles has been commercialized by the producers of gym equipment and sportswear. To consult a CAM practitioner in pursuit of health maintenance is not so very different from working with a sports coach or personal trainer or attending a yoga class. Bakx (1991) also linked the rise of folk medicine to the environmental movement and green culture. Some people equate the pollution by drugs produced by biomedical industry with degradation of the environment by the same industries. Concerns about toxicity of chemicals used in agriculture, manufacturing and energy industries can lead to concern about 'chemically manufactured' drugs. Thus one would expect that those who support the environmental movement or eat organic food would also be those using CAM therapies.

The sociological literature on health and illness has shown that people want to understand the meaning of their illness as much as to be cured. Williams' work on 'narrative reconstruction' in people suffering from rheumatoid arthritis shows the ways in which they seek to explain the onset of their disease (Williams 1984). Their accounts of causation are attempts to find a legitimate and meaningful place for the disease in their lives. Complementary and alternative medicine practitioners offer people resources with which to make sense of illness and other aspects of their life experiences by providing frameworks of explanation and the opportunity to reflect on what has happened to them. Sharma (1992) has argued that CAM therapies may be said to 'work', because they provide meanings and interpretations that are more satisfactory than those provided by biomedicine. People seeking a good therapeutic relationship may value the quality of listening, holistic care and the philosophy of partnership that characterize CAM care. While these characteristics are not exclusive to CAM practitioners, or even exhibited by all of them, they represent an ethos that is widely known. Orthodox practitioners may attribute the appeal of CAM treatment to the longer consultation times, but time alone is no guarantee of a holistic approach or a respectful attitude.

However, not all those using CAM therapies do so for ideological reasons or to experience rewarding therapeutic relationships; in fact, the main reason is to seek help with symptom relief coupled with a belief in the potential effectiveness of CAM (Thomas 2003). For example, only four of Sharma's thirty interviewees had any long-standing interest in alternative lifestyles or politics (Sharma 1992). The group she labelled 'earnest seekers' were people desperately seeking a remedy for one specific problem without having yet settled on one type of therapy or given up altogether. The group of 'eclectic users' tended to use different therapies for different problems. Most people adopt a pragmatic rather than an ideological approach seeking symptomatic relief and using a wide range of options.

More negative reasons for using CAM therapies include dissatisfaction with orthodox care and the search for a satisfactory therapeutic relationship. Dissatisfaction with orthodox care has four elements: poor communication with doctors; a perceived lack of control or choice in conventional care; ineffectiveness of orthodox care; and the perceived dangers and side effects of some orthodox treatments. Criticisms of doctors' communication may be voiced by those with undiagnosed conditions who feel that their problems are not being taken seriously, but also by those who feel that doctors are over reliant on prescription drugs and unwilling to explore other ways of treating disease. Some patients would prefer discussion of self-management including diet and exercise. Given the fact that CAM users tend to be younger and more highly educated, it might be expected that they wish to feel in control of their health care. In a UK study of people attending a variety of complementary practitioners, most of whom had a chronic health problem, Paterson and Britten (1999) identified three main themes: doctors cannot help much; doctors are hopeless; and orthodox medicine may work but it's not acceptable. The latter reason referred to the fear of side effects from prescribed medicines; some respondents' main aim in consulting CAM practitioners was to avoid or reduce steroid-based medication.

As will be described in the next chapter, there is widespread ambivalence about prescribed medicines and concern about side effects, which motivates some people to seek alternative methods of treatment. A study of men with prostate cancer found that some had chosen to use CAM, because they viewed conventional medical treatments as having significant adverse effects including impotence and incontinence (Boon et al. 2003a). People may feel that doctors and orthodox medicine cannot help them much if treatments offered have been of limited benefit. Professionals' use of prescription writing as a way of terminating consultations may have the unintended consequence of motivating some patients to seek other forms of health care. The various motivations for using CAM treatments are summarized in Table 2.1 as push and pull factors. The reasons for seeking help from CAM practitioners may not be the same as the reasons for continuing to do so: Luff and Thomas (2000) found that while the failure of orthodox medicine may be a reason for seeking CAM, a more positive motivation can develop through the experience of treatment.

The Nature of 'Natural' Remedies

A characteristic of some CAM therapies is the use of 'natural' treatments. As with other aspects of CAM, this concept has a range of meanings. For some, natural treatments are those which are not chemical or manufactured. For others, they are of plant origin such as herbs. Natural remedies may be equated with traditional or home remedies, such as lemon and honey for a cough, or they may merely be weak or less toxic substances (than pharmaceuticals). Finally, natural remedies may be substances originating, or needed by, the human body such as insulin. In a Swedish study in which people on long-term medication for asthma, pain or hypertension were asked about natural medicines, several categories of meaning were identified

Table 2.1 Motivations for CAM use

Evidence-based 'pull' factors	*Evidence-based 'push' factors*
• pragmatism; desire for symptom reduction	• pragmatism; perceived lack of effective conventional treatment for a particular problem
• belief in the effectiveness of CAM	• dissatisfaction with conventional medicine
• lifestyle choice; congruence with values and principles of CAM, especially a 'holistic' approach to health (mind, body, and spirit)	○ poor prior experience with conventional medicine
	○ experience of poor communication with doctors in relation to specific health problems
• desire for increased well-being	
• opportunity to take active part in own treatment and care and gain greater control and choice	• concern about unpleasant side-effects of conventional care
• perceived natural and/or non-invasive nature of treatments	
Other possibilities	*Other possibilities*
• search for a satisfactory therapeutic relationship (especially for continuing CAM use)	• flight from science; rejection of science/gullibility and naivety [sic]
• explanations offered by CAM 'makes sense'	• dissatisfaction with medical care in general
• desire for a more person-centred approach to care approach	• high costs of orthodox care (USA)
• accessibility of CAM	• affluence
• affordability of CAM	• being a member of the 'worried well'

Source: Thomas (2003).

(Fallsberg 1991). Natural products were those made from plants but also those whose naturalness was preserved during processing. A natural product had to be processed as little as possible and the genuine substance had to be kept as intact as possible. Another category of natural product was substances either originating in or needed by the human body. They could also be defined as intrinsically weak, so that because of their low concentration they were either non-toxic or less toxic than drugs. The main properties attributed to natural remedies are first that they are safe and second that they are gentle. This characterization of plants as inherently safe overlooks the fact that many well known poisons, such as mushrooms, are plants. It is easier to understand the attributed properties of natural remedies as part of a belief system in which mass production of chemicals is abhorred, and science is seen as producing problems as well as solving them (Beck 1992).

A study of people using natural drugs in Israel found that a third of the sample had used some form of complementary medicine in the last year, and that nearly a half had used conventional and natural drugs concurrently (Giveon et al. 2004). Although the value of this study is limited by the absence of a definition of natural drugs, the authors found that the majority of patients thought that natural drugs did not cause side effects, and that most users of CAM therapies never, or only rarely, reported CAM use to their physicians. Those who did think that natural drugs cause side effects were more likely to report their use of these drugs to their doctors. The authors speculate about patients' 'failure' to report the use of natural drugs without considering the possible reactions of physicians to such disclosures. Given that the article begins with a list of health risks caused by natural drugs, one can imagine that doctors might not accept such disclosures from their own patients. The common perception that natural medicines are safe, and the unfavourable comparison with pharmaceuticals made by many users, suggests that this discourse tells us as much about the perception of pharmaceuticals as about CAM.

The Critique of Biomedicine

It is thus possible to take different aspects of CAM and examine their implications for attitudes to biomedicine generally and prescribed medicines specifically. At the level of ideology, the concept of holism and its openness to lifeworld concerns signals a different kind of patient–professional encounter. As we have seen, the notion of individual responsibility allows clients to take control of the management of their own conditions and to adopt an active role, which is very different from that of the passive and compliant 'patient'. The appeal to self-healing and the notion of working with rather than against the person's symptoms both leave the client (or their own physiological processes) in the driving seat. The commitment to more equal relationships also provides a sharp contrast with most doctor–patient relationships, which are still a long way from demonstrating 'shared decision making' (Charles et al. 1997). There are, however, aspects of CAM therapies that it seems most of their clients do not sign up to, for example, the theoretical framework of acupuncture. Frank and Stollberg's German study of the patients of medical acupuncturists found that patients had little curiosity about the details of acupuncture or Chinese medicine (Frank and Stollberg 2004). They did not conceptualize Chinese medicine as a holistic or spiritual mode of medicine but incorporated acupuncture into their own mechanistic models. Part of the reason for these findings might lie in the fact that the acupuncturists were medically qualified, and those people with a more holistic view of Chinese medicine might have chosen to consult lay practitioners instead. However, Cassidy (1998) also found that people using acupuncture in the United States did not refer to the Chinese concept of Chi when reflecting on their experiences. When writing about those aspects of care that they valued, respondents mentioned symptom relief, warm patient–practitioner relationships, attention to their whole selves, but only rarely used Chinese medicine cue words (such as meridian, yin and yang). Cassidy concluded that these American users of Chinese medicine were choosing practitioners offering a culturally familiar theory of holism rather than selecting acupuncture because it was exotic or foreign. Paterson and Britten's longitudinal study of users of acupuncture in the United Kingdom found that nearly half the respondents used Chinese medicine terms, but they usually qualified this by saying that they did not fully understand them (Paterson and Britten 2004). Sharma (1992) concluded that CAM users were not an eccentric group of people with idiosyncratic criteria for assessing bio-medical care, but rather that they were voicing fairly general discontents.

In relation to the treatments offered by biomedicine, the emphasis on 'natural' treatments suggests that modern pharmaceuticals are not per-ceived (by at least some users of CAM) as either natural or safe (see Chapter 3). The emphasis on the perceived safety of natural medicines probably says more about the perceived dangers of pharmaceuticals than about any literal belief in the safety of the entire plant kingdom. In par-ticular, some users of CAM are fleeing the side effects of pharmaceuticals. Criticisms of pharmaceuticals also include the idea that it is dangerous or unhelpful to mask the symptoms of disease. Some people criticize modern pharmaceuticals on the grounds that they are not individualized but reflect a 'one size fits all' mentality. Indeed, it is only since the latter part of the twentieth century that prescribed treatments have been targeted at specific diseases and diagnoses rather than individual patients. As we will see in Chapter 6, the challenge for the prescriber is to apply the findings of population-based studies to the individual patients in front of them; this gap between generalized scientific findings and clinical practice is precisely the gap that such criticisms identify.

While people using CAM therapies may be motivated by dissatisfaction with biomedicine, they themselves are criticized by some members of the medical profession (Baum 2004).The argument is particularly heated in relation to cancer, a disease which itself produces strong emotions, although the data suggests that the proportion of people with cancer who use CAM is no greater than the proportion in the general population (Boon et al. 2000, 2003b). Verhoef et al.'s systematic review of the reasons for using CAM by adult cancer patients found that the most often stated reason given by over a third of users was perceived beneficial response (Verhoef et al. 2005). Other reasons included wanting control, a strong belief in CAM, CAM as a last resort, finding hope, and disappointment with conventional treatment. This last reason was, however, only mentioned in two studies which comprised less than 5 per cent of the total. Some of the CAM treatments used by people with cancer are onerous and expensive in their requirements such as the Gerson diet, which is based on regular consumption of freshly juiced fruit and vegetables as well as frequent coffee enemas. Baum in particular has deplored the use of CAM therapies when they are used by people who have rejected orthodox treatments (Baum 2004). Beyerstein (2005) has characterized those using CAM therapies as generally ignorant and gullible, suffering from scientific illiteracy, anti-intellectualism and self-serving biases. Verhoef, on the other hand, characterizes CAM use for cancer as an intelligent response (Verhoef et al. 2005). In the final analysis, it is a question of choosing the manner of one's life and death, and those who prefer to use therapies they experience as empowering and respectful while avoiding the often debilitating effects of chemotherapy and radiotherapy are exerting their own right to self-determination.

Lay Assessment of CAM Therapies

We can learn much about the ways in which CAM therapies do or do not help people by asking them what effects they experience. In the already mentioned US study of people using acupuncture, Cassidy (1998) identified three main kinds of effects. These were first the alleviation of symptoms, including physical and emotional pain, or a decrease in their frequency, intensity or duration. She also identified what she called two kinds of 'expanded effects of care' to refer to holistic effects of acupuncture. She found that people reported physiological improvements such as increases in energy as well as reduced reliance on prescription drugs and the minimization of the side effects of drugs. In relation to the latter, she gave examples of people suffering from asthma, epilepsy and Crohn's disease who were all able to reduce or eliminate altogether their use of prescription medicines with concomitant financial savings. Lastly, Cassidy found that acupuncture improved psychosocial coping and adaptive ability, such as increases in self-awareness and self-efficacy, feeling more balanced and centred, or even life changing experiences. These findings support the notion that people experience CAM as enhancing their own sense of control over their lives rather than feeling blamed for their illnesses. Her findings do not, of course, imply that this is always the case. They emphasize the individualistic aspect of users' experiences and say little about their social contexts or responsibilities.

In a British study, Paterson (2002) also examined the effects of acupuncture using a longitudinal research design in which she interviewed people three times over a period of six months. Like Cassidy, she found two main kinds of effects: symptomatic effects and more holistic 'whole person' effects. The symptomatic changes included changes in the presenting problem as well as changes in other health problems. The whole person effects included a sense of relaxation, changes in energy and strength, as well as changes in self-awareness, self-acceptance, self-confidence, self-responsibility and self-help. As a result of increased energy and self-confidence, some people developed self-help strategies such as changes to their diets, which they discussed with their acupuncturists. As Cassidy also found, some of Paterson's respondents were enabled to reduce or stop their prescribed medication either because this was why they had chosen acupuncture in the first place or because their symptoms improved or they felt more self-confident.

These whole person effects may be seen as pertaining to the lifeworld as they refer to individuals' abilities to manage their lives. To the extent that people can talk about their 'whole selves' in CAM consultations, it means that the lifeworld is allowed in. To refer to this as 'holism' suggests that the barrier between system and lifeworld, evident in many medical consultations, has been lifted. If the system and lifeworld are to be joined in individual consultations, perhaps this is sufficient, in the context of equal relationships and mutual respect.

Conclusion

Some, but by no means all, of those people using CAM remedies are also using prescribed medicines; in this sense they are themselves 'integrating' CAM and orthodox treatments. When this happens, the evidence suggests that patients may not inform their biomedical practitioners about their use of CAM therapies. Sharma (1992) noted that the contradiction between being a 'consumer' of CAM therapies and a 'user' of the National Health Service (NHS) could be avoided if people did not tell doctors about their use of CAM. Writers such as Giveon et al. (2004) have identified the potential risks of using natural and prescribed medicines together including the replacement of prescription medicines; compromising the efficacy of prescription medicines; masking or precluding correct diagnoses; interactions between natural and prescription medicines; causing adverse effects or serious illness; and the dangers of contaminated products. While these dangers may be overstated, or may not be dangers at all (if, for example, a medicine with debilitating side effects is replaced by acupuncture), they represent the main biomedical rationale for greater professional awareness of patients' self-medication.

The discourse about safety illustrates the gulf between advocates and critics of CAM therapies. Each side of this debate focuses on the other's safety problems. Individuals consulting CAM therapists are sometimes motivated by the wish to avoid the side effects of prescription medicines; critics point to the potential dangers of CAM or of rejecting biomedicine in favour of CAM. Complementary and alternative medicine therapies may produce side effects, but these tend to be neither serious nor common (MacPherson et al. 2001, White et al. 2001). In contrast, adverse drug reactions (ADRs) are a major cause of hospital admissions and a leading cause of death (Pirmohamed et al. 2004). While there is less evidence available about the safety of many CAM therapies, making direct comparisons difficult, it is unlikely that they are responsible for the magnitude of harm attributable to prescription medicines. For individual clients and patients caught up in this argument, it is probably more important that all professionals attend to the 'mote in their own eye' than criticize the others. As we shall see in Chapters 5 and 7, biomedical professionals tend to emphasize the benefits rather than the harms of pharmaceutical medicines; this fails to attend to patients' lifeworld concerns about safety.

The two sectors of health care discussed in this chapter, the popular and the informal, are part of the lifeworld rather than the system. In particular, CAM is not part of the dominant health care system in the industrialized countries. Some people advocate the integration of CAM and dominant systems of health care to make it more accessible to those who cannot afford private medicine; there is, however, some evidence that CAM therapies provided within the National Health Service change character when they become part of the system (Paterson 2007). In Chapter 3, we will examine Kleinman's third sector, the formal sector of health care. We will look at the ways in which people use the medicines prescribed for them, and the nature of their lifeworld concerns, already touched on in this chapter. Prescribed treatments, although obtained via the formal health care system, are used – or not used – in the lifeworld.

Box 2.1   Example: Penny Brohn Centre, formerly the Bristol Cancer Help Centre

What is the Bristol Approach?

The Bristol Approach, developed by doctors, nurses, therapists and people with cancer, is a unique combination of complementary therapies and self-help techniques. It is designed to work alongside medical treatment and is supported by leading oncologists and others in the health care field.

The Bristol Approach:

- is a programme of lifestyle advice, information, complementary therapies and self-help techniques
- provides support through your treatment and recovery
- supports positive health, physical and psychological wellbeing

Through the courses at Penny Brohn Cancer Care we can help you:

- Cope with the emotional aspects of a cancer diagnosis
- Manage fear and anxiety
- Deal with the specific problems and challenges a cancer diagnosis brings
- Manage and reduce symptoms and treatment side effects
- Improve your health and energy

With all of this support we have seen that it is possible to change the way you live with cancer. Individual elements of the Bristol Approach are shown below:

Specialist support:

- Psychotherapy/counselling
- Doctor sessions
- Nutritional advice
- Group work

Self-help techniques:

- Relaxation
- Meditation
- Imagery
- Breathwork
- Natural pain management
- Gentle exercise

Complementary therapies:

- Massage
- Shiatsu
- Healing
- Music therapy
- Art therapy

Source: http://www.pennybrohncancercare.org,
accessed 1 May 2007.

3

Medicines in the Lifeworld

Introduction

In this chapter I consider the ways in which prescribed medicines, obtained from the formal health care sector, are perceived and used in the lifeworld. Most medicines are taken in people's homes, places of work, or leisure settings; the exceptions are mostly people in hospital or other forms of residential care who take medicines in institutional settings. As van der Geest and colleagues (1996) have noted, people use medicines in a different epistemological framework from the one in which medicines are licensed and produced. Cohen et al. (2001) have also pointed out that various legitimate rationalities motivate medication use, which we need to explore if we want to understand the place of medicines in society. In subsequent chapters I will explore system rationalities, but in this chapter I focus on the lifeworld. Sociological, psychological and anthropological studies have explored how people think about prescribed medicines, and how they use them. These studies are mostly qualitative, and are based on interviews exploring people's accounts, and include some observational studies.

Lifeworld Metaphors and Meanings

As we saw in Chapter 1, the use of medicines goes back to antiquity and reflects a deep-seated urge to 'take something' in response to troubling symptoms or distress. Over the course of several millennia, medicines and medicine use have acquired a range of symbolic and cultural meanings. The diversity of these meanings still reflects the ancient Greek word *pharmakon*, which denoted cure, poison and magical charm. Montagne (1988) has argued that although modern medicine is portrayed as scientific and rational, the metaphors of 'magic, mysticism and life envelop the drugs

45

that health professionals use'. These metaphors are widely used in all sorts of contexts. Ehrlich, who pioneered the use of chemical therapies at the beginning of the twentieth century, coined the term 'magic bullet' to refer to the ways in which these new substances targeted specific organisms in the body. The magical promise of this metaphor still lingers on in terms such as 'miracle drug', 'magic cure' and 'wonder drug'. Metaphors reflecting the curative aspects of medicines include 'remedy', 'tonic' and 'food' (and in some languages, the word to consume drugs is the same as the word to eat food). The harmful aspects of medicines are reflected in metaphors such as 'poison', 'death' and 'devil'. The common use of such metaphors influences the social contexts in which medicines are used and provide access to shared meanings for individual users. Van der Geest and Whyte (1989) argue that in both metaphoric and metonymic senses, medicines serve to make illness tangible and, therefore, open to intervention. Even when they are used in domestic and lifeworld contexts, medicines retain metonymic associations with doctors and the institutions within which they work; in this way the prescription comes to represent the doctor.

The symbolic aspects of prescription medicines are well recognized. Smith (1980) distinguished between the manifest and latent functions of the prescription. He identified seven manifest functions which included the following: means of communication; legal document; record source; method of therapy; and means of medical control of therapy. He identified 27 latent functions such as a visible sign of the physician's power to heal, symbol of the power of modern technology, sign that the patient is 'really' ill, legitimation of long-term illness without cure, concrete expression that physician has fulfilled his/her contract, and reasonable excuse for human contact with physician. The one that patients may be most familiar with is 'satisfactorily terminates the visit', although Smith may have been mistaken in his presumption that such a method of termination was satisfactory. More broadly, the concept of the 'total drug effect' refers to factors beyond the pharmacological properties which may be responsible for its effect. These factors include physical attributes of the drug such as its colour, shape and branding; attributes of the prescriber such as their enthusiasm for the treatment and their authority; attributes of the recipient such as their psychological state and personality; and attributes of the setting, such as hospital or domestic environment (Helman 1990). The recognition that not all the effects of pharmaceuticals are due to their pharmacological properties and that pharmacologically inert substances may also have beneficial (and deleterious) effects is linked to the idea of the 'placebo effect'. Beecher (1955) claimed to show a placebo effect of roughly 30 per cent; his work was influential for many years but is now discredited (Evans 2003). In particular, few studies showed that people receiving placebos had better outcomes than those receiving nothing, as 'no treatment' groups were rarely included.

Moerman and Jonas (2002) have argued that it is more accurate to refer to 'meaning responses' than 'placebo effects'. They define a meaning response as the physiological or psychological effects of meaning in the origins or treatment of illness; meaning responses elicited after the use of inert or sham treatment can be called the 'placebo effect' if desirable and the 'nocebo effect' if undesirable. They eschew the phrase 'non-specific' effects on the grounds that many elements of the meaning response or placebo effect are often quite specific in principle after they are understood. Even though the meaning response is not an acknowledged part of evidence-based practice, and may even be regarded as a nuisance factor when evaluating the efficacy of medicines, it remains a potent force in the lifeworld.

In most industrialized countries, prescribed medicines can only be obtained from licensed health professionals, usually doctors, nurses and pharmacists. These professional groups thus control access to medicines, determining the types of medicine, the doses and the quantities in which they are supplied. Thus, from the lay person's point of view, medicines and health professionals are intimately connected. The use of the same word 'medicine' to denote both the medical profession and the treatment underlines the historically close relationship between doctors and pre- scribing. Health professionals' knowledge of therapeutics is gained through many years of training and experience, which may make it diffi- cult for them to appreciate that patients might have their own experien- tial knowledge and a different belief system. While lay knowledge may well be informed by professional knowledge, the two are by no means synonymous. Even the terminology can lead to misunderstandings. For example, it is clear that lay understanding of the terms 'addiction' and 'dependence' extend beyond the pharmacological meanings of these terms. Lay people express fears about becoming addicted to antibiotics, drugs for epilepsy, hypertension and rheumatism as well as tranquillisers and other psychotropic medicines. For some people, the terms 'medicine' and 'drug' are interchangeable, while for others the word 'drug' has only negative connotations. This suggests that in any discussion about medi- cines, apparently obvious terms may need to be clarified.

The early promise of the 'magic bullet' and the discovery of drugs with seemingly near-magical properties, such as the sulpha drugs and antibi- otics, led to correspondingly unrealistic expectations of what medicines could achieve. Since then, the overprescribing of antibiotics has led to a situation in which effectiveness is compromised by widening range of resistant organisms. For individual patients diagnosed with chronic dis- eases requiring lifelong treatment, the promise of the magic bullet has been broken. If the magic bullet really worked then the cure would be instant and long lasting, like a magic spell. To be prescribed a lifetime of medicine taking is to know that the treatment is not a cure. Long-term medicine use therefore implies a problematic relationship with efficacy.

People with acute problems, such as respiratory infections, may still hope for a magic cure which will put an end to their symptoms (even if such hopes are not consistent with scientific explanations). Those with chronic problems know that their existing treatments are no such thing, and their only hope of a cure remains in the discovery of new drugs. These hopes underlie the campaigns for access to new drugs. In the meantime, patients have to learn to manage their condition and its treatment and develop their own expertise in the process. People living with chronic illnesses are the main consumers of prescription drugs.

Sociological analyses of chronic illness are concerned with the social role of the sick person, the meanings of illness and people's coping strategies of which treatment is just one part. Barbara Paterson (2001) described a 'shifting perspectives' model of chronic illness on the basis of a meta synthesis of nearly 300 qualitative research studies. In this model, living with chronic illness is described as a continually shifting process, moving between illness-in-the-foreground and wellness-in-the-foreground. The former perspective is characterized by a focus on the sickness, suffering, loss and burden associated with living with a chronic illness; the latter includes an appraisal of the chronic illness as an opportunity for meaningful change in one's relationships with others. The major factor in shifting from wellness to illness-in-the-foreground is the perception of a threat to control. In relation to treatment, the paradox of living with wellness-in-the-foreground is that, although the illness is distant, its management must be foremost. The illness requires attention even if the person does not want to pay attention to it. In a Scottish study of middle-aged people living with four or more chronic illnesses, Townsend et al. (2003) found that the experience of multiple morbidity was characterized by fluctuating symptoms, fear, uncertainty and lack of control. Their medication management required constant self-assessment and monitoring.

Particular illnesses are associated with particular meanings, which affect the self-image of those who suffer from them as well as the reactions of those around them. Charmaz (1983) showed how people with physical disabilities experienced a 'loss of self' as their former self-images were damaged. While physical disabilities may be visible to strangers, whose reactions may aggravate the sense of loss, many diseases are not immediately obvious. Someone taking a medicine is, however, labelled as having a medical problem if other people notice and realize what the medication is for. Thus medicine taking can contribute to the assault on an individual's public identity.

The use of medications can also contribute to the ways in which the individual understands their illness. Nichter and Vuckovic (1994) have shown that explanatory models for illness are often framed in terms of the strength, type and quantity of medications taken. A person who accepts a medication shows, by doing so, both to themselves and to others that they accept the illness for which it is prescribed. Conversely, if a diagnosis is not accepted, the treatment is unlikely to be taken. Adams et al. (1997) showed how people who had been prescribed medications for asthma, but who did not accept the diagnosis, used the medications in a very different way from those who accepted the diagnosis. Those who denied the diagnosis had very negative images of what 'asthmatics' were like; they did not take the pre-scribed prophylactic medication but instead overused their reliever medica-tions. Those who accepted the diagnosis of asthma had redefined the social identity and thus the meaning of being asthmatic, and expressed almost evangelical opinions about the importance of controlling their symptoms. They used both prophylactic and reliever medication. Thus the accepters found medication to be an aid to normalization, while for the deniers it was an obstacle to normalization. A third group, referred to by the authors as pragmatists, were struggling to come to terms with the social identity of being 'asthmatic' and used medication in idiosyncratic ways. A diagnosis is a label, and a medication is a tangible sign of that diagnosis. Thus for those prescribed certain neuroleptic medications, the involuntary limb move-ments produced by the drugs betray the fact that they are psychiatric patients (Rogers et al. 1998). Those prescribed antidepressant medication may find that because this signals their inability to cope, it undermines their personal autonomy (Grime and Pollock 2003).

Montagne (1996) has identified the assumptions on which sociological theories of medicine use in the lifeworld are based. Medicine users must observe changes in their mental or physical states, as without this there cannot be any exploration of how medicines are perceived (except to note that in this case they would probably be seen as not doing any-thing). The changes must also be attributed to the medicine, because if not, they will not contribute to that person's understanding of what the medicine does. In fact, lay people as well as professionals can have diffi-culty in knowing whether to attribute a particular effect to a medicine, to the underlying condition(s) or to something else altogether. Pinder (1988), in her study of people with Parkinson's Disease, found that, as the disease progressed, they had increasing difficulty in distinguishing between the symptoms of the disease and the effects of the drugs. While the drugs could mask some of the illness symptoms some of the time, they could also produce other symptoms and various forms of fluctua-tion. Some symptoms were both illness- and drug-related and were increasingly difficult to disentangle.

Lay Perspectives on Medicines

Studies of lay beliefs about medicines have shown that people have a range of positive and negative views that recur across different populations, disease groups and countries. When interviewed, people have less to say about their positive views, perhaps because these represent a taken-for-granted perspective about the necessity, effectiveness and safety of prescribed medicines. Views which are taken for granted do not normally require explanation or justification, being 'obvious'. In a questionnaire study conducted in south London, the majority of respondents agreed that modern medicines have improved people's health (69 per cent) and that medicines help recovery from illness (74 per cent; Britten et al. 2002). For many people, taking medicines is not problematic if they trust the clinician and are willing to do as he or she recommends.

There is, however, a range of commonly expressed negative attitudes about prescribed medicines. Some of these represent non-specific dislike of medicines and medicine taking expressed by people both with and without chronic conditions requiring long-term medication. Clearly, for some people, dislike of medicine taking is closely bound up with a dislike of being ill. Over 86 per cent of respondents in the same south London study agreed with the statement 'I prefer not to take any medicine if I can avoid it' (Britten et al. 2002). This general aversion to medicines is a common finding. For example, one study found that more than four-fifths of a sample of people attending a rheumatology clinic spontaneously expressed dislike at having to take drugs at all (Donovan and Blake 1992). Townsend et al.'s study of multiple morbidity in mid-life found that their respondents showed an aversion to taking drugs, although they acknowledged the necessity of doing so (Townsend et al. 2003). Most of the respondents in Britten et al.'s study of patients consulting in general practice expressed aversion to taking medicines (Britten et al. 2004). Fears about dependency and addiction are widespread and cannot be assessed easily. These fears refer to addiction and psychological dependency as well as concerns about tolerance. People may take 'drug holidays' (during which time they stop taking prescribed medicines) if they are worried that their medicines will cease to be effective if taken over a long period of time. Such concerns are not necessarily related to the known pharmacological properties of the medicines concerned and point to the need for communication and accurate information to inform people's decision-making processes. Other concerns which affect medicine taking include the fear that symptoms may be masked in the process.

A more specific theme is the view that manufactured medicines are unnatural. This perceived 'unnaturalness' has been expressed in relation to oral contraception, benzodiazepines, childhood vaccinations, antidepressants, antihypertensive medication and many other medicines. This concept of unnaturalness is closely linked to that of harm, and as we saw in Chapter 2, substances perceived as natural are often also perceived as safe. Unnatural chemicals may also be contrasted with natural experiences such as the menopause contributing to some women's preference not to take hormone replacement therapy. However, the distinction between natural and unnatural medicines is not clear cut, as some people recognize that natural medicines may also be manufactured, and they are not always regarded as safe.

These positive and negative views are often expressed by the same people. Horne and Weinman (1999) developed the Beliefs about Medicines Questionnaire to assess the prevalence of patients' beliefs about the necessity of prescribed medication for controlling their illnesses and their concerns about the potential adverse consequences of taking it. Their research provides an insight into the balance between positive and negative beliefs for groups of people living with asthma, kidney and heart problems, and cancer, recruited from hospital clinics in the United Kingdom. The majority of the sample (89 per cent) had strong beliefs in the necessity of their medication while over a third (36 per cent) reported strong concerns about potential adverse effects. The authors calculated the differences between individuals' necessity and concerns scores, which they called the necessity-concerns differential; they described it as the result of a cost-benefit analysis for each patient. Compared with oncology and dialysis patients, those with asthma and cardiac problems were significantly more likely to perceive that the costs of their medication outweighed the benefits.

Thus people living with chronic illness have many challenges in relation to prescribed medication. Most of them have to live with the fact that there is no cure: a life sentence of medicine taking makes this plain. Taking medicines labels them as sick, potentially undermining their efforts to keep wellness in the foreground. People express a range of views about medicines in general, as well as specific medicines, so that ambivalence is widespread. Like professionals, lay people often have difficulty in distinguishing symptoms from the effects of medicines.

Lay Testing of Medicines

Clearly, if people have such ambivalent ideas about medicines, the question arises: how does this affect their medicine taking? It is well established that up to a half of prescribed medication is not taken as directed; this finding applies to most disease areas, population groups and geographical locations (Vermeire et al. 2001). Qualitative research helps us understand how their attitudes to medicines inform the ways in which people actually test and use their medicines. I will first explore the testing of medicines.

A recent synthesis of ten years of qualitative literature about lay perspectives on medicines found considerable evidence about the ways in which patients test their medicines, although few studies set out to address it explicitly (Pound et al. 2005). The studies included in the synthesis were concerned with drugs for a range of conditions including HIV/AIDS, hypertension, diabetes, digestive disorders, rheumatoid arthritis, mental illness and asthma. A range of different approaches to testing medicines was noted; for many people this centred on the lay evaluation of side effects.

People have concerns about the side effects of medications taken for many different types of illness including rheumatoid arthritis, cancer, asthma, digestive disorders, high blood pressure and schizophrenia. As Etkin (1992) has pointed out, the interpretation of signs and symptoms is deeply embedded in cultural meanings, and patients and healers in the same society do not necessarily agree about what are primary and secondary effects of particular therapies. She shows that classifying therapeutic outcomes 'into "primary action" and "side effect" implies an intuitive and universal logic that simply does not obtain, even in biomedicine' (Etkin 1992, p. 102). Thus a drug may be marketed for one indication at one point in time and for another indication (and effect) at another. The drug thalidomide is one example of having been originally licensed as a sleeping pill, banned in the 1960s due to its teratological effects, and relicensed over 40 years later as a treatment for leprosy. Patients, like professionals, may have difficulty in deciding whether to attribute a particular symptom to their illness or to the drug. In Pound's review, people with HIV taking antiretroviral therapy reported a wide range of adverse effects, including rashes, dizziness and neuropathy, to the extent that they instilled fear and distrust of the medicine (Pound et al. 2005).

A key aspect of the lay evaluation of medicines is their impact on people's daily lives. Adverse effects make a significant impact on the lifeworlds of those taking them; social activities, friendships, relationships, work and family life may all be affected. Similarly, people with schizophrenia experience a wide range of side effects including feeling like a 'zombie', tiredness, weight gain and blurred vision (Rogers et al. 1998). For some, the most significant aspect of these side effects is their impact on everyday social interaction such as the ability to sustain an ordinary conversation or hold down a job. Thus, people taking antiretroviral medications may have to alter their eating and sleeping habits to fit in with the demands of the drug regimen to the extent that drug taking could become 'the central organizing principle' (Stone et al. 1998, p. 589). These experiences may be gendered: as McDonald et al. (2000) found, men fitted their social worlds around their drug regimens while for women the social world took priority. Women's concerns about their drug regimens focused on the impact on their relationships while men were concerned about the impact on themselves. Women who are carers may find rigid drug regimens particularly hard to follow (Johnston et al. 2000). Thus for some people, medicine taking creates particular problems in relation to their lifeworld responsibilities and roles. These concerns mean that many people weigh up the benefits and costs of medication taking and, depending on their own particular situations, reach different conclusions. For some people, the side effects of the medicines and the damage to their social lives are such that they are not prepared to continue taking the medicines (Siegel and Gorey 1997). In other contexts, people may decide to continue taking their medication after weighing up the unwelcome side effects against the reasons for taking the medication. Benson and Britten (2003), in a study of people receiving repeat prescriptions for antihypertensive medication, found that interviewees balanced their reservations (for example, preferences for an alternative to drugs) against reasons for taking medication (such as feeling better or gaining peace of mind) in ways that made sense for them personally (see example at the end of the chapter).

One clear method for evaluating a medication is to stop taking it and see what happens as a pragmatic assessment of people's own theories about how a medicine works. Siegel et al. (1999) found that if people taking antiretroviral treatments felt worse as a result, then they were more likely to resume their medication. If they felt no different or even better after quitting their medication, they had less incentive to resume (Dowell and Hudson 1997). People using this method may stop taking their medicine without giving it enough time to work, but may not realize this (Donovan and Blake 1992).

Other methods of evaluation included obtaining information from others or observing other people using the same medication. This method of evaluation is likely to increase as more people use the Internet to communicate with others in their own situation (Saukko in press. While people may rely on monitoring by health professionals to help them decide if the medication is working, as in the case of hypertension, these so-called objective measurements may not convince everyone. For those on antiretroviral therapies, if the results of objective measurements conflicted with their own subjective assessments, the latter might be more powerful influences (Pound et al. 2005).

One of the difficulties that people experience when testing their medicines is in knowing which effects are due to the medicine and which are due to the disease. If symptoms of the disease are attributed to the treatment, then people may quit their medicines as a result. There is clearly an important role here for health professionals in helping patients assess which effects are due to which causes; this requires, of course, that the whole question of effects and side effects is discussed openly. In one study, doctors substituted patients' usual brand of Proton Pump Inhibitor for a cheaper brand and reduced the dose at the same time. This made it very difficult for patients to test the efficacy of the new drug as they had not been told about the reduced dose (Pollock and Grime 2000). If patients are not given adequate information about their medicines, it is very difficult for them to assess them appropriately and they may make poor decisions as a result (see Chapter 5). Some concerns are not amenable to testing. A particular worry, for those prescribed a variety of medicines, is that about dependency. Grime and Pollock (2003) found that people prescribed with antidepressants were concerned about psychological as much as physical dependency. In their longitudinal UK study of people recently diagnosed with mild to moderate depression, they found that doctors made a point of reassuring patients that antidepressants were not addictive. These reassurances did not address patients' concerns about psychological dependence. Some people felt that taking regular medication affected their identities: 'I just feel that it is not really you, is it, if you have to get through each day by taking pills really' (Grime and Pollock 2003, p. 518).

Thus the ways in which people evaluate the medicines they are prescribed reflect their lifeworld concerns. The taking of medications may require people to alter their daily routines, potentially impacting on their family and work responsibilities. Friends, family, social activities and work may all be affected by medication regimens. These lifeworld criteria are very different from the outcomes used in most clinical trials, which are developed within the rationality of evidence-based practice and aim to answer narrowly based questions about efficacy and effectiveness. Compared to the criteria used in the lifeworld, these system-based outcome measures are addressing only part of the question.

Ways People Take Medicines

People take different approaches to their medicines and, when interviewed, offer different types of account. Pound et al. (2005) produced a model of medicine taking which distinguished four groups of medicine takers: passive accepters, active accepters, active modifiers and rejecters (see Box 3.1). These groups are not necessarily static, as people may take different approaches to medicines in different contexts and at different times. People who have accepted medicine taking without necessarily giving it a great deal of thought may be characterized as passive accepters. They may well have relinquished control of their illness to their doctors, and when asked, may say that they trust their doctors and will do whatever their doctors recommend. The lack of reflection associated with passive acceptance means that, when interviewed, they may not have very much to say. Their stories may illustrate occasions when their normal taken-for-granted routine is disrupted. By contrast, active accepters are people who have thought about taking their medicines, and may have tested them, and who take them as prescribed. Some

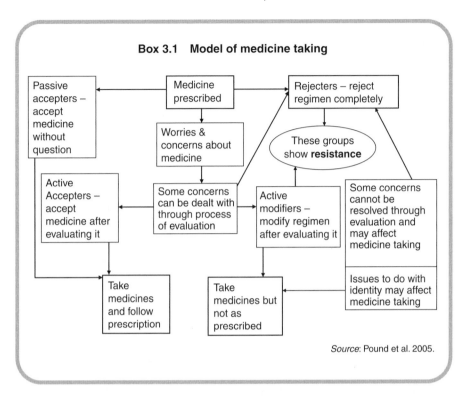

Box 3.1   Model of medicine taking

Source: Pound et al. 2005.

writers refer to this group as showing *purposeful adherence* (Johnson et al. 1999). They may have concerns and worries, or they may not, but in either case they have made a conscious decision to pursue the prescribed regimen. Other people may reject their medicines, either after a period of testing, or not. These rejecters or sceptics may prefer to remain in control by using alternative therapies or by tolerating their symptoms. This group is likely to include people who are critical of both modern medicine and doctors, and who describe pharmaceuticals as damaging and unnatural. They may be more likely to use complementary and alternative medicine (CAM) therapies.

Most research has focused on those who modify their regimens, as those who accept their medication are not considered to be a problem, and those who have rejected their medicines may also reject the invitation to participate in research. Very little longitudinal research has been carried out on this topic, so we do not know the extent to which people's views and behaviours change with time. Grime and Pollock (2003) conducted follow-up interviews with people who were prescribed antidepressants and found that their attitudes were modified by their experiences with the drugs. Some of those who had been initially reluctant found the medication effective, while others who had been optimistic initially were put off by unpleasant side effects. It seems very likely that views about medicines are context specific, and that someone who has rejected the treatment of a minor complaint may then accept treatment for a life threatening condition. However, anti-drug attitudes can remain powerful even in extreme circumstances (see Box 3.2).

Studies of people taking medicines for a range of conditions including rheumatoid arthritis, hypertension, HIV, epilepsy and asthma have shown that self-regulation (in which people make their own decisions about how to take medicines) is common. This may result from a process of testing and balancing costs and benefits of taking medicines. Such modification may also give people a sense of being in control of their disease and its treatment rather than being controlled. People use a variety of ways of modifying their regimen. A common strategy is to minimize medicine intake, and indeed the stronger the drug, the greater the desire to reduce the dose. In a study of middle-aged people diagnosed with four or more chronic illnesses, Townsend et al. (2003) found that respondents adopted a 'minimax' strategy: minimal (thus 'responsible') use of drugs and maximum use of other strategies, such as going to bed or avoiding certain activities, to restrict the amount of medication used. People even try to minimize their consumption of drugs such as proton pump inhibitors and benzodiazepines which professionals think are overused. Other strategies, which also have the effect of reducing consumption, include using medicines symptomatically rather than regularly. Even in conditions such as hypertension, regarded as an asymptomatic condition, some people will take their medicines when they feel the need to and not otherwise. The same has been found for rheumatoid arthritis and bipolar disorder. People also modify their medication regimens in relation to their social activities,

---

Box 3.2   Reluctant pill use

I am a reluctant pill-user, but I am beginning to be more reasonable about it. Pain-killers, I am always astonished to learn, do work. Pain is neither ennobling nor necessary. I can do without it, so I no longer fight what I used to think was a siren song of pills. I even get up at night, out of my warm but hostile bed, to take a pill because I'm finally persuaded it will take away the pain and let me sleep.

(From the diary of Regina Reibstein who was dying of breast cancer, cited in *Staying Alive: A Family Memoir* by Janet Reibstein, Bloomsbury 2002, p. 171).

particularly alcohol consumption. Fears about potential interactions between prescribed medicines and alcohol can lead people to leave off their medicines when partying. This may account for the observation that drug holidays occur more often at weekends. Those taking proton pump inhibitors may adjust their medication as necessary on the basis of what they have eaten or are about to eat. Another strategy of self-regulation is informed by the desire to decrease adverse effects. People may reduce or skip doses in order to reduce adverse effects, sometimes waiting until these effects have passed before starting to take their medicines again. Those on multiple medication may decide to take medicines separately to stop them interacting with each other. Those concerned about the build up of toxicity in their bodies may take drug holidays in order to 'cleanse their systems'. Drug holidays can consist of a short or long period of abstinence, or they can take the form of a regular drug free day once a week. People may also modify their medication to fit in with their daily lives including work and family life. All these methods of self-experimentation are liable to come under the professional rubric of 'non adherence'.

Managing Everyday Life

For many people having to cope with chronic disease, the ability to live a normal life and meet their social obligations is more important than symptom control. In other words, lifeworld considerations often come first. Pinder (1988) found that the main priority for people with Parkinson's Disease was normalizing family relationships. She noted that her respondents struggled to regain the taken-for-granted use of their bodies that other people enjoyed. Arluke (1980) noted that people with rheumatoid arthritis judged the efficacy of their drugs in terms of enabling them to live normal lives. Prescribed medicines may help people to meet their various obligations but at the same time serve as evidence of an inability to perform such roles. The demands of family life and paid employment are the highest priority for many people, and medicine use may be tailored around these competing demands. Studies of the use of tranquillizers have shown how these medicines help women to maintain their roles as wives, mothers, homemakers and employees (Cooperstock and Lennard 1979). For those unable to change their work situation, taking tranquillizers could be the only way of alleviating sometimes incapacitating symptoms and allowing them to hold on to their paid employment. Similarly those taking antiretroviral treatment may alter their regimen to fit in with their daily schedules, so that they continue their lives without too much disruption. Some may feel that strict compliance is neither attainable nor realistic. In a study of English speaking people of Pakistani origin diagnosed with type 2 diabetes, Bissell et al. (2004) found that respondents had most difficulty in modifying daily patterns of living to accommodate their illness. There were a number of constraints on regimen integration, the principal one being poverty. Families found it difficult to buy the recommended foods, and the need to cook separate meals put an extra burden on family life. As people taking insulin are banned from driving certain classes of vehicles, the diagnosis of diabetes threatened the livelihood of two of their male respondents.

The cost of medication is, unsurprisingly, associated with medicine use. In a study based on a nationwide panel of adults living in the United States, Piette et al. (2004) found that medication underuse due to cost was common among older adults living with a range of chronic illnesses such as asthma, heart failure and depression. The findings showed that such underuse was part of a consistent pattern of behaviour rather than something infrequent. Underuse was associated with respondents' incomes and out-of-pocket medication costs but not their race or ethnicity, gender or educational attainment. In another US study by the same team, Heisler et al. (2004) found that cost-related medication underuse was associated with an increased risk of subsequent decline in self-reported health status among middle aged and elderly Americans. For those with pre-existing cardiovascular disease, underuse was associated with higher rates of angina and non-fatal heart attacks or strokes. In a small qualitative study in North West England, Schafheutle et al. (2002) found that the cost of medication influenced participants' decisions about medicine use although it was not the dominant factor.

Putting together what we know about lay evaluation of medicines and the ways in which people take them, it is possible to formulate an underlying list of questions asked by patients (see Box 3.3):

Box 3.3 Patients' questions about their medicines

- What will happen if I don't take anything for this problem?
- How can I manage this problem myself?
- Can I take a natural or other non-pharmaceutical remedy for it?
- Is this medicine really necessary and, if so, what benefits will it bring?
- How can I tell if it's working?
- What is the minimum effective dose?
- What are the known side effects of this medicine?
- (How) will this medicine impact on my daily life?
- How much does it cost?

The Problem of 'Non-compliance'

It is clear that, for some people at least, medicine taking constitutes a threat to their autonomy. Conversely, managing one's own medication can provide a sense of control (Rogers et al. 1998); those using CAM therapies may do so as a way of taking responsibility for their own conditions. Those diagnosed with chronic conditions, whether they like it or not, usually have to manage their own medication regimens on a daily basis. As we have seen, the long-term use of medication in chronic illness also creates a problematic relationship with efficacy. If the drug works at all, there is a danger of becoming 'addicted' over the course of time. Another possibility with long-term or repeated use is that one becomes 'immune' to the drug, so that it no longer works. If the drug has at some time controlled symptoms, the patient may need to stop taking it to find out if it still works, as in the case of epilepsy (Conrad 1985) or rheumatoid arthritis (Arluke 1980).

People living with long-term conditions are likely to develop expertise in their condition and its management. Possibly the greatest impediment to the development of patients' sense of autonomy is the professional concept of 'non-compliance', also referred to less judgmentally as 'non-adherence'. This concept, referring to the extent to which patients do not follow the instructions they are given (if indeed they have been given instructions), has been dominant in the professional literature. An enormous literature, over a period of at least three decades, has attempted to explore this professionally challenging phenomenon (Vermeire et al. 2001). It is a concept which reflects system and professional perspectives on medicine use. All non-adherence is a potential threat to pharmaceutical sales and to professional dominance. Depending on the benefit-harm profile of the particular drug, non-adherence may either threaten the achievement of professionally defined health outcomes or it may reduce the likelihood of adverse effects.

The literature on non-adherence makes little reference to patients' own expertise. As we have seen, the literature on lay experiences of medicine taking illustrates that it is other concerns, such as the impact on everyday life and side effects, which preoccupy patients. In the context of mental health services, psychiatrists may interpret non-compliance as a manifestation of mental illness, despite the fact that it is a universal phenomenon (Rogers et al. 1998). Trostle (1988) has argued that medical compliance is an ideology, and what clinicians call 'compliance' used to be presented overtly as a matter of physician 'control'. Some years earlier, Stimson (1974) had pointed out that the notion of compliance required patients to be 'passive, obedient *and* unquestioning' (italics in original). Trostle claimed that the preoccupation with compliance is a result of the medical profession's declining authority and represents an attempt to regain control. Donovan (1995) identified a number of assumptions inherent in the concept of compliance: that doctors know what is best for their patients; that they are able to impart medical information clearly and neutrally; that they prescribe effective treatments rationally; and that they are the main contributors to decisions about medicines. As will be discussed in Chapters 5 and 7, these assumptions are questionable. Donovan argues that compliance is a false goal, first because it does not matter to patients, and second because prescribing is influenced by commercial and other factors, as well as patients' needs, in doses determined by average and not individual needs. In fact, as Herxheimer (1998) has pointed out, uncomprehending adherence can be dangerous. A study of people admitted to hospital with acute gastrointestinal bleeding showed that, compared to control patients prescribed the same drugs but not experiencing bleeding, they knew less about their medication and were more compliant (Wynne and Long 1996).

The questions first identified by Stimson (1974), namely the number of people not using their medicines as instructed, their characteristics and the reasons why they do not follow instructions, remain salient for those investigating non-compliance. The answers to Stimson's questions seem to be that up to one half of those prescribed medications for any reason do not take them 'as prescribed', that there are no characteristics which allow the prediction of non-compliance because anyone can be 'non-compliant' at some time or other and the reasons for non-compliance, as we have already seen, lie in patients' own evaluations of their medicines. In the work of Horne and Weinman (1999), people's medication beliefs were stronger predictors of reported adherence than clinical or sociodemographic factors. In a systematic review of interventions to enhance adherence to long-term medication, Kripalani and colleagues (2007) found that although several types of intervention were effective in improving adherence, few significantly affected clinical outcomes. This suggests that improving adherence is an irrelevant and insufficient goal.

Although patients' accounts of medicine taking make little reference to the problem of non-adherence, there is evidence that patients are well aware that their idiosyncratic use of medicines is unacceptable to professionals. The situation is perhaps most clearly exemplified in the context of mental illness. The fear of coercion by professionals, who have the power of compulsory admission and enforced treatment, is a powerful enforcer of adherence (Rogers et al. 1998). Coercive or paternalistic relationships are not ones in which patients feel free to talk about their own decisions. The general issue of how patients' lifeworld concerns are discussed in consultations with professionals will be discussed further in Chapter 7.

Construction of Shared Knowledge

There is much evidence to show that people discuss their experiences of health, illness and treatment with members of their lifeworld in what has been called the 'lay referral network'. The advent of the Internet provides the means for expanding this network well beyond an individual's usual social horizons. For example, Saukko (in press) studied the posts to the main online support group for thrombophilia. The group was established by the moderator, who herself had thrombophilia and had experienced many deep vein thromboses (DVTs). In 2003 the group had approximately 1,000 subscribers most of whom were American women. Saukko analysed 3,600 posts over a six month period and found that the most discussed topic was anticoagulants, which were the subject of 900 posts. The issues discussed were the problems people were experiencing with managing their blood coagulation levels with the medications, side effects of common anticoagulants, what food and medications were safe to eat when taking anticoagulants, the side effects of another type of anticoagulant and the prophylactic usefulness of aspirin. Online participants shared their experiences of their INR numbers (anticoagulant: coagulation levels) and gave each other advice on how to stay 'in range'. Individuals asked for and received emotional support from their online peers. Saukko noted that the conversation revolved very tightly around coagulation levels and that this is a very specific way of relating to thrombophilia.

A prominent subtheme for this online group related to the necessity or otherwise of taking aspirin. A common pattern was for a newcomer, usually someone who had not had a DVT, asking if it was necessary to take aspirin, and the longer term members replying, often in expert language, that it was not. On this thread differing and contradictory views were exchanged, and no firm opinion was formed about the desirability of aspirin, taking natural remedies, resorting to stronger medication or not taking anything. In the same study, Saukko (in press) interviewed a group of English people who had had a test for thrombophilia. This group had only used the Internet fleetingly. Some of those who had joined an online group found it helpful and others did not. Thus the local culture and the online culture did not necessarily enter into true communication or community with one another but negotiated with each other. The Internet thus provides the opportunity for those who want to take it, of building up a body of experiential knowledge about medications for a particular condition. Saukko's research also suggests that groups may develop their own identity and focus of interest. The group she studied has a medical advisor, but it is not clear if the group's focus on medications was influenced in any way by this.

Conclusion

The lifeworld, and patients' own perceptions of their symptoms, influence the ways in which medicines are evaluated and taken. There is widespread ambivalence about medicines, some of which is reflected in concerns about safety and the perceived unnaturalness of pharmaceuticals. This ambivalence is reflected in the dichotomy between the desire for access to medicines, especially new and promising treatments, and concerns about safety and the impact on everyday life. People with chronic illness wanting to keep wellness in the foreground of their lives may only be able to do so by paying attention to medicines, which label them as 'ill'. Lay views are at odds with the professionally dominated notion of adherence, which reflects system imperatives. Pound et al. (2005) found that the main reason why people do not take their medicines as prescribed is not because of failings in patients, doctors or systems, but because of concerns about the medicines themselves. The findings of their review pointed to considerable reluctance to take medicine and a preference to take as little as possible. They characterized this reluctance as 'resistance' to medicine taking as it encapsulated the ways in which people take medicines at the same time as attempting to minimize their intake. The tension between wanting access to medicines and resistance to medicine taking is one I will return to (see Table 7.1). Pound et al. concluded that the policy emphasis, instead of attempting to enforce adherence, should focus on developing safer medicines. This brings us into the world of the systems in which medicines are developed, licensed and regulated. In Chapter 4 I will move from the lifeworld to the system starting with the ways in which drugs are licensed and regulated. In doing so, I will be moving from a context in which lifeworld perspectives dominate the ways in which people use their medicines to a context in which such perspectives are virtually absent.

Box 3.4   Example: balancing the pros and cons of taking antihypertensive medication

Reasons for taking antihypertensive medication (% agreement)

- I take BP tablets because of what happens at the doctors (87%)
- I take BP tablets to achieve some good results (92%)
- I take BP tablets because they make me feel well or better (52%)
- I take BP tablets because they have good side-effects on me (31%)
- I take BP tablets because it feels reassuring (68%)
- I take BP tablets because of other reasons (83%)

Reservations about taking antihypertensives

- I'd prefer to lower my BP without taking BP tablets (66%)
- I wonder whether I still need to take BP tablets (36%)
- I'm concerned my BP tablets might be having bad effects I can't feel (37%)
- I'm concerned my BP tablets might have bad effects on me in the long run (41%)

Balancing reservations against reasons to take antihypertensives

- When I started taking BP tablets, I weighed up any concerns about medicines I might have, with one or more of my reasons to take BP tablets (50%)

Source: Benson and Britten 2003.

Part III
System Perspectives

4

The Development and Licensing of Medicines

Introduction

In Chapter 3 I explored the ways in which medicines are perceived, evaluated and used in the lifeworld. Individuals taking prescribed medicines are not only concerned about the efficacy of treatments; their criteria include the ability to lead a normal life, retaining a sense of control and the minimization of side effects. Anyone who takes prescribed medicines has to trust, or at least accept, that there are systems in place to ensure that they are pure, safe and effective. Most people have only the haziest idea about these systems, presumably making the assumption that it would be illegal for anyone to prescribe or sell substances which were adulterated, harmful or ineffective. In fact such confidence is not entirely well founded as this chapter will illustrate.

In this chapter I will examine the systems which underpin the provision and prescribing of medicines and consider the extent to which technical decisions reflect lifeworld values. At the level of the state, national governments set up these systems to ensure, as far as possible, that the medicines people consume are effective for their particular health problems as well as being safe. In countries with state or social security health care systems, governments also have systems for regulating the prices of medicines or for sharing the costs of medicines with patients, the so called co-payment systems. Systems of drug regulation mostly exist at the level of the nation state, although harmonization of European regulatory systems has introduced systems covering the member states of the European Union. It is only narcotics and related substances which have been controlled at the international level. At the level of the economy, most pharmaceutical companies are multinational organizations beyond the control of individual governments although constrained by national systems locally. This illustrates Beck's point that economics is not responsible for something it causes (the effects of pharmaceuticals, for example), and politics is responsible for something over which it has no control (Beck 1992). While pharmaceutical companies are held responsible to some extent for the adverse consequences of medicine use, the responsibility for setting up regulatory systems lies with governments, whose powers to constrain these companies are limited. The tension between the profit motive of the pharmaceutical industry and the need to ensure the provision of effective, safe and affordable medicines is one that runs through every stage of medicine use. The need to protect manufacturers' commercial interests is used as an argument against providing consumers with information about the testing and licensing of the medicines they take.

Cohen et al. (2001) have described the life cycle of medications from conception to over-the-counter withdrawal (see Box 4.1). Each drug follows

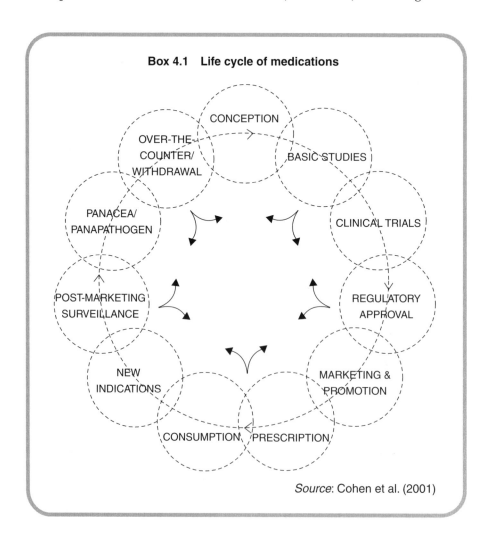

Box 4.1   Life cycle of medications

CONCEPTION

OVER-THE-COUNTER/ WITHDRAWAL

BASIC STUDIES

PANACEA/ PANAPATHOGEN

CLINICAL TRIALS

POST-MARKETING SURVEILLANCE

REGULATORY APPROVAL

NEW INDICATIONS

MARKETING & PROMOTION

CONSUMPTION   PRESCRIPTION

Source: Cohen et al. (2001)

a long and unpredictable trajectory in which each stage of the life cycle is a mini system with its own dynamics and key players. The further into the life cycle of a drug, the more is known about it, partly because drug development is protected on the grounds of commercial sensitivity and partly because the longer a drug is used, the greater the number of people taking it. The rarer the side effect, the larger the population required to detect it.

The Development of Drug Regulation

The purpose of regulating medicines is to ensure their quality, safety and efficacy (but not their price or value). The state carries out this task using information produced by the manufacturer before the medicine is licensed. Such information is necessarily incomplete, as a full assessment of a drug's safety and efficacy profile can only be made once it has been taken by large numbers of people over a period of time. The manufacturer is primarily interested in profits and only secondarily in safety and efficacy inasmuch as they affect sales or if share prices fall. The state is caught in a conflict of interest between the need for a strong economy supported by a profitable pharmaceutical sector and the need to protect and promote the health of its citizens.

Historically, the first of the three elements of drug regulation to attract attention was quality. The adulteration of drugs, meaning alterations to their purity or strength, was a widespread problem in the nineteenth century. This was a result of urbanization, fierce competition and the influence of the trade in patent medicines, which were usually based on secret recipes. Currently the quality of drugs is no longer as pressing an issue as safety and efficacy, although there are concerns about the purity of some generic drugs and Chinese herbal preparations and about counterfeit medicines.

In terms of safety, the earliest forms of drug regulation in the United Kingdom arose out of concerns about the use of cocaine by soldiers in the First World War (Berridge 1999). Soldiers on leave in the West End of London were evidently using cocaine, and fears grew for the effect this might have on the efficiency of the army. As a result, the use of cocaine was included in the Defence of the Realm Act (DORA 40B), which came into force in July 1916. The Act made it an offence for anyone other than medical doctors, pharmacists or veterinary surgeons to be in possession of cocaine, sell it or give it away. The drug could only be supplied on prescriptions which themselves could only be dispensed once. Similar regulations applied to opium but without the detailed prescription requirements. Thus cocaine became the first prescription only drug. This Act was shortly followed by the Dangerous Drugs Act of 1920 which extended DORA 40B to cover a wider range of narcotics especially medicinal opium and morphine. The issue of the safety of non-narcotic medicines took several decades longer to reach public attention in the United Kingdom prompted by the thalidomide tragedy in the 1960s. Thalidomide was a hypnotic drug taken by pregnant women for sleeping problems, and which caused the birth of thousands of deformed children in Europe and the United Kingdom. It had not been used in the United States of America because a medical officer at the Food and Drug Administration (FDA) had delayed approval due to concerns about safety. Following the tragedy, the UK government set up the Cohen Subcommittee to consider the testing and regulation of new drugs. In formulating its proposals, the subcommittee consulted closely with the Association of the British Pharmaceutical Industry (ABPI) due to government awareness of the importance of the pharmaceutical industry to the economy. The Cohen Subcommittee recommended the setting up of the Committee on the Safety of Drugs (CSD) (later to become the Committee on the Safety of Medicines) arguing that it should be independent of industry and that a formal machinery for evaluating the safety of medicines was required. It also recommended the setting up of a centralized system for monitoring adverse drug reactions (ADRs) (see below). The 1968 Medicines Act retained the blanket approach to confidentiality which had characterized the work of the CSD and led to the setting-up of the Medicines Commission in the following year with Dunlop as its first chairman. This Act set the British context for over forty years.

In the United States, interest in the safety of medicines was stimulated by the earlier tragedy of Elixir Sulfanilamide (Abraham 1995). This was a new liquid formulation of an established drug, which killed over a hundred people in the 1930s. The new formulation had not been tested but had been prescribed by doctors. Shortly after this incident, the 1938 Food, Drug and Cosmetic Act became law requiring manufacturers to test new drugs for safety and to report the results to the FDA. Thus, in both the United Kingdom and the United States, requirements about the safety of new drugs were prompted by widely publicized tragedies; the earlier experience in the United States did not seem to alert the UK authorities to the problem, who did not give serious consideration to drug safety until prompted by the thalidomide disaster over twenty years later.

The last element of drug regulation is efficacy; in other words, whether medicines work or not. In the United Kingdom the government, since it paid for most prescribed drugs, had a close interest in their efficacy. In 1929 a government appointed Committee classified 165 prescribed medicines into three categories: those which were sometime drugs, those which were never drugs and those of unknown composition (the so called patent medicines). Doctors were discouraged from prescribing substances in the second and third categories. This was, as Abraham (1995) points out, the first time that a central authority had attempted to set out standards of efficacy. This attempt, however, preceded the explosion of new drugs following the Second World War. In 1966 the FDA commissioned a Drug Efficacy Study of over 4,000 drugs approved and marketed in the United States between 1938 and 1962. Only half were found to be effective; substantial numbers of drugs were found to be either possibly effective or ineffective and a significant number were banned. The list of ineffective drugs affected the products of most manufacturers; shortly afterwards the FDA Commissioner who had supported the removal of ineffective drugs from the market was replaced by someone more friendly to industry. In the United Kingdom, the Committee on the Review of Medicines (CRM) was set up in 1975 in compliance with an EEC directive to review all medicines. This included thousands of drugs which had predated the 1968 Medicines Act and had been allowed to remain on the market as of right. The CRM introduced the criterion of comparative efficacy, meaning that a drug had to be demonstrably superior than comparable products in order to be given a license. This led to a more adversarial relationship with industry than that experienced by the CSD, but the changing economic climate of the 1970s put pressure on the regulatory authorities to speed up their procedures.

Abraham's detailed analysis of the historical development of drug regulation concludes that it can best be described as a process of regulatory capture (Abraham 1995). In such a process, regulatory bodies are set up to protect the interests of consumers from the potential abuses of the regulated industry. Although these bodies may start their work in an aggressive and adversarial manner, the initial enthusiasts are eventually replaced by people who share the industry's perspective. In other words, the regulatory body is progressively 'captured' by the regulated industry. Abraham concludes that regulatory capture is more comprehensive in the United Kingdom, because the regulatory authorities have depended on industry for expertise, because of the 'revolving door' phenomenon in which employees of industry and the regulatory bodies frequently move from one sector to the other, and because the UK authorities have worked in conditions of extreme secrecy. Reforms have benefited the industry rather than consumers' interests, and legislation to protect patients has been weak and compromised. Abraham also concludes, on the basis of research carried out in the 1990s, that corporate bias in the moulding of regulation has been more comprehensive in the United Kingdom than in the United States. In the European context, he has argued that national regulatory agencies have become heavily dependent on industry fees, and that they find themselves competing with each other for regulatory work. In such a competition, agencies win business by approving drugs at an ever faster pace (Abraham 2002). In the United States, Angell (2004) has asserted that the FDA has become extremely accommodating to the pharmaceutical industry. Both the Medicines and Healthcare products Regulatory Agency (MHRA) in the United Kingdom and the FDA in the United States are partially funded by the industry they regulate.

Development of Medicines

As we saw in Chapter 1, many medicines in current use have their origins in traditional plant-based treatments used by pre-modern communities over many years. As such, they provide an example of scientific knowledge arising from the lifeworld. The modern pharmaceutical version may differ from traditional treatments in the way they are manufactured and packaged, but the active ingredients may be the same or very similar. Such medicines include aspirin from willow bark, digoxin from foxglove, and sodium cromoglycate for asthma which is derived from the plant *Ammi visnaga*. The development of new medicines may still be based on natural sources such as plants. Some ethno pharmacologists work in traditional communities to 'discover' previously 'unknown' traditional remedies in much the same way as Livingstone 'discovered' the Victoria Falls on the river Zambezi. Plant substances which look promising will be purified in the laboratory to see if they have any biological effects and, if so, attempts will be made to synthesize them. The benefits of a synthetic product for the manufacturer are that mass production ensures a constant and probably cheaper supply, and that in synthesizing a molecule, small alterations may bring benefits such as fewer side effects or a longer duration of action. Most importantly, in synthesizing a new chemical substance, the manufacturer can apply for a patent. The patenting system provides one of the most powerful influences on the whole pharmaceutical industry by protecting the interests of patent holders while also time limiting their commercial advantages.

There are other ways of developing new medicines. Some are the result of targeted research by pharmaceutical companies and universities aiming to design substances with specific medicinal effects. These discoveries are theoretically based in the sense that they are developed to address a specific problem and to influence a particular physiological mechanism. Collier and Dwight (1997) give the example of beta blockers which were specifically designed to slow the heart by blocking the beta-adrenaline receptors on the surface of heart cells. Beta blockers have subsequently been shown to be useful for other conditions such as glaucoma. Another approach is random testing of large numbers of slightly differing chemical compounds to see if they have medicinal effects. This is time consuming but has yielded many antibiotics and tranquillisers such as Valium and Librium. Perhaps the most promising source of new drugs is the biotechnology industry. New drugs may mimic, replace or otherwise build on naturally occurring substances with the body such as hormones. Pharmacogenetics is the study of individual genetic differences in response to medicines. Such studies may lead to the abandonment of potential new drugs if, for example, a drug is metabolized by an enzyme for which there are common mutations. Pharmacogenetic research may lead to drugs which are targeted at genetic variants of disease, such as the drug trastuzumab (Herceptin) which targets the Her-2 protein in patients with breast cancer.

Another class of ostensibly new drugs is the 'me-too' drugs which are variations on existing profitable medicines, sufficiently different to avoid infringement of rivals' patents and to allow the establishment of new patents. In this way, manufacturers aim to avoid the heavy expenditure and time taken to bring a genuinely new product to market while capitalizing on the possibility of a new patent. Me-too drugs may be clinically very similar to the original drug and are not as profitable, as by definition there is already a successful rival treatment on the market. Manufacturers also bring out new formulations of existing medicines, for example, by producing a formulation which can be taken by another route (oral rather than injection) or fewer times per day. This is one of the reasons why there are so many drugs on the market, and why there may be several potentially useful treatments for any one condition. Overall, the development of new drugs is not informed by consumer preferences or consumer-defined need, as potential users of medicines are not usually consulted.

Having identified or isolated a potentially promising new substance (referred to as a new molecular entity or NME), drug companies have two mechanisms for establishing monopolies and protecting themselves from competition. The first, and much earlier, is to obtain a patent, and the second is to obtain a license for exclusive marketing rights from the appropriate regulatory authority. Once awarded, a patent protects the company from imitation by its rivals for a period of 20 years from the date the application is filed with the US Patent and Trademark Office (USPTO), or the European Medicines Evaluation Agency (EMEA). Prescription drug patents can apply to the substance itself, the method of use, the formulation or the manufacturing process. The method of use refers to the condition that the drug is intended to treat, such as depression or hyperlipidaemia. Formulation refers to both the physical characteristics, for example, capsule or liquid form, and to the method of administration, for example, by mouth or injection. The 20 year patent period includes the development of the new substance, preclinical and clinical testing, and the application for licensing. It can take 10 years to bring a product to market. The longer it takes the shorter the period of monopoly sales enjoyed by the drug company. While the monopoly lasts, drugs generate huge profits for the pharmaceutical companies. There is thus an enormous commercial incentive for companies to carry out the development and testing as fast as possible, to emphasize benefits over harms, and to lobby licensing authorities to process their applications quickly.

In the United States, patentable inventions were originally supposed to be useful, novel and non-obvious. However, in 1980 the US Supreme Court relaxed the requirement about usefulness by stating that the inventions did not have to have practical implications if they were useful for further research. Examiners for the USPTO are paid bonuses partly determined by the number of patents they process, and as it is faster to grant a patent than to deny it and risk having the decision appealed this provides an incentive to grant patents. The Court of Appeals for the Federal Circuit was created in 1982 to hear appeals of patent denials and has been lenient, for example, in applying the standard of non-obviousness. Angell (2004) points out that these changes made it easier for pharmaceutical companies to obtain patents for highly obvious uses of drugs such as successive patents for Prozac, first for depression and then for obesity.

Once the patent for a medicine has expired, other manufacturers are free to produce a generic version of it. The manufacturers of generic medicines do not have to bear the development costs of the original medicines, and the prices of generic medicines are therefore lower than those of patented medicines. Generic medicines are usually identical to the originals but may have different physical properties (such as size and shape) and different filler substances. New licenses are needed for generic medicines, as the licensing authorities need to establish that they have the same clinical effects as the originals. Manufacturers of branded medicines have a number of methods of 'evergreening' their products, that is, extending the patents on existing medicines and thereby delaying the production of generic, cheaper, alternatives. It has become common in the pharmaceutical industry for companies to replace successful products whose patent is nearing expiry with a slightly different one that has the same effect but can be claimed to be an improvement. This may be a slightly different molecule, or a different formulation of the old drug with slower or faster release of the active ingredient, or made by a different ('better' or cheaper) manufacturing process, or combined in the same tablet with another substance that is supposed to improve the properties of the medicine. On expiry of the first patent the company stops promoting the original product, often then marketing the new product at a lower price to make the old one unattractive. Examples include the replacement of omeprazole (inhibitor of gastric acid secretion) by esoprazole, loratadine (antihistamine) by desloratadine, citalopram (antidepressant) by escitalopram. The replacements offer no real therapeutic advance, but they have been heavily and successfully promoted; they have cost patients and health services an enormous sum that is essentially wasted.

Testing and Licensing of Medicines

Once a new molecular entity has been identified which appears to have desirable biological properties, it needs to be tested first on animals and then on humans (House of Commons Health Committee 2005). There are three phases of clinical (human) trials before licensing (phases I to III) and one post-licensing phase (phase IV). The stages of drug development are shown in Box 4.2. The results of these tests are scrutinized by licensing authorities and will determine if the license application is successful or not. Given the heavy costs of drug development, the data from animal and human trials are, therefore, crucial to manufacturers' commercial success.

Studies in animals are carried out to establish a substance's pharmacodynamics, pharmacokinetics and toxicology. Pharmacodynamics refers to the action of the drug on biological processes relevant to the disease in question. This is tested in animals with diseases which resemble the target disease for the drug or on relevant specimens of animal tissue such as blood vessels. In practice, animal models do not often provide reliable predictions of the value of drugs for treating human illnesses, a point which is emphasized by the animal rights movement. Pharmacokinetics refers to the way in which the drug is handled by the body including absorption and excretion, and animal studies can show if the medicine is metabolized in the liver, how long it lasts in the blood, how it is excreted and so on. It can also show the blood concentrations required for the drug to have an effect. Lastly, toxicology refers to the potential for harm, and animal studies can be used to assess if any organs are damaged, whether the drug alters behaviour, whether the drug causes symptoms or alters bodily functions, whether the animal's reproductive organs are damaged or if the drug is carcinogenic. Toxicology tests are carried out on several animal species using different dosing regimens to increase the possibility of identifying adverse effects. These preclinical and non-clinical tests are carried out either by the pharmaceutical companies or by industry funded contract research organizations (CROs), and generally it take about three years. Although most of these tests are completed before the new substances are tested in human populations, not all of them are. In particular, long-term animal studies to test for carcinogenicity of new molecular entities may be ongoing when clinical studies begin. This means that there is a possibility that healthy volunteers, and sometimes even patients, are taking carcinogenic substances. Tests for carcinogenicity are only carried

Box 4.2 Stages of drug development

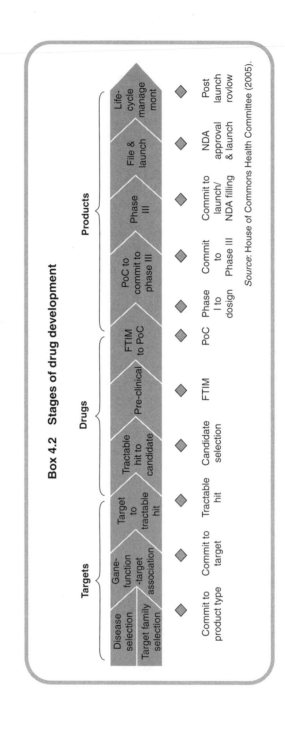

Source: House of Commons Health Committee (2005).

out in animals, because the time frame for the development of cancer in humans is longer than clinical trials; this means that the results of the animal tests are particularly important, and that if, for whatever reason, they provide false reassurance, it can take many years before the mistake is noticed.

If animal studies do not reveal any serious problems, the drug is then tested in humans (clinical trials) in a four phase process. In phase I clinical trials (known as First Time in Man or FTIM), drugs are first given to 100–200 healthy volunteers to test different dosages and frequency of administration as well as the risk of side effects and interactions with other drugs. This phase determines the dosage of the drug to be tested in subsequent trials and can take up to two years. In 2006, the phase 1 trial of the superagonist anti-CD28 monoclonal antibody TGN 1412 hit the news when six healthy volunteers experienced life threatening reactions. An hour after they were given the drug, five of the volunteers developed severe headaches, and all six then developed low back pain, severe gastrointestinal disturbance, and a systematic inflammatory response with rapid heart rate and falling blood pressure (Mayor 2006). The incident raised the possibility that the new generation of 'biotech' medicines may behave differently from their predecessors.

However, if all goes well, phase II trials (known as Proof of Concept or POC) may begin in which the drug is tested on 200–500 patients with the target disease, and these can also take two years. Phase II trials usually take place in hospitals and involve doctors who are not working for the company. As the NME has usually been patented by this phase, this does not risk the company's intellectual property rights. Phase II trials are carried out to determine the safety and efficacy of the drug in the relevant patient group. Phase III trials involve larger groups of patients (between 2000 and 3000) and can take four years. At this point, there is more accurate testing of the drug's efficacy and safety on a larger population, as well as the dose necessary to achieve the desired effect. The testing of doses is crucial for licensing purposes, as licenses stipulate the approved doses. Dosing levels also determine prices, and post-licensing changes in dosage can have an impact on manufacturers' profits. In phase III trials, drugs are compared either to an existing treatment for the same condition or to a placebo (such as a sugar pill). Comparison with a placebo is clearly a less demanding test, as it merely asks the question of whether the drug is better than nothing, but does not guarantee that a new drug is any better than the old one(s). By the time a license application is submitted, the drug may have been tested on over three thousand patients and healthy volunteers. These trials provide the first scientific evidence about efficacy and safety, that the medicine works, and preliminary evidence of its risk profile. They also define how the drug should be used in practice. However, even human trials have limited predictive value for real-life practice, as the people taking part in clinical trials are often very different from those eventually prescribed the licensed drug.

It can take as long as ten years for a drug to progress through these three phases. It has been estimated that of every 100 drugs entering phase I trials, 70 will go into phase II, 33 into phase III, 25 to regulatory submission and 20 to final approval (House of Commons Health Committee 2005). From the industry point of view, this high rate of attrition places a heavy burden of expectations on those medicines which are eventually licensed.

Because the number of patients and healthy volunteers on whom a drug is tested is tiny in comparison to the millions of patient-years over which a drug may be used once it is licensed, phase IV studies are carried out after licensing to monitor the safety and efficacy of a medicine in larger, and more real-life, populations. These trials are referred to as post-marketing surveillance trials. In this phase, older patients with more than one disease and those taking a range of different medicines will be included, who may have been excluded from pre-licensing trials. In 2001, an estimated 80,000 clinical trials were underway in the United States involving about 2.3 million people. Given these kinds of numbers, the difficulty of recruiting patients can lead to delays in the licensing of new medicines. As a result, pharmaceutical companies use several methods for recruiting patients and have also developed relationships with patient advocacy groups to help them with recruitment to trials. Although patients may be paid to participate in trials, the amounts offered are usually much smaller than the amounts offered to doctors.

Having assembled the results of animal trials and phase I–III human trials, the manufacturer is in a position to apply for a product license. Licensing requirements are detailed and elaborate and change frequently. In the United Kingdom, a product license application can be submitted to the Medicines and Healthcare products Regulatory Agency (MHRA), to the EMEA or to another EU country via a mutual recognition system. In the former case, applications are reviewed by the MHRA which is supported by the Commission for Human Medicines (which took over the responsibilities of the Committee on Safety of Medicines (CSM) and the Medicines Commission). Companies may apply directly to the EMEA under a centralized approval system covering biotechnology products and range of drugs. Companies may also seek approval in one EU country and then receive marketing authorization from other EU countries willing to recognize the initial approval under a mutual recognition arrangement. Once licensed, the drug is protected by patent for ten years, although as referred to above, there are ways of extending drug patents.

The MHRA is part of the Department of Health, but is entirely supported by fee income paid by pharmaceutical companies for licensing and inspection.

In assessing product license applications, the MHRA examines the safety, quality and efficacy of the drug. When a license is granted, the license stipulates the name of the medicine, its nature, dose, the method of manufacture and the quality of the medicine, its properties and the terms on which it can be manufactured, distributed, promoted and sold. The license also lists the wanted and unwanted effects, and the advice to be given to prescribers and patients about how the medicine is to be used, in the Summary of Product Characteristics and Patient Information Leaflet respectively. Both these documents list the conditions or diseases that the company can claim the medicine is to be used for (these are the licensed indications). Although prescribers are free to prescribe medicines for whatever indications (diseases) they judge appropriate, manufacturers are not allowed to make claims for non-licensed indications. The Commission for Human Medicines advises the Licensing Authority which in turn is composed of the four UK Ministers of Health in England, Northern Ireland, Scotland and Wales. The Licensing Authority grants the license on the basis of the medicine's effectiveness, quality and safety. Under the terms of the Medicines Act, it is not allowed to consider the medicine's comparative efficacy in relation to existing treatments.

For a European license, a similar kind of relationship exists between the EMEA, the Committee for Proprietary Medicinal Products (CPMP), and the European Commission. A company applies to EMEA for a product license, which is considered by the CPMP. The CPMP contracts out the initial assessment of the application to one of the appropriate bodies in one of the member states, and on the basis of this assessment gives an opinion to the Commission. The Commission makes the final decision. In the United States of America, medicines are licensed by the Food and Drug Administration, which is supported by several advisory committees of outside experts.

Post-licensing

When a license is granted in the United Kingdom, the initial marketing authorization lasts for five years (House of Commons Health Committee 2005). The company then has to apply for another license to keep the product on the market for an indefinite period of time. The stated criteria for relicensing are the same as for the original assessment, but in practice the level of scrutiny at this stage is much less. In fact, the amount of data potentially available to the regulatory bodies is much greater five years post-license than at the time of the original application, which would in theory enable a more robust and reliable review of a medicine's safety and efficacy. This is rarely done, and there is no specific policy about the ongoing evaluation of licensed medicines. At this five-year mark, the potential contribution of patients is greatest due to the much larger numbers of people with experience of the medicine in real-life (rather than clinical trial) settings. There are, however, no mechanisms to tap into patients' experiences as part of the relicensing process.

The Vigilance Risk Management section of the MHRA is responsible for conducting post-marketing surveillance, which involves scrutinising the results of phase IV trials, monitoring the medical literature for any information about safety in particular, and evaluating spontaneous reports of suspected ADRs. In 1963 the Cohen Subcommittee had recommended the setting-up of a central registry of adverse drug reactions to act as an early warning system for new drugs. The system set up at this time, called the Yellow Card system, is still used. Drug companies are required to report all suspected ADRs, and doctors and other health professionals are encouraged to do so by sending in Yellow Card reports. The Yellow Card ADR reporting system is the main tool of the UK pharmacovigilance system for investigating the safety of prescribed medicines. The system relies on volunteer health professionals (doctors, pharmacists, nurses, dentists, coroners, radiographers, optometrists, health visitors and midwives) to complete a Yellow Card if they suspect that a patient's symptoms might have been caused by an ADR, particularly if the drug is new (new drugs are identified by an inverted black triangle in the British National Formulary). It is widely accepted that ADRs are under reported, and that only a minority of health professionals ever submit a Yellow Card. For this reason, the data from Yellow Cards are not used to estimate the incidence of ADRs but rather to signal potential safety problems. Cohen et al. (2001) have argued that the lack of attention to the iatrogenic effects of drugs is part of a powerful bias towards a taken-for-granted view of medications as primarily essential, lifesaving products. The Yellow Card system was reviewed in 2004, and it was recommended that patients, for the first time, should be able to report their own suspected ADRs directly to the MHRA; this recommendation was implemented in 2005.

After a drug has been licensed in the United Kingdom, it may be reviewed by the National Institute for Health and Clinical Excellence (NICE), which provides guidance to the NHS about public health, health technologies including medicines, and clinical practice. It advises the government about the effectiveness (including cost effectiveness) of both old and new medicines. Only a minority of new drugs are scrutinized by NICE, either if its availability varies across the country or if there is confusion or uncertainty about its value. Its role brings it into frequent conflict with the pharmaceutical industry, because an adverse decision (from the industry point of view) means that a drug may not be available on the NHS. The view has been expressed that the industry is trying to destroy NICE (Coombes 2007).

In all countries, the task of evaluating license applications is a time consuming process given the vast amount of material submitted. The EMEA sets a 210 day limit, although applications for generic products are likely to take less time than applications for new chemical entities or new active substances. In the United States, under industry pressure, the FDA has moved from being the slowest regulatory agency in the developed world to being one of the fastest (Angell 2004, p. 209). The first few months after licensing are the most important from the promotional point of view, as this is when the drug companies are trying their hardest to persuade doctors to start prescribing it. This is also the time when least is known about a licensed medicine, as there is as yet no information about the effects of the drug in large populations or over extended periods of time. Depending on the drug's indication, it may also be the time when patients' hopes are at their highest.

Involvement of Patients and the General Public

The regulation, development, testing and licensing of medicines all involve patients and lay people to a lesser or greater extent. Taking them in reverse order, the work of testing and licensing is carried out by the manufacturers (or other companies, such as CROs, on their behalf). Patients are involved as experimental subjects whose interests need to be protected by robust procedures for informed consent. This protection is provided by Research Ethics Committees in the United Kingdom and Institutional Review Boards in the United States. There is some evidence to suggest that patients taking part in clinical trials receive better care than other patients, because there are standard protocols for treatment which have to be observed and because patients need to be assessed frequently. The main interest of patients and the general public in the processes of testing and licensing is one of access to the data they produce. Patients need to know what evidence there is (or is not) to show that a new drug works and that it is safe. Given the relative paucity of information ever available about new drugs, and the extremely high expectations patients may have that a new drug will cure their condition, it is a particularly important situation for transparency.

In particular, patients may want to know which outcome measures were used to judge effectiveness, as the measures chosen may or may not reflect their own goals and aspirations. In life threatening conditions, survival rates may be the obvious outcome measure to choose, but in other conditions where quality of life is more important, there is a wider choice. The choice of outcome measure(s) is crucial to understanding claims about efficacy; manufacturers will be keen to choose measures which maximize the claims they can make, while patients may want to know if the new medicines actually improve their lives. Professionals have their own criteria for choosing outcome measures, which are often based on methodological concerns or to maximize comparisons between different treatments. Researchers increasingly recognize that outcome measures ought to reflect patients' priorities, but methods for achieving this are not yet well developed. In the United States, data about newly licensed drugs is available on the FDA website (http://www.fda.gov/cder). In the United Kingdom, the MHRA publishes Public Assessment Reports for medicines (http://www.mhra.gov.uk). These are available for all newly licensed drugs with commercially or personally confidential information removed. Thus for the first time since the 1968 Medicines Act, the dead hand of secrecy in relation to the licensing of medicines in the United Kingdom is finally lifted. These reports give health professionals, patients and the general public access to some of the information on which they can make their own judgements about the safety and efficacy of prescribed medicines.

In the development of medicines, patients and the public have a limited role. In the particular context of ethnopharmacology, when traditional remedies are investigated for their commercial potential, lay knowledge forms the starting point for scientific investigation. However, in these situations, the people involved may well be members of indigenous groups, whose intellectual property rights may not be recognized or rewarded, and whose environments may be at risk if rare substances need to be extracted in large quantities. Another potential role for public involvement might be the identification or prioritization of diseases for which new treatments ought to be developed. This is an unlikely scenario for drug development carried out by pharmaceutical companies (unless, of course, their shareholders pressurize them to do so); in university or other publicly funded institutions, a good case could be made for public and patient involvement in priority setting.

It is in the context of regulation and post-marketing surveillance that patients have most to contribute in relation to safety and efficacy. Abraham and Sheppard (1997) suggested the setting-up of a public interest subcommittee of the CSM (now taken over by the Commission on Human Medicines), and this will be discussed in Chapter 9. In relation to post-marketing surveillance, the scientific study of the safety of medicines comes within the academic discipline of pharmacovigilance. In the United Kingdom, its main tools are the Yellow Card system (spontaneous reporting) and Prescription Event Monitoring (prospective follow-up of certain newly licensed drugs). Medawar and Herxheimer (2003) estimated that only about 1 per cent of all ADRs are reported, but that the rate varied greatly depending on the severity and type of reaction, and the nature and age of the drug. Only a minority of NHS doctors ever send in a Yellow Card, and a small number of doctors submit most of the reports.

Until very recently in the United Kingdom, as in many other countries, patients have not been allowed to contribute Yellow Cards directly. Following a high profile Panorama television programme broadcast in 2002 and entitled 'Secrets of Seroxat' about the SSRI antidepressant paroxetine, Medawar and Herxheimer (2003) analysed 1,374 viewers' subsequent emails. They also analysed 862 emails posted to an interactive discussion group managed by Charles Medawar. Nearly half of the Panorama emails were negative about the drug; only 17 per cent were positive, with the remainder being uncertain or ambivalent. The discussion group emails were critical of how the drug was promoted, recommended, tested and described. Most of the Panorama emails did not provide data that would facilitate judgements about suspected ADRs, such as the patient's age or sex, the dosage or duration of treatment, or the patient's diagnosis and any concurrent treatment with other drugs. Despite the inadequacies of individual reports, Medawar and Herxheimer concluded that the collective weight of evidence was profound. They found that immersing themselves in a large body of data provided them with a detailed understanding of patients' experiences, and they suggested that this was more valuable than reading a trickle of Yellow Card reports over a period of years. One of the phenomena experienced by patients attempting withdrawal from the drug was variously described as having an 'electric head', 'electric misfirings' or 'an electric zap [which] gets fired off in my brain' (see Box 4.3). Medawar and Herxheimer identified three main reasons for users wanting to stop taking Seroxat: changing circumstances such as the ending of a stressful situation or wanting to become pregnant; unwanted effects; and fear of dependence.

Medawar and Herxheimer (2003) compared patients' reports from the emails and discussion group with Yellow Card reports from professionals. They were able to do this because, for the first time since the setting-up of the CSM in the 1960s, the MHRA gave them access to anonymized Yellow Card reports. These reports are known as Anonymised Single Patient Printouts (ASPPs). The use of medical terminology in the ASPPs made them briefer than the user reports, but this was often at the expense of detail and meaning. Reports from patients in their own words can communicate essential information which professional reporters can never be expected to provide. Medawar and Herxheimer concluded that the major limitations of the Yellow Card system arise not so much from the reports themselves as from the ways in which they are interpreted, analysed and presented. For example, some ASPPs had been classified as 'electric shock' in the category 'Injury and poisoning', suggesting that the source of the injury was mains electricity. But comparing the ASPPs with the patients' reports suggests that at least some of these were inappropriately classified withdrawal reactions. Thus, the loss of the detailed description of patients' experiences led to misclassification of adverse drug reactions. More generally, the authors concluded that miscoding and flawed analyses of Yellow Cards have led to underestimation of the risk of suicidal behaviour in people taking Seroxat and a failure to recognize the relationship between suicidal behaviour and changes in drug concentration.

Users reported difficulties in telling doctors about their experiences, as doctors sometimes denied the existence of withdrawal symptoms or attributed them to some other cause, often the underlying illness. These difficulties demonstrate that relying on doctors and other health professionals to report ADRs is bound to lead to under reporting. Understandably, professionals may be unwilling to entertain the notion that the medicine they prescribed is actually harming their patient. Patients' accounts of their experiences, if reported by doctors, will be filtered through the sieve of doctors' own expectations, knowledge and interpretations of what is credible, serious, relevant and worth reporting. This filtering then produces distorted data. Medawar and Herxheimer also found evidence of patients' unwillingness to tell doctors about suspected ADRs, because they felt that doctors would not take them seriously. The result of this is that doctors do not get to hear about the experiences that patients are afraid to tell them about, which also has implications for the collection of data. It is not only health professionals who do not take patients' concerns seriously; the regulators also regard patients' testimonies as anecdotal, unreliable and unscientific. Medawar and colleagues (2002) concluded that until some form of patient reporting of adverse drugs reactions becomes the norm, the so far unidentified but potentially avoidable harm that patients suffer will continue. This places a burden on patients, their families and the health services but is also morally unacceptable.

Blenkinsopp and colleagues (2006) carried out a review of patient reporting of suspected ADRs using data from six countries having patient reporting systems. Only two of these systems were set up in the twentieth century: the Swedish system based on indirect reporting was set up in 1978, and the US system of direct reporting was set up in 1993. Twenty-first-century systems have been set up in Australia, Denmark, the Netherlands and Canada. The UK system had not been running long enough to be included in Blenkinsopp's review. The review noted the lack of research into patient reporting of suspected ADRs, and most of the evidence they included was based on small studies which did not involve spontaneous reporting. The authors concluded that although patient reports might be more time consuming to process than professional reports, they identified potential new ADRs not previously reported by health professionals, and that the quality of patient reports appeared similar to that of professionals. There was also some evidence that patients report an ADR when they consider their health professional has not paid attention to their concerns.

Conclusion

As noted in Chapter 1, the casting of decisions about the licensing and regulation of medicines as technical issues can serve to remove them from public debate. Such decisions depend on value judgements about the balance between harms and benefits, and between benefits and costs, which are not purely technical issues. In the United Kingdom, the House of Commons Health Committee concluded that 'The consequences of lax oversight is that the industry's influence has expanded and a number of practices have developed which act against the public interest' (House of Commons Health Committee 2005, p. 3). Members of regulatory and licensing authorities, acting on behalf of the societies they serve, have to reflect social interests if they are to retain legitimacy. The systems I have examined in this chapter have little input from patients and the public, although the situation is changing. On balance, the evidence suggests that the interests of industry outweigh those of patients, which is achieved by the process of 'regulatory capture', regulators' financial dependence on industry, the consequent emphasis on speed and the lack of input from patients. In particular, more attention is given to efficacy than to safety (see Box 5.1 for the example of the drug Vioxx). Given the nature of the patent system, there are tremendous incentives on industry to bring their products to market quickly, which militate against thorough investigation (or even honesty) about adverse reactions. From the point of view of individual patients, the drugs produced are not necessarily the ones they want or need; outcomes of the research trials do not necessarily reflect their lifeworld concerns. The patients on whom the drugs were tested may not be typical of those for whom the new drug is eventually prescribed.

Given that most of the activities discussed in this chapter are carried out behind closed doors, the question arises about how professionals and the public obtain information about medicines. Chapter 5 is about information available to professionals and patients and suggests that much of it is biased in favour of the benefits of medicines. Those in the lifeworld may be concerned about the safety of medicines, but the system has other imperatives.

Box 4.3   Example: withdrawal effects

'Twenty four hours after the last dose I begin to feel extremely strange reactions in my brain, which have proved extremely hard to describe to the GP. A slew of weird sensations in my brain gather pace as time wears on. It feels like little electric misfirings going off in there which resulting [sic] in a feeling of disorientation. It's almost like the brain is having its version of goose pimples! It took me ages to figure out that this feeling was the result of not taking the pill. It was and is hard to get across to the doc that these strange feelings are not because of taking the pill but the lack of it.' (10/06/00)

'I too am experiencing the 'electric head'. What an appropriate name. My Dr. told me that it was simply my anxiety returning. I explained that my eyes felt jumpy when I looked from side to side, but he still attributed it to returning anxiety. It's good to see others having the same symptoms, so I know I'm not imagining things!'. (13/07/00)

Source: Medawar et al. (2002).

5

Information about Medicines

Introduction

Medicines are nothing without information. Regulators cannot license medicines without information, prescribers cannot prescribe nor patients consume medicines without information. In this chapter, I will look at the variety of sources of information available about medicines and consider whose needs they serve and how medicines information could be improved. In particular, professionals and patients both need to understand how information about medicines is produced and made available, if they are to judge its suitability for their own needs. In Chapter 4, we saw how the licensing and regulation of medicines is not informed by the lifeworld. In this chapter, I aim to show how the same problems run through the production and dissemination of information about medicines. I will consider information for professionals and for patients in turn.

Information for Professionals

Before and after the licensing of drugs, clinical trials are carried out to establish their efficacy, safety, dosing regime and other parameters. The results of pre-licensing trials are often kept secret on the grounds of commercial sensitivity. Once a drug is licensed, however, publication in prestigious journals can enhance its prestige and credibility. Research papers are a useful tool in the pharmaceutical representative's armoury provided, of course, that they tell 'good news' stories. Professionals rely on the reporting of drug trials in medical journals, and secondary publication in professional journals and magazines, to keep them up to date. Given the high financial stakes, it is only to be expected that the industry would wish to influence and even police the ways in which its products are presented to the world. In fact, a number of concerns about conflicts of interest, publication bias and sponsors' roles in the design and conduct of drug trials have been voiced. The question for all prescribers is, can they trust the information they receive about the medications they are prescribing?

Bekelman et al. (2003) carried out a systematic review of the extent, impact and management of financial conflicts of interest in biomedical research. They found that about a quarter of biomedical investigators in academic institutions received research funding from industry, and that authors who had financial relationships with the pharmaceutical companies were significantly more likely to reach supportive conclusions than authors without such affiliations. They concluded that there was strong and consistent evidence that industry-sponsored research tended to draw pro-industry conclusions. Lexchin et al. (2003) reached similar conclusions. Melander et al. (2003) compared the studies submitted to the Swedish regulatory authority about five selective serotonin reuptake inhibitors (SSRIs) with the studies actually published. This study was unique in having access to all the relevant material about the drugs in question, putting the authors in a strong position to investigate publication bias. They found evidence of selective publication, selective reporting and duplicate publication; selective reporting was the major cause of bias in overall estimates based on published data. Melander et al. concluded that without access to published and unpublished studies and without access to alternative statistical analyses (specifically intention to treat analyses as well as per protocol analyses), any attempt to recommend a specific drug is likely to be based on biased evidence. While their research focused on a narrow range of drugs, there is no reason to believe that the results would be markedly different for other drug classes.

Bodenheimer (2000) commented on the spectacular growth of a new model of research, which is no longer primarily carried out by universities and medical schools, but increasingly by Contract Research Organizations (CROs) and Site Management Organisations (SMOs). Contract Research Organizations offer manufacturers a range of services, from managing entire trials to developing networks of collaborators, implementing trial protocols at study sites and so on. They may subcontract part of this work to SMOs, who may organize networks of collaborating physicians and enrol patients. These organizations compete with academic institutions for money and may offer faster delivery and fewer awkward questions. Some trials have as many as four layers of organization: the manufacturer, the CRO, the SMO and the collaborating physicians. Both Bodenheimer (2000) and Bekelman et al. (2003) identified a number of methods used by industry to produce favourable results. These included trials of younger patients, inactive control substances such as placebos, controls with lower doses than the manufacturer's drug, inappropriate controls and surrogate outcomes. Bodenheimer concluded that while academic–industry drug trials at least have the potential for balance between commercial and scientific interests, trials conducted in the commercial sector are heavily tipped towards industry interests.

Editors of medical journals are aware of these kinds of problems, and in 2007 the International Committee of Medical Journal Editors (ICMJE) published an updated set of uniform requirements for manuscripts submitted to biomedical journals (ICMJE 2007). The revisions included the requirement that sponsors disclose their role in the research as well as assurances that investigators are independent of the sponsor, are fully accountable for the design and conduct of the trial, have independent access to all trial data, and control all editorial and publication decisions. However, Schulman et al.'s survey of US medical schools suggested that these institutions routinely participated in clinical research that did not adhere to the ICMJE standards (Schulman et al. 2002). Failures occurred in relation to trial design, access to data and publication rights. Several of their respondents said that they felt powerless in contract negotiations with sponsors. Schulman et al. concluded that a re-evaluation of the process of contracting for clinical research was urgently needed.

Bodenheimer (2002) identified the paradoxical problem of the 'non writing author–non author writer' in the scientific literature, in which the authors of journal articles are not who they claim to be. There are two main characters in this charade – ghosts and guests. On the one hand, articles are ghost written by professional medical writers employed by drug companies or CROs; the names of these non-author writers are not included in the published paper. On the other hand, non-writing clinical investigators appear as guest authors even though they did not analyse the data or write the paper. Such guest authors may be well known in their field and are chosen to enhance the paper's credibility. Clearly they do not satisfy the ICMJE requirements. Although journal editors may require authors to sign declarations, it is difficult for them to detect dishonesty.

These results suggest that publication bias is a real problem, in other words, that results favouring a particular drug are more likely to be published than negative results. If this is the case, it means that prescribers' decisions, to the extent that they are evidence based, may be biased. If prescribers cannot trust the information published in the scientific literature, they are left in a difficult position. Prescribers who read the scientific literature at first hand are in a position to note any statements about financial conflicts of interest, but even if they remain more sceptical about authors with declared conflicts, this may not help them make decisions. Others who read reports in secondary sources may not know which trials were commercially sponsored and which were not.

Prescribers may be as likely to read advertisements for particular drugs as to read scientific articles. Herxheimer et al. (1993) studied 6,710 drug adverts which appeared during 12 months in 23 leading national medical journals in 18 countries. Their findings showed that indications were mentioned more often than negative effects of medicines and that adverts gave less pharmacological than medical information. They also found that important warnings and contraindications were missing in about half of the adverts.

If prescribers cannot always trust the published information about clinical trials, research participants have also been betrayed. People taking part in clinical trials may accept that they themselves may not benefit from the results, and many do so on altruistic grounds. Selective publication of positive results runs the risk of violating investigators' responsibilities to protect the interests of research participants, whose consent is based on unbiased reporting of the results. Schulman et al. (2002) note that in two cases brought by research participants in the United States, the courts ruled that sponsors and investigators had a legal obligation to honour commitments made to participants, and that promises of benefits offered to them became contractually binding once the participants had fulfilled their obligations.

Information for Patients

Purposes of Information

Information about medicines, like information of all kinds, can serve a variety of purposes. In analysing a range of patient information leaflets, Dixon-Woods (2001) identified two main discourses: the patient education discourse and the patient empowerment discourse. The patient education discourse reflected a biomedical perspective in its choice of outcomes and was based on an assumption of patient incompetence and a mechanistic model of communication. In this discourse, leaflets were seen as advantageous to health professionals by, for instance, reducing the length of consultations or providing medico legal protection. The intended outcome of leaflets was often to increase patients' compliance with medication – in other words, to persuade patients to take their medicines 'properly'. The patient empowerment discourse, a much smaller body of literature, explicitly rejected the professionally driven agenda in favour of enhancing patient choice and supporting patients as active partners in their health care. Research in the latter perspective has identified the kinds of questions that patients ask about their medicines (Raynor et al. 2007). These include questions about the nature of the medicine, the condition it is being prescribed for, the dosage, the name of the medicine, its intended purpose, how and when to take it, and how soon it is likely to work. Patients also have concerns about medicines which they ask about, such as side effects, lack of efficacy, dislike of the medicine, its cost, preference for a branded rather than generic medication and alternative treatments. These questions are narrower than the questions listed in Box 3.3 arising from research about lay views of medicines. The EU requirements for Patient Information Leaflets specify a much shorter list of questions as follows:

- What the medicine is and what it is used for
- Before taking the medicine
- How to take the medicine
- Possible side effects
- How to store it.

Without good information, it is difficult for patients to make decisions about medicine taking or to take an active part in discussions with health professionals about treatment choices. Lack of information puts patients in a weak position, in which their main choice is between doing as they are instructed (being compliant), or not. In particular, patients need information to support their own evaluations, which is described in Chapter 3. Herxheimer (1994) has pointed out the distinction between information and education: people who do not understand the key principles needed for applying and using drug-specific information cannot use it adequately or appropriately. These principles include the dose–effect relationship, determinants of the duration of effect, inter-individual differences and the need to weigh up benefits against harms and inconveniences. The central issue for professionals is whether they want to help patients make informed choices, or whether they want to improve adherence. Although these may well have the same result, in some cases they will not.

Professionals as Sources of Information

People taking prescribed medicines come into contact with various health professionals in the course of doing so. These include the prescriber, who may be a nurse, pharmacist or doctor. The person dispensing the medicine may be a pharmacist or, in rural areas, a dispensing doctor. For those receiving domiciliary or nursing home care, their medicine taking may be overseen by a nurse or other member of staff. All of these people are potential sources of information about the medicine.

When patients are asked about their preferred sources of information about medicines, they usually say that they regard their doctors as the best sources of information (Makoul et al. 1995). For some people, their doctor is the only source of information about medicines. It seems likely that people prefer information given by their doctors because the doctors know the diagnoses, and possibly because they regard doctors as more trustworthy than some other sources, such as industry. Yet studies of consultations between patients and doctors show that doctors may give little information about the medicines they prescribe and certainly less than patients say they want. In some cases, the medicine is not even named, being referred to, for example, as 'the blue one', 'something to help with this cold', 'the oldest one' or even 'these little fellas' (Stevenson et al. 2000).

Makoul and colleagues (1995) carried out a careful and detailed study in the United Kingdom in which they asked general practitioners to rate the importance of communication about prescription medicines and also to estimate the extent to which they actually accomplished this. They found that doctors placed most importance on providing complete instructions for taking the medicine, involving patients in deciding upon a treatment plan and providing patients with enough information to make a choice. Least importance was placed upon explaining all the benefits, risks and all possible side effects. Doctors' ratings of the extent to which they accomplished these tasks reflected the importance they attached to them. The explaining of the benefits of medication was rated as slightly more important than the explaining of risks or side effects. In the same study, doctors' consultations were videotaped, and the extent to which they actually carried out communication tasks was compared with their estimates of accomplishment. In general, they overestimated the extent to which they accomplished specific tasks. There was a large gap between the actual discussion of the benefits and risks of medication, with benefits being discussed in over half the consultations and risks in only 3 per cent of consultations. The possible side effects of medication were discussed in less than a third of consultations. In over two thirds of consultations, side effects, precautions and risks were not mentioned by either doctor or patient.

Following the study consultations, patients were asked to estimate the extent to which their doctors had discussed adverse reactions associated with the prescribed medications. Worryingly, nearly a quarter of the patients left the consultation thinking that important topics had been discussed when, on the evidence of the videotapes, they had not been discussed at all. It is possible that doctors' reluctance to discuss potential adverse reactions was interpreted by the patients to mean that there were none. Nearly a quarter of the patients in the study also reported to the researchers that they had experienced a side effect from the prescribed medicine, of whom nearly a half said that they were unaware of this possibility when it happened. Those patients who were aware of the possibility of side effects were asked how they knew this; fewer than half said that they had learned about possible side effects from their doctors. Thus, the lack of importance attached by doctors to explaining side effects fully does lead to problems for those patients who experience them, including non-adherence. The study by Makoul and colleagues (1995) is further discussed in Chapter 7.

Pharmacy research has shown that some people do not want pharmacists to give them information about medicines because they feel that they have been given this information by their doctors (Cox et al. 2004). Salter and colleagues (2007) analysed home-based medication reviews by UK pharmacists and found that the pharmacists found many opportunities to give information and advice about medications to their elderly patients. However, patients rarely solicited the advice, but rather demonstrated their own competence and expertise. The advice given by pharmacists was often resisted by the patients, and the authors concluded that it had the potential to undermine and threaten patients' management of their medicines. In contrast, a household survey in the United Kingdom found that when people did have a view of pharmacists' area of expertise, it was perceived to be related to medicines rather than to health (Hassell et al. 1998). For many of their respondents, the pharmacist's particular expertise about medicines related to their knowledge of potential adverse effects, dosage information and information about the contents of medication. Similarly, in a study of pharmacy clients in the United States, Chewning and Schommer (1996) found that nearly two thirds of them wanted information about side effects. These findings, if more widely applicable, suggest that pharmacists may be well placed to deal with clients' lifeworld concerns about safety. A focus group study of pharmacy customers in Iceland found that they wanted more information from pharmacists than was often provided, and that customers had actively to ask pharmacists for information (Traulsen et al. 2002). These studies suggest that pharmacists have to steer a difficult course between providing customers with appropriate information when required, without offending those customers who do not perceive pharmacists as sources of expertise about medications, and not undermining patients' competence and self-governance.

Turning to nurse prescribing, Rycroft-Malone et al. (2001) investigated communication between nurses and their patients in eight clinical areas, focusing on information-giving. They found that nurses did not appear to be fostering informed choice, and that they tended to dominate the dialogue. The exceptions to these findings were the rehabilitation ward and mental health, where more of a partnership approach was observed. There was little evidence of information-giving about the side effects of medication, although patients appeared satisfied with relatively superficial information. As part of the same study, the researchers conducted focus groups with carers in the same geographical areas who were caring for those with similar clinical conditions as the study participants. In contrast to the patients' reports, carers expressed a strong preference for information about side effects of medicines and said that professionals had not provided this.

Overall, if professionals do not provide patients with the information they seek, then other sources will become increasingly important.

Written Sources of Information

In many countries, manufacturers are now required by law to provide Patient Information Leaflets (PILs) with all dispensed medication. In addition, written information about medicines may be provided by individual pharmacies, hospitals or health centres. The distinction between written and verbal information may be less important for patients than it is for professionals and industry. Raynor and colleagues conducted a systematic review of written information about medicines and found that patients do not want written information to substitute verbal information (Raynor et al. 2007). Clearly, if contradictory messages are being given, this is unhelpful; on the other hand, written information can reinforce what has been said face to face and can be kept to read again later on. Participants in stakeholder groups conducted by Raynor and colleagues stressed that the source of information is more important than whether it is written or verbal. Some people regard information produced by manufacturers as being the most useful on the grounds that manufacturers are best placed to provide information on their own products. Others distrust such information on the grounds that the manufacturer's main purpose in providing information will be to increase sales. Leaflets produced in accordance with EU recommended terminology may have the unintended consequence of leading people to overestimate the probability that side effects will occur.

Not all written information is helpful to those receiving it, nor does it necessarily address the questions they may want answered. In fact, Raynor and colleagues concluded that most people do not value the written information they receive about medicines (Raynor et al. 2007). They found that many leaflets are of poor quality and do not increase patients' knowledge, satisfaction or adherence. One study of written prescription information provided in US community pharmacies found that most leaflets did not adhere to legally defined criteria of usefulness. These criteria included being 'scientifically accurate, non-promotional in tone and content, sufficiently specific and comprehensive as to adequately inform consumers about the use of the product, and in an understandable, legible format that is readily comprehensible and not confusing to consumers expected to use the product' (cited in Svarstad et al. 2003).

Svarstad and colleagues found that, although the leaflets were generally unbiased in tone and content, they often lacked acceptable information about important contraindications, specific precautions and how to avoid harm while using the medication.

Patients and professionals often have different views about the value and purpose of written information. Patients do not see improving adherence as a function of PILs; some professionals see this as the prime function. For these professionals, providing information is clearly an example of concealed strategic action (see Chapter 1). Professionals may also hope that providing written information will save them time in the consultation (another strategic goal), whereas patients do not want this kind of substitution. Some professionals fear that information about risks and side effects could deter people from taking medicines and use this as an argument against providing information. They may also be concerned about overloading patients with too much information, and there is evidence that professionals underestimate the amount of information that patients need and want. Short and oversimplified leaflets produced by professionals may not be at all helpful to patients. Raynor and colleagues (2007) identified the paradox that professionals value the provision of information about over the counter (OTC) medicines, information that consumers often do not want as they regard OTCs as being safe, while professionals are reluctant to provide the information about prescription medicines that patients do want. The issue of information about side effects is perhaps the most crucial for patients. On this issue, Raynor and colleagues concluded that

> Health professionals worry about the possible negative impact of side effect information on patients, but the findings of the role and value strand [of their review] suggest that some patients prefer to be 'worried and aware' rather than the reverse. Overall the evidence from the trials reviewed showed that providing information about side effects does not increase the side effects experienced or reported, but does mean that they are more likely to be attributed to the medicine. The role of medicines information in enabling patients to recognise side effects is potentially important in improving safety by enabling patients to alert a health professional to the side effect, or reporting it directly to the MHRA. No evidence was found to confirm professional concern that providing information on side effects will lead to patients erroneously reporting side effects. (Raynor et al. 2007, p. 82)

Thus, it is clear that written information provided about prescription medicines does not, on the whole, support people in making decisions. This is partly because the professionals designing and producing this information do not see this as its prime purpose, and few leaflets are produced in consultation with those likely to be using them. The justification for withholding information about side effects, that this will produce side effects by the power of suggestion, is not supported by the evidence. People want to have leaflets that are tailored to their own circumstances, although health professionals are more likely to provide this than are leaflets. People want information to help them make decisions, first about whether to take a medicine or not, and second for ongoing decisions about medicine taking. Leaflets to help people make decisions about whether to take a medicine or not would need to be available at the time of prescribing, and would have to include information about the whole range of treatments available (including self-treatment and complementary and alternative treatments), as well as the benefits and harms of the medicine being prescribed. Leaflets intended to support people already taking a medicine would need to include information about acceptable doses, what to do if a dose was missed, symptoms attributable to side effects and advice about when to seek medical attention. A good example of this kind of information is provided in Table 5.1. Unlike most patient information leaflets, tables of this type provide some indication of the

Table 5.1 Erythromycin: possible adverse effects

Symptom/effect	Frequency		Discuss with doctor		Stop taking drug now	Call doctor now
	Common	Rare	Only if severe	In all cases		
Nausea/vomiting	●		■			
Diarrhoea	●		■			
Rash/itching	●			■	▲	
Deafness		●		■		I
Jaundice		●		■	▲	I
Unexplained fever		●		■	▲	I
Skin blisters/ulcers		●		■	▲	I

Source: Peters (2004).

likelihood of experiencing adverse reactions and the appropriate responses. If people do experience side effects, as many are bound to, accurate information will help them make correct attributions and respond appropriately.

Herxheimer (1999) reviewed leaflets provided with 29 non-steroidal anti-inflammatory drugs (NSAIDs) to see how far they explained the safe use of these drugs and warned about gastrointestinal side effects. He found great inconsistencies in the information and warnings given in the leaflets and serious deficiencies in the content of most of them. The idea that the benefit/risk relationship changes with the dose of most drugs was not explicitly explained beyond the routine warning not to exceed the stated dose. Herxheimer concluded that 'most doctors and pharmacists still seem to doubt that patients are capable of changing the dose of prescribed medicine on their own initiative – if they have the requisite knowledge' (Herxheimer 1999, p. 560).

In fact, as we saw in Chapter 3, patients regularly change the doses of their prescribed medicines often without the knowledge of the prescriber or necessarily with the 'requisite knowledge'. Such knowledge is not provided in most patient information leaflets and indeed may not be available. Little research is carried out to enable patients to individualize their own medication regimens or to determine the minimum effective therapeutic doses of licensed medications. I will discuss this further in Chapter 9.

News Media as a Source of Information

Health and illness provide a rich source of media stories with their potential for dramatic life and death narratives spiced with human interest. Media portrayal of medicines tends to be highly polarized between the two extremes of 'miracle cure' and 'poisonous chemical'. Some of the same criteria that are applied to leaflets can also be applied to the media, such as questions of accuracy, balance, intelligibility and commercial interest.

Entwistle (1995) interviewed ten medical journalists in the United Kingdom, most of whom were their newspaper's health correspondent, to explore the reporting of medical research. Journalists claimed that they were aiming for balanced reporting to avoid producing unwarranted optimism or pessimism. They claimed to have a sense of responsibility about reporting medical research and to be keen to get their stories right. They acknowledged that they were constrained by their inability to evaluate the quality of the evidence reported in medical journals, relying on the peer review system to filter out poor quality research. A study carried out in the Netherlands explored the question of journalists' sources for stories about medicines more widely. Van Trigt and colleagues (1994, 1995) found that medical journals were the most important sources of information because of their insistence on originality. This meant that journalists could be confident that articles in medical journals were newsworthy and had not previously been covered by their rivals. Although, when interviewed, journalists claimed that the pharmaceutical industry was not an important source of information, it was the third most frequently cited source of information in newspaper articles. Whenever a pharmaceutical company was mentioned in an article, another source was often mentioned as well, so that journalists were not relying solely on industry for their information. In terms of balance, van Trigt and colleagues found that the 'good news' agenda of newspapers was similar in coverage to the 'good news' agenda of the scientific literature, with 58 per cent of scientific publications being characterized as positive or neutral compared with 75 per cent of newspaper stories. The same was not true of bad news, as 26 per cent of the scientific publications focused on the negative consequences of medicines, and only 14 per cent of the newspaper articles did. Thus, on both counts the newspaper coverage was more favourable in its portrayal of medicines than the scientific literature, which as we have already seen is more likely to report positive than negative results.

Moynihan and colleagues (2000) examined the coverage by the US news media (newspapers and television) of the benefits and risks of three medications: pravastatin, alendronate and aspirin. These particular medications were chosen because they have important preventive benefits, potentially large markets and have attracted considerable media attention. At the time of writing, pravastatin and alendronate were relatively new patented medicines for the prevention of cardiovascular disease and osteoporosis respectively. Aspirin is an older off-patent drug also used for the prevention of cardiovascular disease. Aspirin and alendronate are associated with gastrointestinal side effects, and pravastatin was considered to have a relatively low rate of adverse effects. While all the articles and reports mentioned the benefits of the drugs, less than half mentioned the potential harms, and less than a third mentioned the costs. Most of the stories reporting only benefits provided information on relative benefits, with only 15 per cent of stories providing information on both relative and absolute benefits, thus providing an overoptimistic assessment. Half of the 170 media stories which reported experts or scientific studies, cited at least one expert or study with financial tie(s) which had been disclosed in the scientific literature, but only 39 per cent of these media stories disclosed these ties to their own readers. Overall, Moynihan and colleagues concluded that the coverage of the three study drugs was overwhelmingly positive, focusing mainly on benefits reported in relative terms. They suggested that when reporting new treatments, journalists and editors should review the evidence using the following series of questions:

● What is the magnitude of the benefit in both absolute and relative terms?

● What groups of patients can be helped?

● What are the associated risks and costs?

● What are the possible links between the sources of information and those who promote the therapy?

Thus, these studies suggest that media coverage of medicines is unbalanced in favour of positive reporting, and that although the scientific literature is an important source of information, so too is the pharmaceutical industry.

In contrast, Gabe and colleagues' work on media coverage of tranquilliser dependence suggested that it was not dominated primarily by medical definitions of health (Gabe et al. 1991). The two ideological frames used by journalists when covering this topic were first the portrayal of women as weak and dependent, and second the portrayal of consumers as knowledgeable individuals capable of challenging the authority of the medical profession. People experiencing dependence, usually women, were portrayed as having lost control and being passive. However, those who were stopping their medication were portrayed as active consumers, on a return journey to normal life. Gabe and colleagues (1991) argued that the use of consumerism allowed journalists to feel that they were 'empowering' or enabling their readers to take action against powerful others rather than exploiting those individuals whose stories they are telling.

The Internet as a Source of Information

Health Policy documents and academic articles frequently comment on the rise of well informed 'consumers' of health services: those who become knowledgeable about their own condition and seek genuine partnerships with their health care providers. It is assumed that the Internet plays a large role in redressing the imbalance of knowledge between patients and professionals. In a study of web based information on the risks and benefits of mammographic screening, Jorgensen and Gotzsche (2004) found that information presented on websites by professional advocacy groups and governmental organizations was selective, biased and failed to mention major harms. In contrast, websites from consumer groups were more balanced and comprehensive. The work of consumer groups is discussed in more detail in Chapter 8. Certainly, the Internet provides an unparalleled and seemingly infinite source of all kinds of information. As Ziebland and colleagues (2004) found, the range of uses to which such information is put is also very broad. In their study of people with cancer, reasons for using the Internet included

- finding second opinions
- seeking support and experiential information from other patients
- interpreting symptoms
- seeking information about tests and treatments
- helping to interpret consultations with health professionals
- identifying appropriate questions to ask their doctors
- checking their doctors' advice covertly
- making anonymous private enquiries
- raising awareness of the cancer.

In relation to treatments, people used the Internet to

- obtain information about treatment options and side effects
- obtain information about treatments still at the experimental stage
- research into new treatments
- find out about complementary and alternative treatments.

Such information is well beyond anything included in most leaflets or discussed in most consultations with professionals, although some of it is covered by the news media.

Nettleton and colleagues (2005) have characterized the structure of the Internet as either a juxtaposition of epistemologically incommensu-rate sites all vying for attention or as structured in ways congruent with more traditional forms of media (the media convergence theory). They identified three types of response to the Internet which they have termed celebratory and empowering, concerned and dangerous, and contingent and embedded. The celebratory response highlights the potential of the Internet to empower patients and to provide a forum for resisting professional dominance. Hardey (1999) notes that the unregulated electronic space of the Internet echoes the diversity of the market for health that existed before medicine secured its professional status. The concerned response, mainly emanating from professionals, focuses on the quality of information and the existence of dangerous and misleading material. Dangers include the availability of prescription drugs, fake or poor quality drugs and the undifferentiated mass of information with no way for the lay person to judge its quality. The contingent response characterizes Internet use as both embedded and embodied: embedded in users' actual use of health services and embodied in their own symptoms and experiences. Nettleton and colleagues (2005) concluded that there is an emerging concordance between lay use of the Internet for health and illness, and dominant conceptions of what constitutes good quality health information. In their study of UK families in which children had been diagnosed with asthma, eczema and/or diabetes, they examined the ways in which people accomplished the legitimacy of information sources. They found that interviewees were well aware of concerns about quality of information on the web and identified six rhetorics of reliability. These were a range of rhetorical devices which parents used to articulate why they trusted some sources and not others. Devices included distinguishing between real and virtual organizations, UK and non-UK based sources, commercial and non-commercial sources, and professional or official and non-professional sources. Interviewees presented themselves as responsible users of the Internet, in contrast to others who might be duped by unreliable information or false claims. They used the information to enhance their experience of health care by deciding when it was appropriate to seek help, formulating appropriate questions and making sense of what they had been told. From their data, Nettleton and colleagues drew out the implicit rules about the appropriate use of health care: that patients should not waste their doctor's time; that patients should become informed but not overly so; and that patients should ask appropriate questions during consultations and be reflective about the answers. Thus, the rhetorics of reliability are reinforcing discourses of professionalism and biomedicine.

An Australian study specifically examined the ways in which consumers searched for and appraised information about medicines on the Internet (Peterson et al. 2003). Participants used a variety of search procedures and had a range of opinions about the credibility of sources. Some thought that pharmaceutical companies provided the 'official' information on a medicine, while others preferred what they regarded as impartial sources such as governments and educational institutions. They viewed the Internet as an important source of information about medicines but were sceptical about its value. It is likely that with the passage of time, the importance of the Internet as a source of information will grow; this is likely to increase consumers' exposure to advertising even in countries where direct advertising is forbidden.

Industry as a Source of Information: DTCA

In most countries, direct advertising of prescription medicines to consumers is illegal. However, in the United States and New Zealand, Direct to Consumer Advertising (DTCA) is allowed, and there is continuing pressure within the EU for the rules to be relaxed. The use of advertising on the Internet may provide a back door method for DTCA, and as use of the Internet expands, it may come to replace DTCA. While some patients may be sceptical about the influence of advertising on their own decisions, they may (like doctors) be unaware of the role it plays in their own lives.

There are different kinds of advertisements, the two main kinds being spreading disease awareness and product awareness. The former is designed to increase awareness of a disease and the fact that it is treatable, while the latter names a drug and makes claims for it. Direct to consumer advertising has been a major part of pharmaceutical marketing in the United States since 1992, and the relaxation of Food and Drug Administration (FDA) rules about television advertising in 1997 increased spending on this medium (for an example, see Box 5.1).

The arguments in favour of DTCA, advanced by the pharmaceutical industry, are that it meets consumers' need for more information; it empowers patients to play a more active role in their own health care; it addresses public health disparities in underserved populations; it can improve rates of diagnosis and treatment for those with untreated or undiagnosed conditions; it can lead to healthier lifestyles (Holmer 1999). The arguments against DTCA are that it bears little relation to public health needs, as there are no adverts for generic drugs used to treat chronic conditions such as hypertension; that there is an inevitable conflict of interest between pharmaceutical companies' financial interests and the need for balanced information; that it is wrong to advertise goods that cannot – or should not – be purchased directly; that putting something on sale suggests that it is fit for the intended purpose; and that TV and radio are inappropriate media for the communication of complex information. The potential effects of DTCA, for its promoters, include quicker diagnosis. For its opponents, potential effects include the production of unwarranted demand. There are also claims that DTCA can harm the patient–professional relationship and that, paradoxically, it can reduce the time spent on diagnosis if the practitioner has to explain why a particular drug is inappropriate or unnecessary. It is argued that DTCA can turn patients into agents of the pharmaceutical industry, that it promotes the idea that newer is better, and that it will increase the cost of health care.

Evidence in favour of these claims is limited. However, the large sums of money spent by the pharmaceutical industry demonstrate its commercial effectiveness. Having reviewed the available evidence, Lexchin (1999) concluded that DTCA would probably have negative consequences for patients' expectations of disease management. He judged that patients would be likely to ask for and receive newer medications, with less well established safety profiles, and may change doctors if their requests are denied. He felt that this could erode patients' confidence in their physicians and the health care system. Two studies which examined the effect of DTCA on primary care consultations in Canada and the United States are discussed in Chapter 7.

The question of DTCA has been debated within the United States. During a public hearing about DTCA held in Washington DC by the FDA in November 2005, Dr Cranston of the American Medical Association raised a number of questions (http://www.fda.gov/cder). He asked if television adverts exhibited fair balance and cited the practice of showing distracting visual material while risk information is discussed on the audio channel. He asked if consumers can understand and accurately assess claims about efficacy of prescription drugs made in DTCA. He also considered the impact of DTCA on the doctor–patient relationship. Dr Cranston concluded that TV adverts were not balanced, that the educational value of adverts could be improved by presenting benefits more objectively, and that there were both positive and negative effects on the doctor–patient relationship, although more research is needed.

The question of consumers' ability to assess claims made in DTCA is similar to the question of their ability to assess information on the web. But it is not clear that any conclusions about consumers' assessment of web-based information is transferable to DTCA if we do not know whether the people watching TV adverts and seeing DTCA adverts in print journals are the same people who surf the Internet. TV ownership is more prevalent than computer ownership, although the digitalization project may well change that. It is possible that TV watchers include the disadvantaged groups that industry wants to reach; if so, these may be the same people who have no health insurance and would have difficulty paying for their prescription medications.

Conclusion

Overall, there is a general bias towards information about the benefits of prescription medicines and away from information about harms and potential side effects. This applies to professional and commercial sources as well as news media and the Internet. It is despite the fact that professionals need unbiased information and patients want to have information about side effects. For patients, there are several layers of pro-drug bias: the initial publication of trial results in medical journals; the provision of written information; media reporting and, as we will see in Chapter 7, face to face communication with health professionals. There are some campaigning organizations which aim to redress this imbalance: for example, the US-based website www.nofreelunch.org and the Australian-based website www.healthyskepticism.org.

Professionals' fears – that information about side effects is a self-fulfilling prophecy – are unfounded, and there is no justification for withholding this information from patients. Most sources of information about medicines would seem to fall into the 'patient education' category, except for DTCA with its explicit and potentially misleading appeal to 'patient empowerment' and the less prominent parts of the Internet. The pharmaceutical industry's main interest in patient empowerment is increased consumption of its own products. There are few sources of unbiased information which aim to help patients first to make informed treatment choices and second to manage their medicines. Both industry and professionals tend to provide information in order to achieve their respective strategic goals of higher sales or adherence. There is little support for the ways in which patients make decisions about whether to take medicines or not, or how they actually use their medicines, which is to adapt the timing and doses to their own lifeworld circumstances. It would seem likely that patient involvement in the production of medicines information could fill this gap, but only in genuinely participatory circumstances.

In Chapter 6, I will consider the factors influencing prescribers of medicines and the various ways in which system imperatives influence professional behaviour, before going on to examine patient–professional communication in Chapter 8.

Box 5.1   Example: Vioxx and DTCA

Vioxx is the brand name of rofecoxib, a drug claimed by its manufacturer Merck to be an effective and safer alternative to non-steroidal anti-inflammatory drugs (NSAIDs) for the treatment of arthritis. It was introduced in 1999 supported by an article in the *Journal of the American Medical Association* and an accompanying but less enthusiastic editorial (Langman et al. 1999, Peterson and Cryer 1999). In 2000, the results of the Vioxx Gastrointestinal Outcomes Research (VIGOR) study were published in the *New England Journal of Medicine*. These findings raised the possibility that the use of Vioxx was associated with an increased risk of heart attacks and other cardiovascular complications. This possibility was eventually confirmed, and the drug was withdrawn from the market in 2004. It was subsequently established that Merck's chief scientist had concerns about the drug before the VIGOR results were published, and that the published results had obscured the cardiovascular risk in several ways. The report contained data from an interim analysis in which adverse gastrointestinal events were counted for one month longer than adverse cardiovascular events. The use of this biased analysis was not reported in the paper and had the effect of favouring the drug's effect on gastrointestinal events (a major problem with rival NSAID medications) and understating the drug's effect on cardiovascular events.

Meanwhile, despite the fact that the company already had data which suggested that the drug was associated with increased cardiovascular risks, Merck spent millions of dollars advertising the drug directly to the American public. One print advertisement showed a smiling woman teacher in a classroom of children under the heading 'I won't let arthritis pain keep me from teaching'. In 2000, Merck spent more than $160 million on DTC adverts, about $20 million more than the previous record for DTCA expenditure. This enormous figure was dwarfed by the $1.1 billion sales achieved in the same year. The monthly cost to the patient, or their Health Maintenance Organization (HMO) or insurance company, was $100–134 a month. Nearly 107 million prescriptions for Vioxx were dispensed in the United States between 1999 and 2004. As Krumholz et al. (2007) remark, 'none of the people picking up these prescriptions had the opportunity to consider the true balance of its risks and benefits'. One could add that neither did most of the prescribers.

Subsequently, Merck faced legal claims for nearly 30,000 people who had cardiovascular events while taking the drug.

Sources: Abramson 2004 and Krumholz et al. 2007.

6

Prescribing

Introduction

In Chapter 4, I examined the various systems for bringing a new medicine to market. Once a drug is licensed, although manufacturers can only make claims about the stated indications, doctors are usually free to prescribe medicines for whatever indications they deem appropriate. In countries with managed care systems, third party insurers may determine whether a particular prescription is reimbursable for a particular indication. In the United Kingdom, GPs have greater freedom to prescribe than hospital doctors, whose prescribing is constrained by Drug and Therapeutics Committees and influenced by pharmacists (Cotter et al. 1993). If patients want access to prescription medicines, lay people in most industrialized countries need to consult professionals with the authority to prescribe. The need or desire for prescription medicines thus brings people into contact with health professionals. In Giddens' terms, patient–professional consultations constitute the main access point for lay people in relation to the expert systems of the production and consumption of prescription medicines; the professional activities of prescribing and dispensing provide the access (Giddens 1990).

Until recently, prescribing of medicines was a core activity which differentiated doctors from other health care professionals. The fact that the same word (medicine) is used to signify both the profession and the material object underscores the closeness of this association. This is now changing and, for example, nurses in countries such as Australia, Canada, the United States and the United Kingdom now have limited or full prescribing rights, as do pharmacists in the United Kingdom. Thus, in the United Kingdom in 2005, 97.9 per cent of prescriptions dispensed in the community (in other words, excluding those dispensed in hospitals and other institutional settings) were prescribed by general practitioners (GPs) compared with 0.6 per cent written by nurses, 0.7 per cent written by dentists and 0.8 per cent written in hospital but dispensed in the community (Government Statistical Service 2006). At this time, there were about 25,500 nurse prescribers in the United Kingdom (House of Commons Health Committee 2005). By 2007 more than 8,000 nurses in the United Kingdom had been trained as independent or supplementary prescribers with access to the same formulary as doctors; many more district nurses and health visitors were prescribing from a restricted formulary (Avery and James 2007). The proportion of prescriptions written by nurses is likely to rise as their numbers increase and their prescribing rights are extended. This is an example of the threat posed to the medical profession by other health care workers, and this is one of the factors identified by McKinlay and Marceau (2002) in their analysis of the decline of the 'golden age of doctoring'. Certainly the training and competence of nurse prescribers has been questioned (Avery and James 2007). If, as Schwartz et al. (1989) claim, 'the act of prescribing is an enduring sign of professional prowess' one can only assume that the extension of prescribing has the potential to reduce medical prowess on one hand, and increase nursing prowess on the other. The extension of prescribing rights to other professionals especially pharmacists also leads to more complex relationships in which different professionals will need to discuss the medication needs of individual patients. The need for good teamworking is more important than ever.

As Cribb and Barber (1997) point out, prescribing takes places at different levels: at the level of the individual consultation; as part of a professional process of the diagnosis and management of disease; and as part of a policy process. There are many interested parties who stand to gain or lose from specific prescribing decisions at any of these levels including the prescribers themselves, patients, professional groups, third party insurers, health maintenance organizations, governments and, of course, the manufacturers. The aim of this chapter is to explore the ways in which different system imperatives impact on prescribing.

What is Good Prescribing?

Habermas' characterization of the system embraces the economy and the state, which have sometimes conflicting interests in the prescribing of medicines (Outhwaite 1994). A thriving pharmaceutical industry can make an important contribution to national and global economies, while national governments have the role of protecting the health of their citizens, providing legislative frameworks for ensuring the safety of medicines and, in some countries, running a national health service. In this context, any definition of good prescribing is likely to reflect these competing interests.

Pellegrino (1976) identified two polarized philosophies of therapeutics, which he called 'pharmacological license' and 'pharmacological parsimony'. These two schools of thought have different definitions of rationality. Those in the 'license' school believe that pharmaceuticals have achieved more good than harm. Proponents believe that 'chemical coping and the widespread use of medication are tributes to the wonders of pharmacology, which permit so many people to function amid the stresses of modern living' (Pellegrino 1976, p. 629). What society needs, in this view, are more drugs with even more varied effects. The 'parsimony' school, on the other hand, feels that the use of a drug is only justified if it demonstrably alters the natural history of a disease or improves a patient's symptoms. More than this is dangerous. Proponents of this school believe that the use of medication to solve social problems is unethical, and that the goal of therapeutics is to use fewer drugs and only if they can be shown to be both effective and safe. Clearly, the purchasers of medicines are likely to favour the parsimony school of thought while the vendors will favour pharmacological license. Pellegrino concluded that it was the very potency of the symbolism of medicines that required professionals to adopt a more parsimonious strategy, and that society had to move away from symbols and towards substances.

A dominant concept in this field, based in the parsimony school of thought, has been that of 'rational drug use' as a way of dealing with profligate and inappropriate prescribing. Examples of non-rational prescribing include the use of ineffective drugs such as cerebral vasodilators for dementia, inappropriate prescribing such as antibiotics for viral infections or expensive 'me-too' drugs and excessive repeat prescribing of 'as required' prescriptions. Cohen et al. (2001) identified several further types of seemingly irrational prescribing practices including the following:

- Failure to transmit necessary information to the patient
- Failure to obtain informed consent
- Prescriptions for non-licensed indications
- Reliance on commercial rather than scientific sources of information
- Non-adherence to recommendations from controlled studies or clinical guidelines
- Failure to report suspected serious adverse drug reactions to public health authorities.

The reasons why physicians make inappropriate prescribing decisions are various but include the failure to keep up with developments in pharmacology, over promotion of drugs by industry, errors of oversight or omission, ignorance or disdain for cost issues, pressure from patients or their families, the need to be seen to do something for their patients, and as a way of terminating consultations (Soumerai et al. 1989). Definitions of rational prescribing attempt to address these problems. The interests of industry would be better served by a 'pharmacological license' model with which these irrational practices are largely compatible.

An early and influential definition of rational prescribing was that drug treatments should be 'appropriate, effective, safe and economic'. This definition was set out in an article entitled 'Sociology of Prescribing' by Peter Parish who was in fact an academic GP (Parish 1974). For Parish, an appropriate treatment was one which would benefit the patient most, and an effective treatment was one which produced 'proper and intended effects'. Parish was aware that doctors could mistakenly believe that drugs they had prescribed had had the intended effects without knowing if the patients had even taken them. A more recent definition is that a rational prescription is one which is 'an appropriate drug, at an appropriate dose, for an appropriate period, for a specified therapeutic aim', where appropriateness is being considered in terms of efficacy, safety and cost (Bateman 1998). Clearly the dimensions of rationality are fluid, as the earlier definition made no mention of dosage or timeframe, for example.

Definitions of rational prescribing are primarily based on a pharmacological concept of rationality and, to a lesser extent, economic rationality as seen by the state or managed care organization. These definitions serve to constrain the effects of industry but they do not acknowledge the relevance of patients' priorities and preferences. In particular, these concepts of rational prescribing make no reference to adherence, that is, whether and how the patient takes the prescribed medicine. Given the long-standing problem of 'non compliance' and the enormous literature this has generated, this is a surprising omission (Vermeire et al. 2001). A drug which is not taken, or is taken in idiosyncratic ways, may not achieve what the prescriber intends. To assess rational prescribing without considering adherence is like judging the quality of a meal without tasting it. The failure to take adherence seriously as a component of prescribing is mirrored in the general lack of monitoring of patients' use of medicines (the exceptions being potentially dangerous situations such as warfarin clinics or in chronic diseases such as diabetes clinics), and physicians' lack of engagement with patients' perspectives.

A rather different approach to the concept of good prescribing was taken by Cribb and Barber (1997), who argued that prescribing is more than just a technical issue. In the context of the United Kingdom, Barber claimed that prescribers should have four aims: to maximize effectiveness; to minimize risks; to minimize costs and to respect the patient's choices (Barber 1995). His rationale for advocating a broader definition was that in a publicly funded system such as the UK National Health Service (NHS), ethical and practical considerations require engagement with patients' preferences. In describing this model, he explicitly acknowledged the tensions between these different aims, particularly between effectiveness and risk, and between patients' choices and cost minimization. In a later paper, Cribb and Barber (1997) developed this argument further. They identified three components of good prescribing: prescribing drugs which have the right technical properties; prescribing drugs which do what the patients want and prescribing drugs which serve the general good. Again, tensions were acknowledged even within components. The technical component is mainly concerned with pharmacological issues, although economic aspects may also be included here. However, to conceptualize efficacy, for example, as a purely technical issue is to claim that biomedical definitions are the only ones that count. For patients, the relevant outcome measures by which they decide if a medicine is working may or may not coincide with biomedically defined outcomes (as we saw in Chapter 3).

The proposition that good prescribing requires drugs which do what the patient wants is a novel concept in the prescribing literature. Characterizations of poor prescribing often include references to 'patient demand'. Thus, Schwartz et al. (1989) found that patient demand was the most frequently cited motivation for non-scientific prescribing of a specific range of drugs. Similarly, Bradley (1992a) found that patient expectations were the most common reason for prescribing decisions which the prescriber found uncomfortable. In general, yielding to patients' inappropriate expectations has been posited as a key element in poor prescribing. The question posed by Cribb and Barber is 'whether, and to what extent, a patient's "specifications" of the goals and parameters of prescribing should be accorded weight'. This is partly a philosophical question about the extent to which health care goals should be determined by patient wants rather than professionally defined needs; it is also a practical issue in the sense that it is the patient who has to decide whether to have a prescription dispensed, and whether and how to take the drug on a day to day basis. It is a question which follows from policy commitments to patient involvement in health care. This component of Cribb and Barber's model requires prescribers to know why their patients are seeking health care and, if they are in fact taking prescribed medicines, what they are hoping to achieve in doing so. This is often not the case. In Chapters 2 and 3, we explored the ways in which patients use both non-prescribed and prescribed treatments, and in Chapter 7 we will explore the ways in which prescribers and patients communicate about prescribing. The points to note here are that patients have their own criteria for testing the medicines they are prescribed; these criteria are not often shared with prescribers; that patients' goals and priorities may change over time and these may conflict with system goals. Particularly in the context of chronic illness, prescribing is an ongoing process which may extend over many years. As patients' and prescribers' goals may differ, this approach requires prescribers to be able to identify these differences and discuss them with their patients.

The third of Cribb and Barber's components refers to the wider community. Individual prescribing decisions impact on the community in several ways, for example, by using resources that might have been spent on other patients, by labelling a problem such as obesity as a medical rather than a social problem, by affecting community resistance to antibiotics, or by preventing the spread of an infectious disease. Some of these impacts fall within the domain of public health, and any considerations about the greater good are based on value judgements even if these are not made explicit. In a democratic society, one could argue that these value judgements (for example, about the rights of individuals who have contracted highly infectious diseases such as tuberculosis to refuse treatment) should be debated in public. Any definition of appropriate or rational prescribing will reflect certain interests, and the definitions discussed here reflect the interests of funders.

Cribb and Barber argue that these wider considerations are obscured by treating prescribing as a purely technical matter, and in making this argument they acknowledge that the usual objective frameworks against which prescribing is judged are insufficient for these wider purposes. Thus they offer no easy solutions. They conclude that 'prescribing will only improve if individuals' agendas are drawn into the prescribing process at every level', but they do not explain how this might be done. What is clear is that the technical and the non-technical aspects of prescribing are closely intertwined, whether acknowledged or not.

Prescribing Decisions

Cribb and Barber (1997) talk about the context of choice of prescribing and identify two related factors. The first is that prescribing takes place within institutional and cultural settings which have their own normative expectations; these will include the norms inherent in different systems of health care. The second factor relates to the ways in which prescribers' choices will be limited by the drugs available to them via national or local formularies, or the policies of health insurance organizations. The contexts of choice for individual prescribers will be partly determined by the licensing arrangements in their own country and the funding arrangements already described in Chapter 1.

One aspect of prescribing which is implicit in the definitions discussed above has to do with medicalization, which is described by Conrad as 'defining a problem in medical terms, usually as an illness or disorder, or using a medical intervention to treat it' (Conrad 2005, p. 3). Prescribing medication for a particular problem is a powerful way of defining the problem as medical rather than social, and there is an increasing number of problems such as 'attention deficit – hyperactivity disorder' and 'erectile dysfunction' from which prescription medications promise relief. Cohen et al. (2001) argue that medications are both cause and consequence of the medicalization of social problems. Thus any consideration of the appropriateness of prescribing needs to examine whether the problem is in fact a medical one. Those writing about medicalization have argued that it is a means by which professionals exert social control, and feminists have certainly resisted the constraints imposed by medical professionals on childbirth. Pharmaceutical companies, in contrast, have much to gain from redefining social problems as medical and have been accused of disease mongering to create new markets for their products. Conrad (2005) has argued that the pharmaceutical industry is having a growing impact on the boundary between the normal and the pathological thereby becoming an active agent of social control. Practices include the introduction of questionable new diagnoses such as social anxiety disorders that are hard to distinguish from normal life, promotion of aggressive drug treatment of milder symptoms and diseases, promotion of anxiety about future ill health in healthy individuals and inflated disease prevalence rates (Mintzes 2006). However, to understand this phenomenon more fully, one would need to know if and how individuals experiencing such problems were helped by having them diagnosed and treated within a medical framework. For some, the legitimacy of a medical diagnosis might provide reassurance that their problem was being taken seriously as well as access to treatment; for others, as Illich (1976) has argued, such a response might undermine their capacity for dealing with their own problems. The evidence suggests that the emphasis on prescribing medicines serves to divert attention from other, non-pharmaceutical, ways of managing health problems (Waitzkin 1991).

For individual prescribers at the level of the consultation, the first decision is whether to prescribe or not. This part of the prescribing process has been somewhat neglected in comparison with questions about drug choice, efficacy and so on. Bradley (1992b) has argued that from the point of view of both quality and cost, the decision whether or not to prescribe is more important than what to prescribe. His own work showed that clinical and social considerations interact when doctors make decisions about whether to prescribe or not, and that the need to maintain a good relationship with the patient is a major factor in uncomfortable prescribing decisions. If the doctor decides not to prescribe, however, we need to ask what else he or she might offer the patient by way of advice or reassurance. There is some evidence that doctors do not routinely ask patients if they have been treating themselves with over the counter or other remedies before consulting, although the sociological literature shows that most symptoms experienced in the community are self-treated (Locker 1981). If doctors are prepared to discuss and support patients' decisions about non-prescribed remedies and self-treatment, this could make it both easier not to prescribe as well as providing a logical starting point for any pre-scribing decision. If, however, the recommendation of self-care is only deployed to justify the decision not to prescribe, the opportunity for a gen-uinely supportive consultation may be lost (Mangione-Smith et al. 2006). This kind of strategic use of self-care, as a method of reinforcing an unwel-come prescribing decision, may provide an example of distorted commu-nication in Habermas' terms (see Chapter 7). Similarly, doctors rarely ask patients if they are expecting or hoping for prescriptions, and the evidence suggests that their estimates of patients' expectations for prescriptions are not always accurate (Britten and Ukoumunne 1997). However, discussions of patients' self-care or expectations for prescriptions are likely to take time, and a major factor in deciding to prescribe is the fact that it often pro-vides a faster way of terminating a consultation. Toop (2003) has provided a checklist for prescribing decisions, which begins with the reason for prescribing (see Box 6.1).

Box 6.1   Checklist for prescribing decisions

What is the reason for prescribing?

Is drug treatment necessary at this time?

Are there alternative non-pharmaceutical options?

Is the patient prepared to take a drug?

Which drug group(s) would be most suitable?

Which drug is the best choice from this group? (safety, efficacy, compliance, and cost)

Do I need to find out more about this drug?

What formulation, dose frequency, and duration?

How should the drug be monitored and adjusted?

Does the patient understand the potential risks and benefits?

Source: Toop (2003).

Reviews of the literature on prescribing have identified a range of technical and social mediating factors such as medical education, formal regulation and control, doctors' characteristics, demands from society and patients, and advertising (Hemminki 1975). Studies of prescribing in particular situations, such as decisions which make the prescriber uncomfortable, or are deemed unscientific or for new drugs, all demonstrate that social influences are important. Everyday clinical experience involves tailoring prescribing to the individual and psycho-social needs of the patient within the central context of the doctor–patient interaction (Armstrong 2002). Perhaps the most well known wild card in prescribing is the placebo effect, variously perceived as 'noise', part of a psychosomatic response, or an intrinsic aspect of the healing process.

Schwartz et al. (1989) identified the schism between scientific knowledge and clinical experience when investigating the prescribing of three drugs commonly thought to be prescribed at a higher rate than warranted by the scientific evidence. Doctors prescribing these drugs disputed the relevance of scientific research to their clinical practice, and claimed that their clinical experience proved the therapeutic effectiveness of the target drugs. They felt that years of practising in the real world was more relevant to clinical practice than academic studies and, for example, that they had no time to spend on counselling their patients instead of prescribing. In a similar vein, Jones et al. (2001) examined GPs' and consultants' prescribing of new drugs and found that GPs' references to the scientific literature were often vague and not apparently based on critical appraisal. Prosser et al. (2003), also examining GPs' prescribing of new drugs, found that peer-reviewed journals were influential for only 17 per cent of the GPs in their sample, and that non-peer-reviewed journals were cited more often. In contrast, Prosser et al. (2006) found that hospital consultants all rated independent research evidence as the key source of empirical validation for a new drug. Overall, the authors identified four forms of knowledge about new drugs: scientific knowledge, social knowledge, patient knowledge and experiential knowledge. Although there was a consensus in favour of scientific knowledge, it was not always a major influence for prescribing. Social knowledge was derived from comparisons with colleagues and based on trust and socialization. Knowledge of individual patients could temper the influence of scientific knowledge, while consultants' own experience of using new drugs influenced subsequent prescribing. Prosser et al. (2006) concluded that knowledge of new drugs was socially and culturally determined and that prescribing occurred beyond the boundary of scientific epistemology. They argued that the biomedical concept of treatment is too simplistic for ready application to everyday clinical practice.

Thus a number of writers are agreed that prescribing is more than a technical issue, and is influenced by a range of social and contextual factors. Cohen et al. (2001) have argued that the 'rational use of drugs' paradigm is inadequate for understanding the place of medications in society because of the numerous competing and legitimate rationalities about the role and purpose of medications. At present there is no consensus about how prescribing might be judged in this broader perspective. However, Britten et al. (2003) explored the feasibility of using a broader definition of the appropriateness of prescribing in UK general practice by measuring three variables: the pharmacological appropriateness of prescriptions; doctors' assessments of their own prescribing decisions in terms of whether they were strictly necessary or not, and whether or not the patient had wanted a prescription before the consultation. Judgements of pharmacological appropriateness were made by an academic pharmacist and an academic GP using the Pharmacological Appropriateness of Medicines devised for the purpose of the study. Combining all three measures for the 58 prescriptions for which complete data were available, the authors found that none of the prescriptions were judged to be unwanted, unnecessary and technically inappropriate. However, less than half of them were judged to be wanted, necessary *and* appropriate. In over a quarter of cases, there was at least one poor endpoint or outcome (which are discussed in more detail in Chapter 7), and some prescriptions which were both wanted and necessary were nonetheless not taken as prescribed. The study demonstrated the feasibility of using a broader definition of prescribing in research and showed its potential for yielding valuable insights into the nature of general practice prescribing and patients' use of medicines. However, much more work would need to be done before it could be used in routine clinical practice, and any such instrument would need to capture the longitudinal nature of much prescribing as well as the activity of dispensing.

Once a prescriber has written a prescription, it usually has to be dispensed by a community or hospital pharmacist. In a review of the roles of community pharmacists, Guirguis and Chewning (2005) questioned the dominant assumption that there are only two roles in pharmacy practice, which are either professional or commercial. Current pharmacists' role sets included 'clinical, business, dispenser, patient advocate, and manager' (Guirguis and Chewning 2005, p. 499). Thus, pharmacists are in a position to contribute to at least two of the components of good prescribing defined by Cribb and Barber (1997). They can ensure the technical correctness of prescribed medicines by correcting prescribers' mistakes, if necessary, and they are in a position to discuss the acceptability of the medicine to the patient. Pharmacists' responsibilities to patients are emphasized in the concept of pharmaceutical care, which emerged within clinical pharmacy in the United States. There are several definitions of pharmaceutical care which variously refer to rational use of medicines, health outcomes, quality of life for the patient and patient-centredness (Almarsdóttir and Traulsen 2005). The potential for pharmacists to engage with clients' perspectives is limited, partly by clients' low expectations and lack of knowledge of pharmacists' roles. However, Chewning and Schommer (1996) have shown that even brief exposure to a short pamphlet about pharmacists' activities can increase clients' knowledge of the roles of pharmacists. From the point of view of the patient or client, the dispensing of a prescription is their last access point to the system before taking the medicine into the lifeworld. Pharmacists also contribute to the quality of prescribing via 'academic detailing' visits to general practices, as for example in the Australian Quality Prescribing Initiative.

System Imperatives – the Pharmaceutical Industry

A major driver of non-rational prescribing is the pharmaceutical industry. Apart from direct advertising, pharmaceutical companies sponsor medical 'educational' events in attractive locations and provide all manner of branded gifts to remind doctors of their products (see example at end of chapter). The industry is a major influence on prescribing, but one which has been somewhat ignored in the research literature until recently. This influence is accomplished by myriad 'forms of entanglement' (Moynihan 2003) in addition to advertising. Moynihan identifies 16 such forms including visits to doctors from company representatives (see Box 6.2). Angell (2004) points out that industry sponsored 'educational' activities provide a legal mechanism for manufacturers to persuade doctors to prescribe their products for 'off label' uses and to bribe doctors to prescribe their drugs.

Doctors tend to say that their prescribing habits are not influenced by industry, but it seems unlikely that manufacturers would spend as much money as they do if it did not deliver results. Avorn et al. (1982) tested this assertion by interviewing physicians in the Boston area about two drug groups (cerebral vasodilators and propoxyphene products) for which the information about efficacy conveyed by scientific sources (that they were ineffective) differed markedly from that conveyed by commercial sources. The authors asked physicians about their beliefs about these drugs, and the answers were used as markers to indicate the likely source of information. The vast majority of physicians interviewed

Box 6.2   Forms of entanglement

- Face to face visits from drug company representatives
- Acceptance of direct gifts of equipment, travel or accommodation
- Acceptance of indirect gifts, through sponsorship of software or travel
- Attendance at sponsored dinners and social or recreational events
- Attendance at sponsored educational events, continuing medical education, workshops or seminars
- Attendance at sponsored scientific conferences
- Ownership of stock or equity holdings
- Conducting sponsored research
- Company funding for medical schools, academic chairs or lecture halls
- Membership of sponsored professional societies and associations
- Advising a sponsored disease foundation or patients' group
- Involvement with or use of sponsored clinical guidelines
- Undertaking paid consultancy work for companies
- Membership of company advisory boards of 'thought leaders' or 'speakers' bureaux'
- Authoring 'ghostwritten' scientific articles
- Medical journals' reliance on drug company advertising, company purchased reprints, and sponsored supplements

Source: Moynihan 2003.

claimed that they used scientific sources of information and were not influenced by drug advertisements and company representatives, but their beliefs about the effectiveness of the two drugs suggested otherwise. These results were congruent with the fact that, despite little scientific evidence of efficacy, the two drugs were widely prescribed at the time of the study.

Given the nature of the patent system discussed in Chapter 4, it is clear that pharmaceutical companies will focus most of their attentions on newly licensed drugs. By definition, new drugs are less familiar to prescribers than their older competitors; the comparatively high prices of new drugs means that they are more profitable than old drugs, and having invested heavily in developing new drugs, manufacturers are keen to reap the rewards before the patent runs out. Thus an analysis of factors influencing the prescribing of new drugs is likely to illuminate the influence of the pharmaceutical industry. Jones et al. (2001) investigated the prescribing of new drugs by consultants and GPs in Birmingham and found that consultants usually prescribed new drugs only in their own specialty, used few new drugs, and claimed to use scientific evidence to inform their decisions. In contrast, as one would expect from the nature of their work, GPs generally prescribed more new drugs and for a wider range of conditions; there was, however, variation between GPs and between drugs. For both consultants and GPs, drug company representatives were an important source of information, although specialists often asked representatives to provide them with information from the scientific literature. For GPs, drug company material was often the only source of information used before prescribing. General practitioners' references to journal articles suggested that they had not read them critically. Although this study relied on doctors' self-reports, their prescribing of specific drugs was monitored, and the data were consistent with statements they made to the researchers.

Prosser et al. (2003), in their study of GPs' decisions to prescribe new drugs, found that pharmaceutical representatives were the major influence. Other techniques used by industry, such as advertisements and mailings, drug samples and post-marketing surveillance trials, were all less influential than face-to-face meetings with representatives. Most of the GPs interviewed felt that company representatives were a useful source of information enabling them to keep up to date with new products. Congruent with the findings of Jones et al. (2001), Prosser et al. found that GPs made little reference to objective, scientific information about new drugs. In a quantitative study of GPs, Watkins et al. (2003) found that doctors who saw drug representatives frequently were significantly more willing to prescribe new drugs and to agree to patients' requests to prescribe a drug that was not clinically indicated, and they were more likely to feel dissatisfied with consultations in which they did not prescribe and were more receptive to industry advertisements and promotional literature.

Given the profit-making imperative of the pharmaceutical industry, and the resulting informational biases discussed in Chapter 5, it is clear that the influence of industry is likely to result in 'irrational' prescribing. Information from industry is likely to emphasize the benefits of medications and overlook adverse reactions, thus making it biased from a scientific point of view. It is also unlikely to provide patients with the information about side effects that many people want to know about. In this context, governments and insurance companies have developed a range of mechanisms for encouraging rational prescribing.

System Imperatives – Attempts to Rationalize Prescribing

The most potent force for changing and rationalizing medical practice is Evidence Based Medicine, also more inclusively referred to as Evidence Based Practice (EBP) or Evidence Based Health Care. It now forms a powerful international movement which aims to influence the practice of health care professionals by promoting the production and implementation of objective scientific evidence about clinical practice. The international Cochrane Collaboration (www.cochrane.org) organises and publishes systematic reviews of evidence according to strict protocols to determine the value of interventions in health care. Evidence Based Practice is based in the discipline of clinical epidemiology, and its key methodological tool is the randomized controlled clinical trial (known as the RCT). The problems which EBP aims to tackle include clinical variability, the use of health care technologies for which there is no good evidence and conversely the under use of effective treatments.

However, the production and dissemination of high quality evidence (and the rejection of literally thousands of research papers not meeting the strict Cochrane quality criteria) is not sufficient to change clinical practice. Those wishing to bring about such change have devised a wide range of educational and other interventions aiming to improve clinical practice. Soumerai et al. (1989) conducted a comprehensive review of interventions to improve prescribing in primary care, which they classified into seven categories. These were

- the dissemination of printed educational materials
- reports of patient-specific lists of prescribed medications
- group education of different kinds including conferences
- feedback of physician-specific prescribing patterns
- reminders at the time of prescribing
- one-to-one education
- ongoing clinical pharmacy services.

Soumerai et al. (1989) concluded that mailed educational materials alone had little or no effect on prescribing behaviour, although they could be an important component of other strategies. Similarly, the distribution of computerized listings of patient-specific prescribed medications had no beneficial effect on overall prescribing patterns. Effective interventions included ongoing computerized reminder systems, which the authors suggested were acting as 'secretarial reminders' rather than performing educational functions. The authors also concluded that ongoing feedback reports of physician-specific prescribing performance might be effective in improving certain types of prescribing practices such as the use of generic drugs. Finally, they found that brief one-to-one educational outreach visits by either specially trained clinical pharmacists or physician counsellors were effective in substantially reducing inappropriate prescribing. They noted that this is precisely the method which has been used over many years by the pharmaceutical industry. Soumerai et al.'s conclusions were endorsed by Bero et al. (1998) who concluded that passive dissemination of information, in written or lecture form, is generally ineffective in closing the gap between research and practice. They identified four consistently effective interventions:

- Educational outreach
- Manual or computerized reminders
- Multifaceted interventions
- Interactive educational meetings in which practitioners participate in workshops including discussions of their practice.

The interventions discussed by these authors have had the aim of improving prescribing, and other aspects of clinical practice, in relation to scientific criteria. They all promote voluntary activities requiring the willing participation of the target audience. State interventions have been drawn from the same repertoire and may indeed have been influenced by the kind of review carried out by Soumerai et al. (1989). In the United Kingdom, the government has financed the provision of independent information about drugs via several sources. The *British National Formulary* (BNF), which is published jointly by the British Medical Association and the Royal Pharmaceutical Society of Great Britain, is provided free of charge to all medical students and practising doctors. It was the reference which all prescribers used before the advent of computerized prescribing support. For many years, the government also supported the publication of the *Drug and Therapeutics Bulletin* which was published by the Consumers' Association, but this arrangement has been rescinded and the Bulletin has been taken over by the British Medical Association. Similar publications are published in other countries, such as the French *La Revue Prescrire*. In the United Kingdom, other sources of independent information is the *MeReC Bulletin*. General practitioners in the United Kingdom are also sent information on their own prescribing. The Prescription Pricing Authority (PPA) sends all GPs a summary of their own and their practice's prescribing data every quarter year and the summary of local and national figures for comparative purposes. These Prescribing Analyses and CosT (PACT) data come in varying levels of detail showing the costs of prescribing (Level 1), details of therapeutic areas with costs and information on new drugs (Level 2) and numbers of items and percentages of prescriptions written and dispensed generically (Level 3). The UK government, via the Department of Health, has also employed physicians and pharmacists to visit individual doctors whose prescribing habits are out of line with those of their peers. In the early days of the NHS, these were Regional Medical Officers who visited prescribers chosen because of their expensive prescribing habits. More recently, medical and pharmaceutical advisers have been employed by health authorities, and their remit has been both scientific and economic. Hospital prescribing is guided by Drug and Therapeutic Committees which draw up formularies and make policies relevant to individual institutions.

However, there are clear tensions between the scientific evidence produced as a result of randomized controlled trials and the everyday experience of practitioners in their own local contexts. Some of the physicians in the study conducted by Schwartz et al. (1989) disputed the relevance of scientific research to their own clinical practice and claimed that their own clinical practice proved the therapeutic effectiveness of the 'inappropriate' drugs. For these physicians, the real world of clinical practice bore little relation to the experimental settings of published research. Wood et al. (1998) argued that 'health professionals do not simply apply abstract, disembodied scientific research, about which they have only scant knowledge of the context or circumstance of its production, rigidly to the situation around them'. In their study of one NHS Health Authority, they found that practitioners actively engaged with the research evidence in order to assess its relevance and usefulness for their own situations and populations. For Wood and colleagues, the question is not about disseminating research findings to a passive audience of practitioners, but is rather 'how evidence can be *translated within* the assumptive world of practitioners' (Wood et al. 1998, p. 1734, italics in original). Similarly Armstrong (2002) found that GPs' prescribing decisions were geared to the needs and contexts of individual patients and bore little relation to the idealized model of evidence-based practice. He argued that doctors' prescribing repertoires were anchored in a familiarity with individual drugs and confidence in their use based on past clinical experience.

A further difficulty for those aiming to ensure that prescribing is based on good scientific data is that the perception of a drug's properties depends on the way in which the information is framed. Several authors have examined the ways in which doctors' perceptions, or their hypothetical prescribing decisions, are influenced by the presentation of absolute or relative risk information. Bucher et al. (1994) found that doctors presented with relative risk information were more inclined to prescribe than those presented with absolute risk information despite the fact that both sets of risk information were based on the same data. Bobbio et al. (1994), also using data from the Helsinki Heart Study, presented the findings to 148 physicians in 5 different ways: relative risk reduction, absolute risk reduction, differences in event-free patients, number needed to treat to prevent one event, and events reduction and mortality. They found that none of their respondents realized that all five data formats were equivalent, as none of them gave the same answer to all questions. Once again, physicians said that they would be more likely to prescribe the drug whose results were reported in terms of relative risk reduction. In addition, Naylor et al. (1992) found that clinicians' views of drug therapies were affected by underuse of summary measures that relate treatment burden to therapeutic yields in a clinically relevant manner.

The UK government has also used more overt methods to contain the costs of prescribing in primary care. These include the setting of indicative prescribing amounts (the word 'budget' being too politically sensitive) and the GP fundholding scheme in the 1990s. Under this scheme, practices could hold their own budgets for spending on all non-acute hospital therapeutic and diagnostic services, any drugs prescribed or dispensed, and all practice expenses. The scheme allowed practices to move money between elements of their overall budget, and fundholding practices were found to spend comparatively less than their non-fundholding peers on prescribing costs at least in the early years. The early fundholders achieved savings by eliminating unnecessary prescribing, minimizing costs by moving to generic prescribing, by moving to cheaper drugs within the same therapeutic class and by reducing or at least containing the overall volume of prescribing. The overt government emphasis on costs alienated many doctors, and the fundholding scheme was controversial.

Some state interventions have taken a legislative approach notably in the form of 'limited lists' of prescribable drugs. The introduction in the United Kingdom in April 1985 of a limited list restricted prescribing in seven therapeutic areas to a small number of generic drugs. The seven categories were antacids, laxatives, cough and cold remedies, analgesics for mild to moderate pain, vitamins, tonics and benzodiazepines. Despite initial opposition, this list was subsequently extended to restrict prescribing in further therapeutic areas. These various initiatives in the United Kingdom have succeeded in achieving a high rate of generic prescribing for example, and reduced antibiotic prescribing in primary care. In the United Kingdom, prescribing by GPs is now supported by computer programmes which set out the choices of drug, information about doses and interactions. This initiative is consistent with the findings of

Soumerai et al. (1989), although computer support systems represent much more than a secretarial reminder function. Given the opposition of the pharmaceutical industry to such initiatives to rationalize prescribing, this represents a triumph of the needs of the state and the profession over industry. Such computerized support does, however, reduce GPs' clinical autonomy by reducing the judgements required in making prescribing decisions.

These various measures to influence practitioners all involve, to a greater or lesser extent, threats to their clinical autonomy. There is as at least as much focus on professionals' compliance with guidelines as there is on patients' compliance with treatment. Pharmaceutical companies use methods of 'entanglement' with doctors in order to increase sales of their products. Governments use a mixture of carrot and stick approaches to contain costs and promote rational prescribing. Elite sections of the medical profession promote EBP in order to promote best practice, although practitioners on the ground do not always see this evidence as relevant for their own purposes. There is very little in this literature about patients' perspectives or even about the adverse effects of prescribed medicines. If patients' preferences are considered at all, they tend to be characterized as a negative influence on prescribing. The literature shows that there are major tensions between scientific evidence and clinical experience, and between scientific and economic interests. Most definitions of rational prescribing do not acknowledge these tensions, perhaps because they represent efforts to rise above them. However, the technical and social aspects of prescribing are interdependent. It is not realistic to regard prescribing as merely a technical issue, as it excludes the actions of prescribers, patients, governments and industry, all of whom have vested interests in the outcomes of prescribing decisions.

Conclusion

The differences between the system perspectives of the pharmaceutical industry and those of EBP may be characterized as the clash between the pharmacological license and the pharmacological parsimony philosophies. There are further tensions between scientific knowledge and clinical experience; methods of promoting EBP face the problem of perceived lack of relevance to clinical practice. The state is interested in containing costs, supporting industry and promoting the health of its citizens; the goal of industry is to increase profits and provide good returns to shareholders. Members of the medical and nursing professions, in the name of EBP, pursue a technical interest in trying to influence prescribing which does not acknowledge the inherent social aspects. In this literature, the main reference to patients' perspectives is negative; patients' lifeworld concerns are not acknowledged but may be taken on board as part of prescribers' clinical experience.

The use of definitions of rational prescribing may be seen as the dominance of the parsimonious view and a challenge to industry-induced irrationality. However, characterization of prescribing as a predominantly technical issue, while it provides a parsimonious tool, also serves to obscure the various conflicting interests and has the effect of excluding the input of patients and the public. It could be argued that the concept of rational drug use is a major vehicle for lifeworld colonization. If, however, patients' lifeworld concerns – particularly those about safety – were taken on board, these could provide support for a more parsimonious approach to prescribing.

Definitions of rational prescribing focus on outcomes, but prescribing is also a process involving health professionals, patients and sometimes their carers. So far we have been considering prescribing as a part of the system. However, when professionals and patients meet each other in consultations, this provides an access point between the expert system and the lifeworld. If the lifeworld has been largely absent from the systems we have discussed so far, the situation in health care consultations should provide much more opportunity for lifeworld and system to interact. This is the topic of Chapter 7.

Box 6.3   Example: industry sponsored 'educational' events

Some years ago I (Nicky Britten) was invited by a well known pharmaceutical company to speak at a weekend conference in a holiday resort on the south coast of England. I was surprised to be asked and did not initially feel very enthusiastic, because I feared that the company would attempt to influence what I said. This fear turned out to be unfounded. Although the company prepared my slides beforehand, they did not alter any of the content. I accepted because I was intrigued to find out at first hand what an industry-run event would be like. I imagined that there would be a heavy emphasis on the promotion of individual products, and again I was wrong. There was very little, if any, obvious product promotion.

Instead, the event appeared to be run on familiar lines for anyone accustomed to postgraduate teaching in UK general practice. The local postgraduate office had approved the event on the condition that it included a certain amount of small group teaching, possibly thinking that this would require the services of local GP tutors. Accordingly, the hotel ballroom in which the conference took place was set out in café style tables with about eight people per table. At the centre of each table was a computer which performed the role of tutor. The seating arrangements, I came to realize, were far from random. Each company representative had personally invited those GPs with whom he or she had, or wanted to establish, a good relationship. Each table was occupied by that representative and 'their' GPs, so that relationships could be consolidated over the course of the weekend. The computer led tutorials were on carefully chosen ethical topics such as contraception for the under 15s, which required illustration with professionally produced videos of mini skirted teenage girls alluding to their sexual activities. The ethical issues thus raised provided plenty of material for the subsequent dinner time conversation for the mostly male GPs.

I had wondered beforehand how my talk on communication about prescribing would be received with its references to patients' aversion to medicine taking. I need not have worried, and I realized that the content of my talk was supremely irrelevant. The whole purpose of the weekend was for the company reps to build relationships with individual GPs and create a sense of obligation or at least reciprocity. The reps were taking trouble to ensure that the doctors enjoyed themselves by organizing free golf, sailing and other activities in the long gaps between the educational events in the ballroom. It was clear that no product promotion was necessary or even desirable, and that the next time any of the reps called up one of their GPs, they would be offered a return invitation to the GP's surgery.

The company wrote afterwards to thank me and to say that my talk had not been well evaluated, and that they would not be inviting me again.

Part IV

The Interface between System and Lifeworld

7
Patient–Professional Communication

Introduction

Having looked at medicine use from both lifeworld and system perspectives, I will now explore the ways in which these perspectives inform each other, or not, during health care consultations. Meetings between patients and professionals are one of the key sites in which lifeworld and system perspectives come into direct contact with one another. In particular, professionals are in a position to help patients weigh up the balance between benefit and harm and make decisions which are relevant to them as individuals. Consultations constitute one set of access points at which lay people come into contact with expert systems (Giddens 1990). Health care consultations are the contexts in which many prescribing decisions are made; the reason they do not account for all such decisions is because repeat prescriptions for chronic conditions may be issued without a consultation. In the United Kingdom, for example, repeat prescribing accounts for about 75 per cent of items prescribed and over 80 per cent of drug costs in primary care (Bradley and Blenkinsopp 1998).

It is easy to consider health care consultations as self-contained and independent of the social context in which they occur. Thus, some researchers have focused on the amount and kinds of information exchanged by patients and doctors (for example, Roter and Hall 1992), and others have measured the extent to which doctors use a patient-centred style of consulting (for example, Elwyn et al. 2003). A few researchers, for example, Waitzkin (1991) and Mishler (1984), have located analyses of doctor–patient communication within their broader social context, to consider aspects of the social structure and the lifeworld respectively.

In this chapter, I will begin by looking at the ways in which different health professionals communicate with their patients about medicines. I will then continue the thread from Chapter 6 about the factors influencing

129

prescribing decisions and examine the ways in which patients' expectations for prescriptions, and doctors' perceptions of these expectations, influence prescribing decisions. I will then build on the findings of Chapters 2 and 3 to characterize the nature of patients' lifeworld perspectives on their medicines; I will explore the extent to which lifeworld concerns inform health care consultations, and I will draw conclusions about the relative role of communicative and strategic action in these meetings. To do this, I need to introduce the concept of concordance in relation to medicine taking and prescribing. First introduced by a working party of the Royal Pharmaceutical Society of Great Britain, concordance is a model of the patient–professional relationship which explicitly recognizes patients' perspectives (RPSGB 1997). It is an agreement between a patient and a health care professional that respects the beliefs and wishes of the patient in determining whether, when and how medicines are to be taken. Although reciprocal, this is an alliance in which the health care professionals recognize the primacy of the patient's decisions about taking the recommended medications (Britten 2003). In Habermas' terms, concordance represents communicative action.

The definition of concordance is evolving, but the main point to note is that it is not a synonym for adherence or compliance, which was discussed in Chapter 3. The two terms refer to different phenomena: concordance is about the relationship between two or more parties, while adherence refers to the behaviour of individuals. A systematic review found little research examining the exchange of views in health consultations, a crucial element of concordance, although patient participation in discussion of medicines was associated with positive outcomes (Stevenson et al. 2004). The question of whether patients' lifeworld concerns are articulated and addressed in health care consultations is, therefore, a question about concordance.

The concept of concordance acknowledges the importance of patients' lifeworlds, but it also acknowledges the potential for disagreement or conflict between patients and professionals. Table 7.1 illustrates possibilities for agreement and disagreement in relation to the writing of prescriptions. If both patient and prescriber agree, either that a prescription is necessary or that it is not, then concordance (at least in relation to the necessity of the prescription) exists. If however, the prescriber thinks a prescription is necessary but the patient does not, then the potential for conflict exists. This scenario is most likely in the case of medication for long-term conditions, and patient resistance may take the form of non-adherence as I discussed in Chapter 3. Similarly, there is also potential for conflict if the patient thinks a prescription is necessary but the prescriber does not. This scenario is most likely in relation to medication for acute illnesses such as antibiotics. If patients want to resist the prescriber's decision, they need to do so in the consultation itself, as I will show later in this chapter. Such resistance can be experienced as 'patient pressure' by the prescriber. In

Table 7.1 Potential scenarios for agreement and disagreement

		Patient	
		Wants prescription	*Does not want prescription*
	Wants to write prescription	Agreement	Disagreement Context: long-term medication Prescriber's problem: patient's non-adherence Patient's problem: resistance to treatment
Prescriber	*Does not want to write prescription*	Disagreement Context: short-term medication Prescriber's problem: pressure to prescribe Patient's problem: access to treatment	Agreement

cases of potential conflict, the task of concordance is to find a mutually agreeable way forward which acknowledges the perspectives of both patients and professionals.

Nurse Prescribing

Given the recent advent of nurse prescribing, much less is known about it than about physician prescribing. Most of this chapter thus inevitably focuses on the latter. There is, however, a small but growing body of research about nurse–patient communication about prescribing in a range of clinical areas. In the United Kingdom, nurse prescribing takes two forms: supplementary prescribing and independent prescribing. In supplementary prescribing, the patient is initially assessed by an independent prescriber (either a doctor or a dentist) who formulates a clinical management plan. Nurses and pharmacists are then able to prescribe in accordance with the plan. Independent nurse prescribers were originally confined to the Nurse Prescribers' Formulary but are now able to prescribe from the whole British National Formulary. Nurse prescribers' courses were originally only open to health visitors, district nurses or practice nurses holding either of these qualifications, but the situation is changing (Skidmore 2002). It remains to be seen what proportion of nurses become nurse prescribers, and what range of medicines they do in fact prescribe; however, nurses with access to the whole formulary do prescribe drugs that were previously restricted to doctors (Avery and James 2007). In their review of the effectiveness of nurse prescribing, Latter and Courtenay (2004) found that nurses prescribed at a comparable rate to GPs writing prescriptions in about two-thirds of their consultations.

On the basis of ten case studies, Latter et al. (2007) examined nurses' prescribing consultations to establish if they were practising concordance. Study sites were chosen on the basis of the type of nurse and practice setting, the relative frequency of prescribing medicines and geographical location. Nurses' consultations were evaluated using a structured observation checklist, and the results showed that nurses much more frequently gave instructions about how to take the medicines than information about possible side effects. Table 7.2 shows the competencies observed when nurses were communicating with patients. When asked after the study consultations, the majority of patients felt that they had not been told about possible side effects or what to do if they experienced one. Nearly all the nurses thought that they were practising concordance, and in at least two-thirds of consultations the researchers judged that nurses had listened to and understood patients' beliefs and expectations, explained the nature of the condition, and had checked the patient's understanding and commitment to their treatment. However, there was less negotiation and information sharing that would enable patients to make informed choices, and Latter et al. (2007) concluded that the nurses' communication was consistent with a compliance approach to practice. Nurses were giving information which would help patients take their medicines and withholding information that could lead to patients making informed decisions not to take their medicines. This is consistent with the review carried out by Raynor et al. (2007) discussed in Chapter 5 and provides an example of strategic action on the part of the nurses, which I will discuss further at the end of this chapter. Comparing Latter et al.'s results with those of an earlier general practice based study, it would seem that the nurses' communication was comparable to that of the study doctors in respect of providing instructions for taking the medicines. However, the nurses in Latter et al.'s study were more likely than the doctors in Makoul et al.'s earlier study to discuss side effects and to listen to the patients' ideas. Table 7.3 shows the extent to which GPs carried out various communicative activities on the evidence of their videotaped consultations; the percentages give the proportion of consultations in which each communication task was actually carried out. Box 7.3 gives an example of problems caused by misunderstandings about side effects.

Table 7.2 Nurses' communication with patients about prescribing

Item	Yes	No	Total
Gives clear instructions to the patient – how to take the medicine (dose, use and duration).	89% (n = 105)	11% (n = 13)	100% (n = 118)
Gives clear instructions to the patient – possible side effects and action to take in event of side effects.	48% (n = 57)	52% (n = 61)	100% (n = 118)
Checks patient's understanding and commitment to their treatment.	73% (n = 86)	27% (n = 32)	100% (n = 118)
Explains the nature of the diagnosis/patient's condition to the patient and the rationale behind it.	66% (n = 78)	34% (n = 40)	100% (n = 118)
Explains the potential risks and benefits of the treatment options to the patient.	39% (n = 46)	62% (n = 72)	100% (n = 118)
Assists the patient in making an informed choice about the management of their health problem.	45% (n = 54)	55% (n = 64)	100% (n = 118)
Listens to and understands the patient's beliefs and expectations.	64% (n = 76)	36% (n = 42)	100% (n = 118)

Source: Latter et al. (2007).

Table 7.3   GPs' communication with patients about prescribing

Task	Videotape (%)
Provide instructions for taking the medicine	87.0 (18.9)
Discuss patients' ability to follow treatment plan	7.9 (12.0)
Find out what patients think about the medication	33.9 (20.4)
Discuss benefits of the medication	56.0 (23.0)
Discuss risks of the medication	3.1 (6.2)
Discuss side effects of the medication	30.7 (18.2)

Source: Makoul et al. (1995).

Patients' Influence on Prescribing

In Chapter 6, I considered a number of influences on doctors' prescribing decisions, but did not explore the influence of patients. This influence tends to occur when patients want prescriptions rather than when they do not; in other words, it represents a patient agenda of access rather than resistance (see Table 7.1). Doctors make reference to patients' inappropriate expectations for prescriptions, particularly antibiotics. As Worthen puts it some time ago, 'Almost every practising physician has a repertoire of stories about the patient entering the office and demanding to be treated with the miracle drug reported in the *Ladies' Home Journal'* (Worthen 1973). These claims are not only made by clinicians as, for example, the Audit Commission (1994) attributed much inappropriate prescribing in general practice to patients' expectations. These claims were not usually based on any detailed evidence, and the mostly quantitative research which has been carried out to investigate patients' expectations has painted a rather more complex picture. Britten and Ukoumunne (1997) measured not only patients' expectations for prescriptions but also doctors' perceptions of these same expectations in a study based in UK general practice. They found that two-thirds of their sample hoped for a prescription before the consultation and that doctors estimated that 56 per cent of patients were expecting prescriptions. While patients' expectations were indeed a major influence on prescribing, and patients hoping for prescriptions were over twice as likely to be given one, doctors' perceptions were an even stronger predictor of the decision to prescribe. In cases where doctors thought that the patient expected a prescription, patients were seven times as likely to receive one. These findings corroborated those of a very similar study carried out in Australian general practice, in which patients hoping for prescriptions were nearly three times as likely to receive one compared to patients not hoping for prescriptions and ten times as likely to if their doctor thought that they were expecting a prescription (Cockburn and Pit 1997). In both these studies, and others since, doctors' perceptions of patients' expectations are the main driving force; thus doctors' claims that inappropriate prescribing is driven by their patients need to be challenged. Doctors' perceptions that patients expect antibiotics or other prescriptions can lead to inappropriate prescribing. Britten and Ukoumunne (1997) found that over a fifth of the prescriptions written in their study were not thought by the prescribers themselves to be strictly indicated on purely medical grounds. Similarly, Macfarlane et al. (1997) found that doctors prescribing antibiotics for patients with acute lower respiratory tract illness judged that nearly a quarter of them were not indicated; they concluded that patients' expectations and requests had a powerful effect on prescribing even when doctors did not consider that an antibiotic was indicated.

The issue of patients' expectations for prescriptions takes on a particular focus in the case of Direct to Consumer Advertising (DTCA), as in these cases it is likely that patients' requests are stimulated by advertising. Mintzes and colleagues (2002, 2003) carried out one of the few studies of this field by surveying patients consulting primary care physicians in the United States and Canada, where US TV advertisements are also broadcast. They found that patients requested advertised drugs in 7 per cent of consultations in Sacramento and in 3 per cent of consultations in Vancouver. These proportions are significant given that overt requests for prescriptions are quite rare (Stivers 2007). The doctors in Mintzes' study fulfilled most of these requests, and patients requesting an advertised drug were nearly 17 times as likely to receive a prescription for the requested drug or alternatives than patients who had not made such a request. However, doctors judged that half of the prescriptions for requested DTCA drugs to be a 'possible' or 'unlikely' choice for similar patients rather than a 'very likely' choice. This provides clear evidence that patients' expectations, when fuelled by DTCA, can stimulate inappropriate prescribing.

One question which quantitative studies have generally shed little light on is how doctors come to form the impression that particular patients are expecting prescriptions. In cases where patients ask for DTCA drugs, it is possible that they come to the consultation with a copy of the advertisement (if it appeared in a print medium), but we do not know if this is what really happens. In other cases, it is much less clear how doctors form their perceptions. Bradley's work suggests that doctors' perceptions may be based on non-verbal aspects of the consultation (Bradley 1990). We do not know whether patients' expectations and preferences are actually articulated in the consultation. Stivers and colleagues (2003) used the method of Conversation Analysis to explicate the findings described above and showed that prescribers' perceptions of patients' preferences are more significant determinants of prescribing decisions than patients' actual expectations. In a study of parents and children being seen for upper respiratory tract infection symptoms, Stivers and colleagues (2003) explored the ways in which prescribers' perceptions were formed. The authors identified four communication behaviours of parents. These were a 'symptoms only' problem presentation, for example, a parent saying 'He has a runny nose and a sore throat'; a 'candidate diagnosis' problem presentation, for example, a parent saying 'He's had a terrible sore throat so I thought maybe it was strep'; diagnosis resistance; and treatment resistance. Parents resisting a diagnosis might, in response to a doctor's statement that the child had no ear infection, say 'He doesn't?'. After the doctor recommended an OTC treatment, a parent resisting the treatment recommendation might say 'So, you don't think he needs antibiotics?' Although parents' expectations for antibiotics were not significantly associated with any of these communication behaviours, physicians' perceptions of parents' expectations were. If the parent offered a candidate diagnosis, doctors were five times as likely to think that they wanted an antibiotic than if the parent did not offer a candidate diagnosis, and if parents resisted the diagnosis, they were over three times as likely to be perceived as wanting an antibiotic. Thus, doctors were forming their perceptions of parents' expectations on indirect communication behaviours. Parents might not have been intending to communicate pressure or even expectations for antibiotics, and they might not have realized that this was how their behaviour was being interpreted. What they might have been wanting, and this study did not measure it, was reassurance about their child's health. The authors comment that doctors may be too quick to interpret certain communication behaviours as indicating expectations for antibiotics. From the point of view of Habermas' distinction between the system and lifeworld, it would seem that these parents were perhaps more oriented to communicative action, and asking for help in understanding and interpreting their child's symptoms and behaviour, while the doctors were oriented to the system solutions of prescribed medication and a 'disposal decision' with which to terminate a consultation.

In a subsequent and larger study, also of children with upper respiratory tract infections, the same authors identified three communication behaviours, one used by doctors and two used by parents (Mangione-Smith et al. 2006). The doctors' communication behaviour was a recommendation against antibiotic treatment; the parents' communication behaviours were first offering a candidate bacterial diagnosis and second questioning the doctor's treatment recommendation. Parents' questioning of the treatment plan was strongly associated with the doctors' communication practice of ruling out the need for antibiotics. In other words, if doctors ruled out the need for antibiotics, some parents would then question the treatment plan. Parents using either of the two parent behaviours were more likely to be perceived by their doctors as wanting antibiotics. The authors noted that positively framed treatment recommendations for either symptomatic treatments or home remedies were met with significantly more parent alignment with the proposed treatment plan. They also noted that although Latino parents of low socio-economic status had higher expectations for antibiotics, they did not use the communication behaviours described and, therefore, that inappropriate antibiotic prescribing for these families did not appear to be driven by doctor-perceived pressure to prescribe.

The work of Stivers and colleagues also illustrates other aspects of patient resistance, particularly how patients can influence prescribing by withholding agreement. This is due to the fact that, unlike diagnostic statements, treatment proposals usually receive some form of acknowledgement (Stivers 2005). Conversation Analysis has shown that treatment recommendations are treated as proposals which are only complete, normatively speaking, when some sign of acceptance is given. If patients do not accept a treatment proposal, Stivers' work shows how this resistance can lead to changes in what the physician proposes and to altered prescribing decisions. Parent resistance can be seen to be initiating a negotiation of the treatment decision. This provides an insight into the ways in which patients can influence prescribing decisions, sometimes by means of silence, since passive withholding of acceptance is heard as constituting resistance to the proposed treatment (Bugge and Jones 2007). It is the micro climate of the consultation, in which the withholding of an expected agreement can shape a prescriber's perceptions, which provides the space for some patients in some circumstances to achieve their own goals. Stivers concludes that it is not only parents' behaviour but also the existing normative constraints that lead physicians to perceive pressure and to acquiesce to what is sometimes inappropriate treatment. These observations are more pertinent in cases where patients want prescriptions than in cases when they do not; in the latter case, patients' resistance can take the form of accepting the prescription without any intention of actually using it.

These studies about patients' influence on prescribing focus on situations in which patients are seeking access to medicines. They can tell us something about the relationship between patients' expectations for prescriptions and physicians' behaviour; they do not tell us very much about their lifeworld concerns or resistance to taking medicines. This is because such concerns are often absent from the consultation, and because they tend to reduce the wish for prescriptions rather than increase it. The desire not to have a prescription is much harder to express, as it may imply criticism of professional judgement, than the opposite. In particular, patients do not usually reveal their self-regulation of medicines (Cox et al. 2004), although there have been no studies that have investigated the proportion of self-regulating patients who have reported this to their doctor. If patients do discuss self-regulation, they may say that they have deliberately not taken their medication as directed, or that they had run out of their medicine, had forgotten or were confused. The evidence reviewed by Cox et al. (2004) suggests that there is no significant relationship between various doctor and patient characteristics and the extent to which patients using long-term medications told their doctor about an adherence problem. A qualitative study indicated that patients were more likely to feel that they could tell doctors about having changed their medication regime if they had done it to alleviate side effects (Meystre-Agustoni 2000). In another study, when patients reported an adherence problem, doctors commonly responded by changing the medication or providing education, although a third of the adherence problems that were raised were ignored (Sleath et al. 2000). When patients were asked how they thought their doctor would respond if they told them about being non-adherent or changing their regime, many felt that they would be told they could come back if necessary or they would be given information. However, some felt that their doctor would not agree with their decision and might be angry. This suggests that the possibility of open discussion and more supportive professional–patient relationships was lost. In addition to reluctance to mention non-adherence, patients do not usually talk about their use of CAM therapies with their doctors. Patients with schizophrenia may feel unable to discuss their use of alternative coping strategies such as prayer or yoga on the grounds that their diagnosis undermines the validity of their views in the eyes of psychiatrists (Rogers et al. 1998). Patients with other conditions may also be reluctant to reveal their use of CAM therapies (Stevenson et al. 2003).

System and Lifeworld in Health Care Consultations

Lay perspectives about prescription medicines go well beyond opinions or preferences about particular drugs. As we saw in Chapters 2 and 3, people may use resources from all three health care sectors when managing their own and their families' health and illness, and decisions to use treatments from one sector may be made in the context of actual or potential treatments from other sectors. Those consulting CAM practitioners may do so because they are dissatisfied with orthodox care, have a preference for natural treatments, want to have treatments that are appropriate for their own individual circumstances, or want to be able to talk about their 'whole selves'. This latter aspect suggests that the inclusion of the lifeworld is a valued aspect of CAM consultations. The use of prescribed medicines is very much informed by the ways in which medicine taking, or the experience of side effects, impacts on everyday life and the ability to lead a normal life. Decisions about taking prescribed medicines are shaped by the demands of family and paid work and the extent to which medication regimens interfere with these. As we have seen, these experiences are gendered suggesting different kinds of concerns for women and men. There are some widespread concerns about medicine taking and a general desire to minimize medicine use rather than increase it. Patients carry out their own evaluations of medicines against their own criteria, some employing a 'minimax' strategy of minimal use of medicines and maximal use of other strategies (Pound et al. 2005; Townsend et al. 2003). All this suggests that lifeworld concerns are relevant topics for discussion in health care consultations.

As early as 1980, Hall characterized prescribing as a social exchange arguing that the act of prescribing has as much to do with social processes as with the management of presenting symptoms. He invoked the principles of exchange theory in analysing consultations and claimed that social, political and economic factors structured participants' expectations (Hall 1980). More recently, Pollock (2005) has argued that the participants in a consultation are constrained by social norms which inhibit the full and open disclosure of information and concerns. As a result, although a consultation may succeed as a social encounter, it may not realize its therapeutic potential.

A recent systematic review of the literature on communication between patients and health care professionals about medicines found both that there was limited research on the extent to which patients express their views about medicines and such research as there was suggested that patients' perspectives are not discussed in most health care consultations (Cox et al. 2004; Stevenson et al. 2004). Those studies which had examined the questions asked by patients found that around half of patients using long-term medications addressed questions to their doctors, and less than 40 per cent addressed questions to pharmacists; most of these were technical questions about the quantity or supply of medication, or when and how long to take it. However, the topic most frequently asked about was side effects. Sleath et al. (1999) investigated patients' demographic characteristics and found that while older patients asked more questions about their medicines even when the number of medications was taken into account, other characteristics such as gender, race, income and perceived health were not associated with question asking. Cox et al. (2004) also found that patients and doctors discussed the benefits of medicines in most consultations, whereas discussions about side effects, risks and precautions were not as common. This was despite the fact that patients felt that discussion of side effects was important if not essential (Frederikson 1995). This imbalance in favour of the benefits of medicines echoes the findings of Chapter 5 in respect of written information about medicines. The review provided a few insights into the lifeworld concerns voiced by patients; these included the desire to stop taking a medicine, wanting to know why someone else with a similar condition had not been given the same drug, presumably after comparing notes with one another, and the effect of antiretroviral therapy on social and sexual relationships. More detailed insight into the ways in which lifeworld concerns are, or are not, addressed in health care consultations come from studies by Waitzkin (1991) and Mishler (1984), whose studies were not specifically focused on prescribing, and by Barry et al. (2001) and Britten et al. (2000), whose research was based on a study of doctor–patient communication about medicines.

Waitzkin (1991) is one of the few writers who has analysed doctor–patient consultations in the context of social problems with the intention of linking micro analyses of talk to the social structure. His work was based on detailed analyses of 336 encounters between patients and doctors in both private practice and hospital outpatient departments in two states in the United States. His analysis of the micro-political structure of medical discourse employed six categories: social issue as context; the patient's personal trouble; the medical encounter; the expression of contextual (lifeworld) problems in medical discourse; countertextual problems deriving from social context; and the management of lifeworld problems. By countertextual problems, Waitzkin was referring to troubling lifeworld issues not easily resolved within the medical encounter, such as a man's imminent redundancy from his job. Waitzkin argued that by not criticizing the social contexts in which patients' troubles arose, medical discourse served to reinforce the dominant ideology and thus the status quo. In this way, social conditions remained unchallenged while the patients, with the benefit of medical advice, did their best to adjust. In this situation, medication is a technical fix which serves to individualize patients' problems and divert their attention from the causes of their distress. Waitzkin provided detailed analyses of 17 encounters in which he analysed problems to do with patients' family and gender roles; ageing; sexuality; leisure; substance use and other 'vices'; and troublesome emotions. In each of these encounters, the expression of lifeworld problems such as marital strife, the need to continue working, and social isolation produced countertextual tensions to which the doctors responded in various ways including interrupting the patient to return to technical matters or marginalizing the lifeworld concern. Although some doctors may listen sympathetically to patients' lifeworld concerns, the traditional format of the medical interview does not make this easy. Waitzkin argued that the management of lifeworld concerns involved reified, technical solutions such as medication or counselling, which reproduced mainstream and ideological assumptions about appropriate behaviour. His argument is, therefore, that medical discourse contributes to social control by reinforcing individual accommodation to the status quo. In identifying medical practice with scientific ideology, Waitzkin does not specify its particular strategic goals apart from the individualization of distress. Thus, his analyses do not link doctors' actions with any specific system goals, such as time pressures in the consultation or the interests of the pharmaceutical industry.

Mishler (1984) used Habermas' concepts of system and lifeworld and Schutz's (1962) concepts of scientific and natural attitudes to develop his own characterization of the voice of medicine and the voice of the lifeworld and their relationship in health care consultations. His work was based on 25 consultations drawn from the same US database as Waitzkin, although they used different subsets of consultations for their detailed analyses. Mishler defined the voice of the lifeworld as

the patient's contextually-grounded experiences of events and problems in her life. These are reports and descriptions of the world of everyday life expressed from the perspective of a 'natural attitude'. The timing of events and their significance are dependent on the patient's biographical situation and position in the social world. (Mishler 1984, p. 104)

In contrast, Mishler defined the voice of medicine as one which:

reflects a 'technical' interest and expresses a 'scientific attitude'. The meaning of events is provided through abstract rules that serve to decontextualize events, to remove them from particular personal and social contexts. (Mishler 1984, p. 104)

The voice of medicine thus reflects system perspectives which reflect scientific and professional definitions. Mishler acknowledged that both parties could speak in either voice, but concluded that patients' attempts to explain their problems in the voice of the lifeworld were interrupted by doctors speaking in the voice of medicine. The patient's story emerged as a series of fragments resulting from the doctor's mode of questioning. These questions were almost always in the voice of medicine and shifted the topic of conversation away from the lifeworld. The effect of the doctors' interruptions was to strip away the context of patients' experiences of their problems. Most shifts in the other direction, from the voice of medicine to the voice of the lifeworld, were initiated by the patient. These shifts took place within utterances where typically patients would answer the doctor's question in the voice of medicine and then continue in the voice of the lifeworld. These lifeworld utterances were viewed by Mishler as efforts by patients to maintain the continuity and coherence of their lifeworld narratives. He characterized the consultations as struggles between the two voices and two different domains of meaning. Continuity of discourse was maintained by two conversational strategies pursued by each party. The doctors used a strategy of selective attention in which they responded to particular elements of patients' accounts and not others. Typically the doctors focused on the patient's symptom, and then referred to it within another context expressed in the voice of medicine. In this way the symptom was transformed by being relocated to a different province of meaning. The patients' strategy was to attempt to stay in touch with the voice of the lifeworld by connecting their responses to doctors' questions to their lifeworld concerns. In this way patients attempted to retain the meaning of their problems in their lifeworld contexts.

Mishler characterized the domains of meaning represented by the two voices. In the voice of medicine, reality was described in terms of its objective physical features in which connections between different parts were not articulated. Although doctors' questions were almost certainly based on underlying conceptual frameworks, these were not articulated and in particular were not evident to the patients. By contrast, features of the voice of the lifeworld included the causally contingent nature of events; they were self-centred and linked past and present, and events were temporally ordered in relation to one another. Mishler summarized these differences by characterizing doctors' questions as being directed towards the definition and classification of each item in turn, while patients' accounts emphasized the relations between items.

Mishler's work has been much cited, but until recently it has not been replicated. Barry et al. (2001) tested Mishler's analysis using a British data set of 35 general practice consultations collected as part of a study of communication about prescribing. This data set was more comprehensive than the one available to Waitzkin and Mishler as it included patient and doctor interviews as well as tape recorded consultations. As a result, the researchers had more information about lifeworld concerns mentioned by patients in the interviews but not necessarily in the consultations. This study also linked communication in the consultations with their outcomes to provide a separate indicator of their success or failure. Ten mainly patient-centred and contextually specific endpoints were combined to produce a composite outcome score ranging from one, the best outcome, to four, the worst outcome. The ten endpoints were wanted or unwanted prescriptions; no prescription when that was wanted or unwanted; another wanted or unwanted action, such as referral to hospital; information or reassurance wanted by patients; presence or absence of major misunderstandings; dispensing of prescriptions; self-reported adherence; problems with medication; patient and doctor satisfaction as reported in post-consultation interviews (see example at the end of this chapter). Thus, if a patient wanted a prescription but did not receive one, this was rated as a poor endpoint from the patient's point of view. If a patient did not want a prescription and did not receive one, this was rated as a good endpoint. If a patient did not have a prescription dispensed or said that they did not take their medication as prescribed, this was rated as a poor endpoint. These endpoint scores were added up to produce the overall outcome for each consultation. Most of the endpoints measured were patient centred, and they were all relevant to the specific content of the consultation.

Barry et al. (2001) identified four different patterns of communication based on the use of the voice of medicine and the voice of the lifeworld by patients and doctors. These patterns were Strictly Medicine, Lifeworld Blocked, Lifeworld Ignored and Mutual Lifeworld. In the Strictly Medicine consultations, both patients and doctors spoke in the voice of medicine. In these consultations, patients presented physical problems, often single acute problems for which they had not made prior appointments. On the whole these consultations had good outcomes, and in particular the doctors were very satisfied with them. The Lifeworld Blocked consultations seemed similar to the ones described by Mishler in the sense that glimpses of the lifeworld, voiced by patients, were immediately suppressed by doctors' questions. Most of these patients were consulting for chronic physical problems, and these consultations had less successful outcomes. In these two kinds of consultations, the voice of the lifeworld is largely absent, but in the Strictly Medicine consultations this does not lead to poor outcomes. In the other two kinds of consultations, Lifeworld Ignored and Mutual Lifeworld, the voice of the lifeworld was much more present, but again these two patterns were associated with different kinds of outcomes. In the Lifeworld Ignored consultations, patients talked in the voice of the lifeworld for much of the time but were ignored by their doctors who spoke exclusively in the voice of medicine. The difference between these consultations and those in the Lifeworld Blocked group was that the patients kept on repeating their lifeworld concerns even when they were ignored. These consultations showed most evidence of active struggle between the two voices as patients repeatedly returned to their lifeworld concerns and doctors repeatedly ignored them. Most of the patients in this group had chronic physical problems such as arthritis and asthma, and this group had the worst outcomes of all. The consultations with the best outcomes were the Mutual Lifeworld group in which both patients and doctors spoke in the voice of the lifeworld. The doctors not only spoke in the voice of the lifeworld themselves but also allowed patients to speak in this voice. Most of these consultations were about psychological problems. Thus it is not necessarily the absence of the voice of the lifeworld that is problematic, but its suppression. Given the grounding of the outcome scores in the context of each consultation, these findings suggest that ignoring or blocking patients' lifeworld concerns can cause difficulty for the medical agenda.

A further analysis based on the same study specifically examined the ways in which patients expressed concerns about medications and how doctors responded. This analysis focused on aversion, in other words, patients' expression of the dislike of taking medicines or its consequences such as minimization of medicine taking or stopping taking medicines (Britten et al. 2004). The ways in which patients talked about medicines during home interviews with researchers was compared with the ways they did so in consultations with their doctors. In the interviews (which were, of course, much longer than the consultations), people expressed a generalized dislike of taking medicines, some rejecting all medicines while others rejected specific medicines. Some people were prepared to take medicines if they had particular symptoms but would not continue doing so once their symptoms had stopped. Some people were critical of doctors' prescribing habits and talked of being 'fobbed off' with prescriptions instead of being listened to. Although all but one of the patients expressed aversion to medicines in the interviews with the researchers, only a minority did so in the consultation using different strategies to achieve this. One way of introducing aversion in to the consultation was to mention it in passing while talking about something else. Thus one patient, while explaining why he had not taken anything for his heartburn, said 'Cos I'm not that keen on taking stuff' as an aside. When people made these asides, the doctors did not respond to them as is often the case in everyday conversation. Other patients introduced aversion as a topic of conversation rather than as an aside in direct or indirect ways. The direct expression of aversion was problematic as it led, in one case, to the doctor's abandonment of responsibility and in another to the doctor criticizing the patient. Other patients used indirect strategies for introducing the topic of aversion such as embedding these statements in stories about their families or blaming other people for their decision to stop taking medicines. Doctors responded to these expressions of aversion not by exploring patients' views or enquiring about the nature of patients' concerns but by exhorting them to take their medicines. In no case in this study did the expression of aversion lead to any discussion of the underlying reasons. The only apparently unproblematic references to aversion were in cases when it was initiated by the doctor, but there are reasons for thinking that these were examples of strategic action (see Box 7.1). This will be discussed further below.

These studies illustrate Habermas' thesis about the colonization of the lifeworld discussed in Chapter 1, by showing the ways in which medical consultations do not often provide a space for the exploration of lifeworld concerns. In some cases, patients seem perfectly happy not to mention the lifeworld while in others the absence or blocking of lifeworld concerns is problematic. Stivers and Heritage (2001) have identified two specific ways in which patients introduce lifeworld concerns: by using 'expanded answers' and 'narrative expansions'. In both cases, the patient provides more information than the doctor's question asked for. An expanded answer is an answer to the doctor's question together with a brief elaboration. Narrative expansions are more extensive responses through which the patient can introduce her or his own agenda; they serve to provide insight into what is on the patient's mind. While it is possible that some of patients' lifeworld concerns are not relevant to the consultation, their concerns about medicines are likely to be relevant even if clinicians do not regard them in this way. But as Frank (1989) has argued, where there is colonization there is also resistance, and the work of Stivers and her colleagues has provided insights into the ways that patients accomplish resistance to doctors' treatment recommendations.

Box 7.1   Concealed strategic action 1 (denying access)

D: (laughs) How do you feel about antibiotics?

P: Yeah. Well I believe in using them as little as possible

D: Yes

P: Really

D: Yes. I-I-I have to agree, he's not got a temperature, he's just ratty and er er-uncomfortable with it. And my feeling would be if you can and you prefer to get away with just adequate pain relief on a regular basis until he clears it himself. Because he's got small passages and because he's – he's tiny, he can't blow his nose.

D: That I really don't think he's a sick sick baby. All right?

P: Good. So we won't bother with antibiotics just yet.

D: I really think we should wait and see.

P: Okay. Good

Source: Britten et al. 2004.

Strategic or Communicative Action?

For Habermas, the system and lifeworld employ different forms of communication. The system is based on purposive-rational action while the lifeworld is based on communicative action. Communicative action is oriented to understanding, and strategic action is oriented to success. Habermas refers to communication pathologies, which are the product of confusion between these two types of action. Concealed strategic action may be either conscious or unconscious and differs from open strategic action in which a speaker openly pursues an action (as, for example, if a nurse or doctor openly asks a patient to do something). In cases of conscious deception, one participant may act with an orientation to success while allowing the other to believe that the conditions of communicative action are being met. Such situations may be seen as examples of manipulation. In unconscious strategic action, also referred to as systematically distorted communication, a participant's actions may be oriented to success even though they believe that they are pursuing communicative action. Scambler considered the relevance of Habermas' theories for doctor–patient communication as follows: 'The main thesis proffered is that one of the most profound implications of system rationalization for physician–[patient] communication is the domination of the voice of the lifeworld by the voice of medicine via open and concealed strategic action' (Scambler 1987, p. 184).

Scambler provides an illustration of the contrast between manipulation and open strategic action in a consultation between a pregnant woman who wants to stay at home and a doctor who wants her to come into hospital (using data from a study by Graham and Oakley (1981)). In an attempt to persuade the patient to do as he asks, the doctor switches from lay language ('I think you ought to come in for the rest and to do some water tests') to technical language ('You see ... on the water tests the oestriols are falling'), and then resorts to open strategic action ('In fact I think you should come in today') when this fails.

In the context of prescribing, we may ask about the extent to which health professionals use open or concealed strategic action and if there is evidence of systematically distorted communication. The difficulty in distinguishing between conscious and unconscious deception is that of attributing conscious or unconscious motivations to health professionals, which is not possible without a thorough knowledge of their emotions and thought processes. It seems safer to restrict our interest to the difference between open strategic action and manipulation without making a judgement if this is conscious or not.

In using the concept of strategic action, one needs to ask what 'success' might consist of. What are the endpoints which professionals strive to achieve? In relation to prescribing, and in the short term, professionals may be seeking to avoid 'inappropriate' or 'irrational' prescribing and to achieve 'compliant' patients. In the longer term, professionals may be striving to improve the health of their patients, establish their own professional credibility with colleagues, maximize their income, manage their own levels of stress or several other objectives. In the short term, two of the difficulties facing prescribers are patients 'demanding' inappropriate prescriptions, very often antibiotics, and 'non compliant' patients. Both of these threaten the achievement of rational prescribing (even though as we have seen, concepts of rational prescribing may not make explicit reference to adherence).

As we saw earlier in this chapter, nurses may be more oriented to achieving adherence than to helping patients make informed decisions (Latter et al. 2007), and this is consistent with the use of written information discussed in Chapter 5. Stevenson et al. (2000) found that doctors sometimes mentioned the side effects of antibiotics as part of an attempt to persuade patients that they were unnecessary but did not necessarily do so when wanting to prescribe. In Stivers' study of doctor–patient communication about medicines described above, there were examples of manipulation in the context of prescribing – or rather not prescribing – antibiotics for children. The overprescribing of antibiotics for children is a worldwide problem due to the associated development of antibiotic resistant bacteria (Stivers 2007). Thus success for the prescriber in such a situation is to avoid prescribing for children with viral infections. If a decision not to prescribe antibiotics can be presented in such a way as to avoid conflict and resistance from the parent, this may also save time in the consultation. In such a situation, Britten et al. (2004) found that one doctor used the technique of asking parents for their views on antibiotics, but only in situations in which she did not want to prescribe. The doctor's strategic goal in these cases was to block the patient's access to inappropriate medication thereby avoiding an irrational prescribing decision (see Box 7.1). In two examples, the parent's response, which revealed their aversion to using antibiotics in the terms already discussed, allowed the doctor to present her prescribing decision as an agreement with the parent's preference. In this study, there were no examples of doctors asking patients how they felt about taking particular kinds of medicine apart from the kind of situation just described (antibiotics for a child). In particular, there were no examples of doctors asking this question when they wanted to prescribe a medicine, and in which case the question is much more appropriate as it has relevance for subsequent medicine use.

Other potentially manipulative strategies were used by doctors to persuade patients of the appropriateness of prescribed or recommended medication, to achieve the goal of overcoming resistance to medicine taking. In one case, a man consulting with indigestion made an explicit statement that he preferred to avoid taking drugs (see Box 7.2; Barry et al. 1999). The doctor wanted to refer the patient for a diagnostic endoscopy, but in the meantime prescribed Gaviscon to manage his symptoms while awaiting the referral. To make the medicine more appealing to the patient, he described Gaviscon as a medicine 'which is actually just made from seaweed'. The strategic goal for the doctor was the patient's acceptance of the prescription. In attempting to achieve this, he first misrepresented the medicine (as Gaviscon, although derived from seaweed, contains much else besides) and second based his manipulation on an assumed preference on the part of the patient for natural remedies. The doctor had not ascertained if this was actually what the patient preferred.

Although Scambler (1987) only examined the behaviour of physicians for examples of strategic action, it is clear that patients also pursue their own goals, at least in the cases where they want prescriptions. Stivers (2002) identified four main types of communication used by parents wanting antibiotics for their children. Direct requests for antibiotic treatment clearly constitute open strategic action. The other methods used by parents were statements of desire for antibiotic treatment, inquiries about antibiotic treatment and mentions of past experience with antibiotic treatment. All four of these methods were rare in her study and constituted less than 10 per cent of the sample of 360 paediatric consultations. Although less direct, these other methods also constitute open strategic action as their purpose is clearly to obtain antibiotics for their child.

**Box 7.2   Concealed strategic action 2
(overcoming resistance)**

D: And and what I would do until then

P: Mm

D: is put you on a a medicine called Gaviscon which is actually just made from seaweed. Okay? It's er you know that jelly-like stuff you get in s- when you tread on seaweed?

P: Yeah

D: Well they've made made it into – they've made it into tablets and they've made it into

P: Yeah

D: suspension

Source: Barry et al. 1999.

One may ask if it is actually possible or appropriate to have purely communicative action in such a tightly constrained institutional setting. Perhaps all communicative action within health care consultations has to be oriented to some system or professional goal. The literature on patient-centred medicine is partly justified in terms of patient satisfaction, which might indicate attention to lifeworld, and in terms of adherence, which reflects system goals. Whatever the professional rationales, it is clear that patients are looking for both communicative and strategic action. Wensing summarized the expectations of over 3500 patients in eight European countries and found that the top priority was that 'a GP should have enough time to listen, talk, and explain to me' (Wensing 2003). In another list based on 19 studies of patients' priorities, he found that the top priority was 'respect and personal interest for the patient as an individual', which he labelled humanity. The patients in these surveys also prioritized many strategic goals, such as the provision of quick services and doctors having adequate clinical knowledge and skills. The challenge of health care consultations is to balance communicative and strategic action. If professionals are solely oriented to strategic action, they will fail to engage the lifeworld. If they aim to achieve communicative action first, they may understand the patient's lifeworld concerns and in the process realize that patients may be seeking other outcomes which are not necessarily incompatible with system goals. Patients may be seeking to understand the meaning of their problem or the reasons behind it; they may want to discuss concerns about medicines; they may want to find out if there are other ways of managing their problem or if their own methods of self-management are adequate.

Scambler and Britten (2001) have drawn attention to the potential for systematically distorted communication in which neither doctor nor patient is aware that strategic rather than communicative action has prevailed, and Stevenson and Scambler (2005) have argued that this may be a result of criticisms of paternalism and open strategic action. In contrast, the concept of concordance represents the ideal of communicative action within an institutional setting, in which patients' lifeworld concerns are respected, if only on the pragmatic grounds that most medicines are taken in the lifeworld. Patients make their own choices about how to take their medicines based on their own criteria. If professionals wish to support patients by helping them to make informed choices, the use of concealed strategic action is unlikely to help.

Conclusion

Health care consultations constitute an interface between system and lifeworld. Although patients' expectations for prescriptions influence prescribing decisions, doctors' perceptions are the more salient influence. System imperatives and professional agendas of both nurses and doctors often dominate, and prescriptions can be used to provide technical solutions to lifeworld problems. The blocking or ignoring of lifeworld concerns can lead to problematic outcomes. Professionals may use open or concealed strategic action to pursue their goals, but micro analysis of consultations reveals patients' power of resistance based on normative lifeworld frameworks and everyday conversational 'rules'. In Chapter 8, I will consider the extent to which lifeworld concerns and patients' resistance are more salient in the activities of patient groups.

Box 7.3   Example: misunderstanding about the cause of side effects

The consultation and home interview partly shown below are taken from the case of a 67 year old retired cleaner. She had had rheumatoid arthritis for seven months and had difficulty walking and getting about. She was taking a range of drugs including painkillers, and had been having gold injections at the local hospital. She was also worried about losing her hair, an important aspect of her lifeworld. The doctor was a female doctor in a single handed rural practice. In the consultation, the patient asked whether her hair loss was due to the drugs, and the doctor replied with a question about steroid injections in the voice of medicine. In the post consultation home interview with a researcher, the patient attributed the hair loss to the gold injections and decided to discontinue them.

Consultation between patient and doctor

Patient: And there's another thing. I'm losing my hair. Erm is it the medication or is it erm arthritis or what? Could it be? I don't know ... Mm. I mean I know I've never had a good head of hair but ...

Doctor: You've just had steroid injections haven't you. You haven't been taking steroids by mouth have you?

Patient: No.

Doctor: No. I doubt if it's the injections. Er ... how many have you had?

Patient: Erm I've had ... I've had four I think.

Doctor: Four altogether.

Patient: Mm. Do you think it's them then?

Doctor: It's ... it's possible but ... erm ... on the other hand it may be again just one of those things ...

Patient: Mm.

Doctor. ... that people do tend to get thinner hair as they get older.

Post consultation interview between patient and interviewer

Patient: well I did mention about losing my hair and she thought it was the injections that I've been having. So I won't be having any more of those.

Interviewer. What were the injections? I don't think we talked about those.

Patient: Well I used to have one every time I went to the hospital ... I think they're called gold injections.

Interviewer. Is that for the arthritis?

Patient: Yes.

Interviewer. So how often have you had that before?

Patient: I've had four altogether.

Interviewer. And she thinks that's what's causing your hair to fall out?

Patient: She thinks that's what it is. She's not sure, but that's what she thinks

Interviewer. Right. And were they helping at all – the injections?

Patient: Cor, they're marvellous. They last a month and you don't get any pain at all

Interviewer. So it's a bit of a shame not to be able to have any more then?

Patient: Mmm ... I'm not having any more, I'd rather keep my hair!

Source: Britten et al. 2000.

8

Collective Action

Introduction

One of the tensions running through any discussion of medicine use is that between 'patients' and 'people'. This may be treated as a semantic issue arising from the connotations of the word 'patient' as implying a passive and uncomplaining role. Other words have been suggested, such as 'consumer', 'client' and 'service user', but they all have their own particular connotations which are not necessarily appropriate to the context of healthcare. However, the problem is much more than a semantic one. It can be argued that the colonization of the lifeworld by the dominant health care system turns people who inhabit the lifeworld into patients who inhabit the system. Within the system, patients have only a limited part to play in which their lifeworld concerns are treated as secondary to system imperatives. As a result, as we have seen in earlier chapters, the involvement of patients in healthcare is often minimal. So far I have been considering individuals in their roles as patients (or, to a lesser extent, carers), but I have not considered collectives or groups of people. Given the lack of attention to the lifeworld in most health care systems, one of the potential functions of patient groups is to champion lifeworld concerns and resist its colonization (Scambler 1987). In this chapter, I consider the extent to which health consumer groups address the 'democratic deficit' in the provision of health care; in other words, the lack of opportunities for patients and carers to participate as citizens and clients. Can self-help and health consumer groups be described as vehicles for resisting colonization of the lifeworld and, if so, what are their achievements?

Types of Groups

There are many contexts in which people can identify common interests with others in similar situations. Self-help groups are those whose main interest is in supporting individual members. Kelleher defined self-help

152

groups as 'groups which place a value on experiential knowledge, thus implicitly challenging the authority of professional health care workers to define what it is to have a particular condition and how it should be managed' (Kelleher 1994, p. 111). The paradox of self-help groups is that while membership is often defined on the basis of having a particular disease, the majority of those with any disease do not want it to constitute their primary identity; some people may want to keep their disease status hidden or at least marginal to their identity. Those individuals who join self-help groups are those who are willing to have their disease entity made public. As Vincent (1992) has pointed out, self-help groups have to find a balance between mutuality and individualism, between reciprocity and either giving or receiving services, and between active involvement and passive membership. She characterized self-help groups as forming a continuum. At one end are groups in which all members are offering and receiving care and support in a reciprocal fashion, and at the other end there are organizations in which a small number of people are providing information and services to a large number of members and non-members, as do charities and voluntary organizations. Self-help groups may meet face to face or on-line, and indeed the Internet has transformed the ways in which people can identify, and communicate with, others with similar experiences. It is possible that one of the appeals of Internet-based groups is the possibility of separating one's life as a member of a disease community from the rest of one's life. Self-help groups tend to be formed by those people whom medicine cannot cure, in other words, those with chronic diseases. These are the people for whom the promise of the magic bullet has been broken: there is no cure, and this fact is driven home by the fact that non-curative treatments have to be taken over long periods of time, possibly for the rest of the person's lifetime. An example of self-help groups are the small groups of people with diabetes meeting face to face who were studied by Kelleher (1991). These groups discussed topics such as diet and complications of diabetes but also shared and legitimated each others' experiences of 'non compliance'.

There is another distinction between inner focused self-help groups, mostly concerned with providing services to members, and outer focused pressure groups aiming to influence clinical practice or health policy. The work of Baggott et al. (2005) was concerned with outer focused health consumer groups, which they defined as 'voluntary sector organizations that seek to promote and/or represent the interests of users and/or carers in the health arena at national level'. The UK-based groups they studied were primarily interested in influencing the policy process. Baggott et al. distinguished between three types of groups: condition-based groups such as CancerBACUP; population-based groups representing particular populations such as Help the Aged; and formal alliance organizations such as the Long-term Conditions Alliance. The distinction between such health consumer groups and self-help groups is blurred, as a group which begins as a self-help group may evolve over the course of time into a more outer focused organization. Baggott et al. (2005) identified the values and ethos of the groups they studied, which constituted an ethic of caring. These values included the following:

- A commitment to the principle of equity within the National Health Service (NHS)

- A concern with enhancing the autonomy of those they represented

- The aim of empowering individuals

- A belief in the value of personal experience

- The desire to encourage the participation of their members and clients, and to respond to their issues.

These values can be seen as an attempt to resist lifeworld colonization by helping to redress the passive role assigned to patients and by valuing the lifeworld experiences of individuals.

Baggott et al. (2005) summarized their research by identifying four potential benefits from the activities of health consumer groups all of which make a contribution to the public sphere. First, groups provide information for a wider public; their activities may generate policy developments and service improvement; they may help sensitize policy makers to the needs and preferences of patients and carers and lastly they may facilitate mechanisms for incorporating patients' and carers' views into decision making. Health consumer groups vary tremendously in size and in the resources available to them. Duckenfield and Rangnekar (2004) examined the websites of 17 UK patient groups to establish if those with greater resources had greater media profiles, and whether those with more accessible and informative websites experience higher levels of Internet traffic. They examined the content of websites under several categories: forums, news, patients, carers, publications, medical professions and research. Members of groups with on-line forums found these to be an extremely beneficial service. Although thè largest patient groups have traditionally had the financial resources and national reputation to reach their target audiences more effectively, Duckenfield and Rangnekar concluded that the smaller groups have disproportionately benefited from the growth of the Internet. These benefits have enabled many of them to close the communication gap between themselves and the larger patient groups.

In addition to health consumer groups, there are general consumer groups whose interests include health-related topics. The US group

Public Citizen has an active Health Research Group (see the discussion on outer focused group on p. 161). In the United Kingdom, the National Consumer Council has set out seven principles which are relevant to the regulation of medicines. These are access, choice, safety, information, equity, redress and representation (National Consumer Council 1993). In an earlier publication they made the case for greater consumer involvement in medicines policy:

> Medicines are probably the most important products we ever consume – often they hold sway between life and death and can dramatically influence the quality of our lives. It is anomalous that consumers have so little market power over such an influential sector, and one so vital to their personal health. Of course there will be difficulties in redressing this imbalance, but much could be done, we believe, to improve the situation for both the individual patient and for consumers generally. (National Consumer Council 1991, p. 49)

A completely different kind of group wishing to influence medical research is the animal rights movement, which is arguably one of the most significant lifeworld influences on the pharmaceutical industry. This movement represents one particular perspective about the status and treatment of animals in scientific research, which goes back to the nineteenth century (Elston 1994). In advocating the rights of animals to be treated humanely, campaigners articulate strong critiques of scientific research and modern medicine. Elston points out that even in Victorian times, anti-vivisection campaigners made links between the scientific research they disapproved of and the reductionist character of medicine. Current critiques are well informed about the ways in which pharmaceutical trials are conducted and draw from a range of academic sources. One of the main arguments is that of species error: that tests carried out on animals have little or no validity for humans. Perhaps in response to this long-standing campaign, medical research involving animals in the United Kingdom is governed by strict rules. However, in recent years the animal rights movement has rejected democratic methods in favour of direct and sometimes violent action, and it has also come into conflict with health consumer groups about the right to treatment. There is a clear conflict of interest between those wanting access to new treatments resulting in part from animal-based research and those wanting to ban such research. There are, therefore, conflicting interests amongst the various lifeworld groups seeking to influence clinical practice and medical research and not only in terms of competing for limited resources.

Prioritizing the Lifeworld

By their very nature, self-help groups and health consumer groups of all kinds have the potential to prioritize and address the lifeworld concerns of their members and clients. Kelleher (1994) has argued that self-help groups reinvigorate the public sphere by means of communicative action to develop mutual understandings which may challenge the authority of medicine. They provide a space within which a range of concerns can be discussed in a non-coercive environment and in which the knowledge of experts can be criticized and resisted. While some of the issues raised by individuals will be specific to their own situations or organizations, such as the use of human or animal insulin for people with diabetes, many of them are generic issues or have more general implications beyond the specific situation they arise from. These general issues fall under a number of headings, but tend to be of a moral and practical nature due to their origin in the lifeworld rather than scientific or technical. Table 8.1 provides an overview of the contents of a few patient group websites paying particular attention to the availability of a chat room, the presence of patients' stories, information about complementary and alternative medicine, other non-pharmaceutical treatments, adverse drug reactions, and campaigning activities.

Normalization

One of the main points to emerge from studies of individuals' experiences and management of chronic illness is the desire to lead as normal a life as possible. A normal person inhabits the lifeworld, while a sick person inhabits the health care system in the role of 'patient' with all that it implies. As we saw in Chapter 3, individuals may be managing the tension between illness-in-the-foreground and wellness-in-the-foreground (Paterson 2001). People living with long-term illnesses often prioritize their families, work and social relationships above adherence to a medical regimen. Thus 'normality' is a lifeworld concern to be judged against lifeworld criteria such as getting children to school, maintaining social networks or holding on to paid work. Kelleher (1994) argued that the importance of self-help groups lay in their lifeworld origins and the opportunity they provide for discussing the experience of chronic illness in moral and practical, and not medical, terms.

The Internet has greatly expanded the opportunities for social support enabling participants to overcome geographical boundaries and other constraints related to ill health and disability. Loader et al. (2002) analysed postings to a newsgroup for people with diabetes and found that the

Table 8.1 Contents of patient group websites, accessed at various times in 2007

Group	Chat room	Patient stories	Complementary and Alternative Medicine	Other non-pharma treatments	Adverse drug reactions	Campaigning
Alzheimer's Society www.alzheimers.org.uk	Alzheimer's talking point	Real lives	Info sheet on CAM (8 different therapies named)	Dietary supplements	Info sheet on drugs mentions side effects	NICE decision re access to treatment
Cancer Backup www.cancerbackup.org.uk			Under Q&A section ten questions, inc Essiac, under Complementary and eight under Alternative	Only CAM questions	269 items under Q&A section	
National Kidney Federation www.kidney.org.uk	NKF Talkline Message Board	Perceptions, patient experiences			Side effects of steroids. Unwanted effects 49 pages	Improvement in provision, lobbying Parliament. NKF Advocacy Officer
Asthma UK www.asthma.org.uk	Discussion forum		Short paragraph on complementary therapies	PDF on 'Non drug approaches to managing your asthma'	Side effects of asthma meds	
JABS: Justice Awareness and Basic Support www.jabs.org.uk	JABS Focus	Yes, not in special section			Focus of whole site	Not clear although potential obvious
Insulin Dependent Diabetes Trust www.iddtinternational.org		one story – diabetes common sense			Yes – to synthetic insulin	Lobbying DH to ensure animal insulin is still available
American Heart Association www.americanheart.org		Survivor Stories		Section on Preventative health care	Drug interactions and side effects, also Medicine Chart	Advocacy network, encouraging people to enroll as advocates, to lobby for more research
Depression and Bipolar Support Alliance www.dbsalliance.org	Live chat room and six dicussion fora	In discussion fora		Talk therapy, peer support, lifestyle strategies	Under Frequently Asked Questions	Advocacy section

newsgroup provided them with the opportunity for mutual support. Participants shared their understandings of what it was like to try and live a 'normal' life with a chronic condition. Loader et al. felt that the future challenge is to ensure that such self-help networks are regarded as valuable spaces for social support and greater understanding of the social conditions of living with chronic conditions and not sites of 'misinformation' to be colonized by medical experts. In a review of health-related computer-mediated support groups, Wright and Bell (2003) found that people were not looking for counsel from professionals but for others who would help them address everyday issues and fears that professionals might have either been unaware of or have insufficient time to explore. Sullivan's analysis of messages posted to two gender specific cancer support groups found highly gendered styles of communication (Sullivan 2003). Female subscribers to the Ovarian Problems Mailing List posted messages which provided emotional support and created a community of similar others; while the male subscribers to the Prostate Problems Mailing list used it as a place to share medical information about the cancer, its treatment and side effects.

In addition to these kinds of groups which provide space for interaction between members, the websites of some self-help and health consumer groups include individuals' stories and experiences (see Table 8.1). These stories provide a lifeworld flavour to the websites and show readers that the group values the experiences of individuals.

Experiential Knowledge

We have already seen in Chapter 6 that there is a tension between scientific evidence and clinical experience, which reflects the experiential knowledge of prescribers and other health care professionals. The same kind of tension between objective scientific knowledge and personal experience exists for lay people and for the same reasons. The daily experience of living and coping with a particular condition is at the heart of lifeworld knowledge, but in consultations with health professionals, patients may find their personal experiences ignored or blocked (Barry et al. 2001). Kelleher (2001) makes the point that doctors have difficulty with patients with diabetes, for example, who want to incorporate their own experiential knowledge into the management of their condition. By contrast, in self-help groups, individuals have the opportunity to share their lifeworld experiences and to gain confidence in their own experiential knowledge through sharing it with others. This sharing is greatly enhanced by the Internet – see, for example, the 'Perceptions' pages on the website of the National Kidney Federation (www.kidney.org.uk) and the 'Real Lives' section of the Alzheimer's Society website (www.alzheimers.org.uk).

In analysing posts to an on-line support group for thrombophilia, Saukko (in press) identified a dominant concern with managing anticoagulation including the discussion of problems that posters were having and their experiences of deep vein thrombosis. Similarly, Baggott et al. (2005) found that health consumer groups endorsed the value of lay knowledge and distinguished between embodied and encoded knowledge. Embodied knowledge is the personal experience of individuals living with a particular condition, while encoded knowledge is the aggregation of such knowledge carried out by the leaders of health consumer groups. This encoded knowledge may take the form of member surveys, analysis of help lines or collecting stories about members' experiences; the collation of such knowledge is highly valued by policy makers (see below).

Challenging the Professionals

Individuals wishing to challenge health professionals may turn to self-help groups or complementary and alternative medicine (CAM) practitioners. Vincent (1992) demonstrates some similarities between self-help groups and complementary medicine. She argues that both serve to empower individuals and provide a challenge to medical orthodoxy without suggesting that they are necessarily linked to one another. Self-help groups can provide a safe context in which medical knowledge is interrogated and compared to lifeworld experiences without risking confrontation with health professionals. Kelleher (2001) contrasts the conversations in self-help groups with those with family members and with health professionals. He argues that self-help groups may be seen as resisting the uncoupling of system and lifeworld, as the dry and one dimensional medical descriptions of what it is like to have a particular condition can be fleshed out with the vivid details of real experience. Self-help groups may also help their members regain a sense of control over their own lives. Kelleher found that in the groups he studied, there was a widely accepted view that living a full life meant developing ways of managing diabetes, which included a degree of non-compliance, and the sharing of this view provided legitimation for individual members. In this way, group members were endorsing each other's right to self-manage their condition in a way that might be unacceptable to professionals.

The health consumer groups studied by Baggott et al. (2005) were those promoting or representing user and carer interests, selected to represent a range of conditions. Their research showed that these groups tended to collaborate with health professionals, because they recognized that the expertise and knowledge of professionals complemented their own. Their study provided little evidence of the challenging of health professionals, perhaps because the target of these groups' activities was health policy at a national level rather than the clinical practice of individual profession-als. The activities rated as important by the groups studied included pro-viding information and advice, publicity, building networks, fundraising as well as influencing national policy. It seems likely that it is easier for inner focused and face-to-face groups to challenge health professionals in their private discussions, and that the aims of outer focused groups require them to maintain good relationships with professionals.

Risks of Pharmaceuticals

Some groups may also have more specific goals in relation to pharmaceu-ticals, particularly in relation to adverse drug reactions and the risks of pharmaceuticals. We have already seen that people are often given written and verbal information that emphasizes the benefits of medicines rather than the harms, and that concern about the dangers of prescribed drugs is one motivation for seeking care from complementary and alternative practitioners. One would expect self-help groups to inform their members and clients about the risks of medicines and to provide a space in which open discussions about side effects could take place. The on-line group studied by Saukko (in press), for example, debated the respective merits of a branded drug (Coumadin) and its generic equivalent warfarin in main-taining blood coagulation levels by avoiding the twin dangers of clotting and bleeding. A quarter of the posts she analysed focused on the use of anticoagulants and themes discussed included side effects of common anticoagulants and other problems in managing medications.

One might expect health consumer groups to be campaigning against products found to be associated with unacceptable risks. Some of the less well known groups are exclusively focused on the risks of pharmaceuticals such as the UK-based Insulin Dependent Diabetes Trust (IDDT), which is concerned with the problems arising from the use of 'human' (genetically engineered) insulin. The IDDT describes itself as performing functions typical of a self-help group (see Box 8.1).

After a large number of people with diabetes wrote to the then British Diabetic Association (BDA, now Diabetes UK) complaining about prob-lems with human insulin, the BDA commissioned Dr Natasha Posner to analyse 384 of these letters. Insulin Dependent Diabetes Trust was set up in 1994 when the BDA did not publish the commissioned report. Insulin Dependent Diabetes Trust devotes a section of its website to the difficulties experienced by some people with human insulin, such as hypoglycaemia

---

Box 8.1   Insulin Dependent Diabetes Trust website

The Trust was set up to look at some of the day to day difficulties of living with diabetes, the worries, fears and concerns that perhaps we don't talk about at the hospital clinic – the ones that many of us experience and understand because we actually live with diabetes. As a charity, IDDT has a Board of Trustees and all our Trustees either have diabetes or have family members with diabetes. So we all know first hand that while diabetes doesn't rule our lives, it is an important part of them. It needs care and attention, it can be a nuisance and it is not without its problems!

The Trust is run entirely by voluntary donations and we do not accept funding from the pharmaceutical industry in order to remain uninfluenced and independent.

Source: IDDT website www.iddtinternational.org, bold font in original, accessed 14 April 2007.

---

and loss of warnings and the 'dead in bed' syndrome. It cites scientific research including a Cochrane review to support its claims and provides advice about what patients should do if their consultant refuses to change them to animal insulin. Insulin Dependent Diabetes Trust's policy of refusing industry funding may be related to the perception that the BDA's position might have been influenced by such funding. The IDDT has since argued that charities and patient groups should declare their sources of funding (Hirst 2003). This example suggests that the more established groups, and particularly those in receipt of industry funding, may be less critical than smaller groups.

The groups listed in Table 8.1 all included information about adverse drug reactions on their websites, but in the absence of a comprehensive survey it is not possible to say how typical this is. Some of these websites included information about CAM and other non-pharmacological treatments either to suggest that members might find these treatments useful (such as the Alzheimer's Society website) or to caution people about unrealistic expectations (such as the Cancer Backup website). In this respect, some of the websites are providing more balanced and broadly based information about potential treatments than the written information reviewed in Chapter 5.

A very different kind of outer focused group, not identified with a particular disease, is the US campaigning organization Public Citizen's Health Research Group, which maintains the website www.WorstPills.org and has published a book *Worst Pills, Best Pills* (Public Citizen 2005). Public Citizen is a non-profit organization which accepts no corporate or government funding or any advertising. The website is entirely concerned with the dangers of prescription medicines, and the organization also conducts research-based consumer advocacy. The Group petitions the Food and Drug Administration (FDA) to ban unsafe prescription drugs, and its warnings have provided an early warning system for a number of drug withdrawals. Readers were warned of the dangers of Vioxx, for example, more than three years before the drug was withdrawn in the United States. The website provides several free consumer guides, including ones on the misprescribing and overprescribing of drugs, and rules for safer drug use (see Box 8.2). A Drug Worksheet which is available on the site provides a tool for people to monitor their prescription drug use, and it is designed in a manner to enhance discussions with health professionals. This Group thus provides a specialist source of information directly addressing one of the main lifeworld concerns about prescription medicines, and the advice it provides emphasizes that there may be non-pharmaceutical alternatives.

While niche groups like Public Citizen Health Group emphasize the risks of pharmaceuticals, Table 8.1 shows that several disease focused groups also include information on potential harms as well as the benefits of medicines on their websites.

Box 8.2   Ten rules for safer drug use

1. Have 'brown bag sessions' [medication review] with your primary doctor.
2. Make sure drug therapy is really needed.
3. If drug therapy is indicated, in most cases, especially in older adults, it is safer to start with a dose that is lower than the usual adult dose.
4. When adding a new drug, see if it is possible to discontinue another drug.
5. Stopping a drug is as important as starting it.
6. Find out if you are having any adverse drug reactions.
7. Assume that any new symptom you develop after starting a new drug may be caused by the drug.
8. Before leaving your doctor's office or pharmacy, make sure the instructions for taking your medicine are clear to you and a family member or friend.
9. Discard all old drugs carefully.
10. Ask your primary doctor to coordinate your care and drug use.

Source: www.worstpills.org (accessed 14 April 2007).

Animal Rights

Although there is a potential for conflicts of interest between members of different patient groups, in terms of media attention or access to scarce resources, these do not usually come to public attention. In contrast, there are clear and well documented conflicts of interest between patient groups and animal rights activists. The issue of animal rights is clearly a moral issue rather than a technical one and takes as its starting point the view that animals are sentient beings with a moral status. DeGrazia (2002) identifies three increasingly strong arguments in favour of animal rights. The first, moral-status, argument holds that animals have at least some moral status and that they should be treated well for their own sake. The second, equal-consideration, argument is that animal suffering matters as much as human suffering. The third position is the 'utility-trumping' argument that animals have certain vital interests that humans must not override even in the interests of society. Although the term 'animal research' covers a number of activities, in the context of this book it mainly refers to the testing of substances which have the potential to be new drugs. There are three standards for using animals in research. The strong animal-rights standard, held by some activist groups, is that animals may only be used in research if they are not harmed or their involvement is in their overall best interests. A utilitarian standard stipulates that animals may only be used in situations where the benefits outweigh the harms, where the interests of all parties including animals are considered. A sliding scale standard is one in which animals may be used only where their use is consistent with giving their interests appropriate moral weight taking account of their cognitive and other capacities. Critics of animal research argue that animal models can be misleading, and even though they may contribute to scientific knowledge, this does not in itself prove that animal research is necessary. Some academics have argued that many animal studies are of poor quality, and that systematic reviews should be employed to ensure best use of existing animal data and to improve the estimates of effect from animal experiments (Pound et al. 2004).

The animal rights movement has influenced the ways in which medical research is carried out using very different methods from the ones used by other consumer groups. Animal rights groups have carried out a number of high profile direct action activities such as breaking into animal houses and setting animals free, detonating bombs near the houses of medical researchers, sending parcel bombs and picketing the building of new research laboratories. The Weatherall report (2006) was set up to examine the use of non-human primates in research. It acknowledged the climate of intimidation created by some opponents of animal research and recommended the investigation of claims that scientists and research companies are moving their non-human primate work overseas. It also advocated a wider public debate:

> Because this is such an emotive topic, and since no civilised society would wish to cause unnecessary suffering to any living thing, the only way forward is to obtain a consensus opinion of the acceptability, or otherwise, of animal research. This should be based on widespread informed public debate, which must rest on a genuine understanding of the current issues involved; since biological and medical research moves so quickly it is not productive to limit these discussions to past events. (Weatherall report 2006, p. 11)

As the report did recommend the continued use of non-human primate research, it would seem that its authors judged that an informed public debate would support their recommendations.

Relationships with Other Stakeholders

One consequence of colonization of the lifeworld is limited discussion in the public sphere. To the extent that patient groups contribute to public debate and open up new topics for discussion, they are in a position to resist colonization. Kelleher (2001) argues that self-help groups are one way of sustaining the public sphere. In the United Kingdom, patients are increasingly being asked to contribute to the planning and delivery of health care under the banner of consumer involvement. Such involvement does not necessarily mean that patient groups will influence public debate or have any effect on health policy. To exert influence, outer focused patient groups develop relationships with other groups and organizations including civil servants and policy makers, industry, professional and academic organizations, the media and researchers and academics. All these players have their own imperatives and interests which may or may not coincide with those of patient groups. The animal rights movement uses direct action rather than collaborations with representatives of the system to achieve its aims.

Civil Servants and Policy Makers

In order to influence civil servants and policy makers, patient groups need to be taken seriously as legitimate contributors. Baggott et al.'s (2005) research showed that patient groups brought two elements to the policy process. First, they were able to represent the interests and views of patients and carers; second, they contributed their expertise in the form of patients' experiences of health conditions and of health services as well as wider issues arising from the lifeworld. Policy makers needed to judge the quality of a group's interaction with its members in order to know how representative their views were. Baggott et al. identified three factors which strengthened a group's case with policy makers: groups who surveyed the opinions of their members or of the public were regarded more highly than those relying solely on anecdote or individual cases; their findings had to be presented clearly with specific recommendations for policy or practice; and they had to be targeted, tailored and timely to fit in with the needs of policy makers. In these circumstances, policy makers valued the experiential knowledge of health consumer groups on the grounds that it helped them develop policies more likely to match the needs of users. Unsurprisingly, the groups with greater resources had greater capacity for engagement with government; Baggott et al. found that population-based groups had the greatest contact with civil servants and ministers, followed by alliance organizations, while the condition-based groups had least contact. Patient groups articulated various barriers to effective consultation including the burden of consultation documents and short deadlines, government rules on confidentiality and the complexity of government departments.

The actual contribution made by patient groups include their influence on the National Service Frameworks (NSFs) in the United Kingdom and on decisions made by the National Institute for Health and Clinical Excellence (NICE). National Service Frameworks are condition-specific national standards for clinical care in the NHS developed by expert panels on which patient groups are represented. The groups interviewed by Baggott et al. did feel that they had drawn attention to issues that would otherwise have been neglected such as quality of life, psychosocial aspects of health and the need for better communication between professionals and patients. However, the civil servants interviewed felt that the medical profession dominated the policy agenda, and Baggott et al. found no examples in which health consumer groups had overcome opposition from professional or commercial interests.

Industry

As discussed in Chapter 4, NICE is an organization set up by the UK government to provide guidance to the NHS on the clinical and cost-effectiveness of some newly licensed drugs and other technologies. Patient groups have the potential to influence decisions made by NICE by providing witnesses and by contributing to the Partners' Council. This Council is made up of doctors and other health professionals, patient and industry representatives. Public input to NICE's work is provided by the Citizens' Council, from which patient groups are precluded, as are health service employees and suppliers. Duckenfield and Rangnekar (2004) investigated the role of patient groups in the work of NICE between 1999 and 2003 by analysing the identity of witnesses appearing before the NICE technology appraisal panel and by assessing their impact on appeals against NICE decisions not to recommend particular drugs. The identity of witnesses provides an indication of the extent to which NICE consulted different interest groups in coming to its decisions, and the analysis of appeals gives an indication of how successful different interest groups are in pressing their priorities in the face of an adverse NICE decision. The data on witnesses showed that the proportion of witnesses representing patient groups (28 per cent) was comparable to the proportion representing medical groups (31 per cent) and somewhat greater than the proportion representing industry (22 per cent). In terms of appeals, when either individual manufacturers or patient groups made appeals, they almost always failed. However, when both a manufacturer and a patient group objected to a NICE decision, they were almost invariably successful in forcing a reappraisal. Thus health consumer groups and the pharmaceutical industry working in tandem make a formidable team.

Although industry is clearly a useful partner in obtaining access to treatments, there is the danger of groups being unduly influenced by commercial interests if they accept funding from pharmaceutical manufacturers. Baggott et al. (2005) found that the groups they researched were very aware of the potential dangers of working with industry; many interviewees expressed uncertainty about the balance of benefits and risks of doing so. Interviewees were mistrustful of industry's motives in funding patient groups and aware of the potential for sponsorship to compromise a group's independence and integrity. Groups adopted one of three positions in relation to industry funding: no contact on principle; no contact because drug treatments were not relevant to their activities; and varying degrees of sponsorship of some groups representing conditions heavily dependent on medicines. A third of the groups studied by Baggott et al. accepted private sector sponsorship, although the authors did not specify if this was all accounted for by the pharmaceutical industry. From the point of view of industry, Baggott et al. identified several reasons for working with patient groups:

- Promoting brand awareness
- Valuable source of information about consumers' views
- Potential ally in the debate about DTCA

- Supporters in campaigning for particular treatments
- Helping to promote an image of industry as generous
- Conferring legitimacy in dealings with other stakeholders.

Baggott et al. found that health consumer groups were mainly concerned about access to new drugs; clearly such an agenda is entirely compatible with a manufacturer's need to maximize the market for new drugs. Access to treatment may perhaps be conceptualized as a lifeworld concern to the extent that it represents a challenge to state and professional priorities at the time of the challenge, and that consumer groups are campaigning for the right to treatments that would otherwise be denied them. However, it could also be argued that groups lobbying for new drugs are a prime example of colonization by industry, which persuades people that the new treatment is the magic bullet they have been waiting for. Successful campaigns by cancer and HIV/AIDS groups lobbying for access to new treatments may have alerted industry to the potential gains from working with patient groups (see Box 8.5 for the example of Herceptin). However, the risk of 'capture', already noted in Chapter 4 in relation to the regulatory authorities, also applies to consumer groups. In the same way that doctors deny that industry advertising affects their prescribing behaviour, patients may be unaware of the ways in which contact with industry influences their view of the world and their evaluation of treatment options. Peter Mansfield of the group Healthy Skepticism has argued that this unawareness may itself increase patient groups' vulnerability to the influence of industry:

> We are now ... understanding the risk of invisible unintended bias from exposure to industry influence techniques. These techniques include manipulation of reciprocal obligation, which can occur without our awareness. Patient groups tend to reciprocate by lobbying governments to pay for overpriced drugs rather than lobbying the companies to reduce their prices. (Mansfield 2007, p. 1020)

One could add that if patient groups lobbied industry about issues of importance to their members, then the issue of drug side effects would be near the top of their agendas. The fact that patient groups' lobbying activities are often about access to treatment and infrequently about resistance to treatment (Box 7.1) does suggest a pro-drug bias consistent with the interests of the pharmaceutical industry. Some groups, aware of these issues, have developed guidelines about working with the pharmaceutical industry (see Box 8.3). The *British Medical Journal* (19 May 2007, p. 1035) ran an on-line poll of its readers in May 2007 on the question 'Should patient groups accept money from the pharmaceutical industry?'

Box 8.3   LTCA guidelines on working with the pharmaceutical industry

Recommended general principles, currently under review

Long-term Conditions Alliance recommends four principles as the basis of your policy:

Principles

- Integrity and openness
- Maintenance of independence
- Equality in partnership
- Mutual benefit for all concerned.

Integrity and openness enable individual members, other funders and the public to know how you get your resources and can be a way of pre-empting queries and criticism from them, or from the press. Funders, too, will feel confident that they know about your other supporters, and on what basis you have obtained that support.

Independence can theoretically be affected by almost any collaboration or donation, not just from the pharmaceutical industry. Independence is substantially easier to safeguard, however, if all concerned in your organisation have signed up to a policy and use this to inform decisions.

Equal partnership should underpin a policy. Spelling this out as a principle can help you identify your special strengths and unique knowledge, and feel more confident about your dealings with large companies. Rather than a situation in which you are largely a passive recipient of money, both sides should be prepared to work towards partnership and joint working, in interests of the people whom the organisation represents.

Mutual benefit should result. You cannot expect companies to hand over money or support simply for philanthropic reasons. Successful partnerships are those where both partners gain something. This does mean though that each should make efforts to understand the internal culture and external pressures on the other. The broad benefits which each expects to gain should be openly set out.

Source: Long-term Conditions Alliance website, see www.ltca.org.uk

---

The results showed that 16 per cent of respondents said yes and 84 per cent said no. The results included readers' comments on the issue including one who had witnessed the use of skilled public relations firms to appeal to patients on an emotional level. One consumer organization which does not accept industry funding is the campaigning group Health

Action International (HAI), which is an independent global network based in the Netherlands. Health Action International has advocated greater transparency in all aspects of decision making around pharmaceuticals, better controls on drug promotion and the provision of balanced, independent information for consumers and prescribers (see www.haiweb.org).

Media

As well as professional and industry organizations, patient groups can also collaborate with the media. Baggott et al. (2005) found that groups pursuing an open strategy, that is targeting the media, government and parliament, were more successful than those targeting the government alone. The authors found that a higher proportion of the groups they studied had contacts with the media than with government or parliament, and that groups saw the media as offering the opportunity to influence policy. On balance, Baggott et al. concluded that the media were seen as allies of health consumer groups, and that groups tended to be portrayed sympathetically. The difficulty for groups was not in attracting media attention, given a high level of media interest in health stories, but in ensuring appropriate coverage. The media's interest in emotional or sensational stories could conflict with the ways in which health consumer groups wished to portray their members. Groups wanting to correct unhelpful stereotypes could find their message undermined by journalists' need to tap into common understandings of a particular condition.

Researchers and Academics

Patient groups also have relationships with researchers and academics. Some self-help and health consumer groups have professional members who may set the agenda or dominate in other ways. For the professionals, self-help groups may seem to provide an ideal setting in which patients can be 'educated'. If, as Seale (2005) has suggested, information on the Internet tends to reflect professional perspectives, the same might be true of self-help groups. Even if groups are not dominated by professionals, they may adopt a professional perspective. For example, Saukko (in press) found that longer-term members of the thrombophilia support group used expert language to explain to newcomers why aspirin was ineffective. Their explanations about how aspirin works on the platelets whereas thrombophilia affects the fibrinogens were perhaps necessarily dependent on expert language given that questions about mechanisms of pharmacological action are not readily testable or subject to lay scrutiny.

However, some patient groups are in the driving seat of academic research. Collectively, the organizations which form the Association of Medical Research Charities fund over a quarter of public domain bio-medical research in the United Kingdom (Duckenfield and Rangnekar 2004). This is unlike the situation in other parts of the world. Patient groups differ from more traditional funding bodies in the way they pri-oritize research topics and appraise grant proposals because of their inclusion of the relevant target community in the funding process. Perhaps the best known example is the UK Alzheimer's Society, which has a consumer-led process to determine research priorities and strong lay representation on their research commissioning panel (see Box 8.4). Research funded by patient groups has a strong clinical orientation. Duckenfield and Rangnekar concluded that patient groups are respond-ing to evidence of mismatch in research agendas pursued by practition-ers and the objectives desired by consumers. Even when research is funded by other organizations, such as the National Health Service, the active collaboration of patient groups may increase academics' success in

---

Box 8.4   Alzheimer's Society research commissioning process

Quality Research in Dementia Advisory Network

The QRD programme is an active partnership between carers, people with dementia and the research community.

The heart of Quality Research in Dementia is the QRD Advisory network: a net-work of 150 carers, former carers and people with dementia who play a full role in the following areas:

- They set the priorities for research
- They provide comments and prioritisation of grant applications
- They select applications for funding
- They monitor on-going projects being funded by the Alzheimer's Society
- They tell others about the results of the research.

Source: Alzheimer's Society website, www.qrd.
alzheimers.org.uk, accessed 16 April 2007.

winning funds. Patient groups thus play an important role in shaping the cognitive development of this area of scientific research. The quality of this research, as judged by journal impact factors, is high and thus likely to command respect.

Academics and researchers have much to gain from closer relationships with patients groups not only in relation to research funding. Those running clinical trials and other research studies may hope that endorsement by well known groups will increase the acceptability of their research thus increasing recruitment as well as its credibility. Recruitment to clinical trials is becoming a problem, and patient groups are very well placed to mobilize their members and encourage them to participate. If the criteria they use to endorse research funded by other organizations are similar to those used by patient groups commissioning their own research, groups are in a strong position to influence the conduct of clinical trials and increase their relevance for the lifeworld.

Conclusion

Self-help and other groups are clearly providing various arenas in which lifeworld experiences are valued and shared and in which medical knowledge can be interrogated and challenged. This is in contrast with the dominance of system perspectives in many health care consultations. The achievements of some patient groups are impressive: providing support and legitimation for members, providing balanced information, funding and shaping medical research, campaigning for access to new drugs and influencing policy makers. The Internet is an important tool for patient groups and has disproportionately benefited the smaller ones. All these provide evidence of resisting the colonization of the lifeworld, and in some cases, bringing lifeworld considerations to the activities of the system. In relation to the distinction made in previous chapters between access to new treatments and resistance to old treatments, patient groups are perhaps more active in the former than the latter. In many ways it is easier to campaign for access to a new and promising drug than against one that is already established. When patient groups collaborate with industry, they make a formidable team, but this, of course, raises many questions. The risk of 'capture' by industry interests applies to patient groups just as much as it does to regulatory authorities, and many groups are aware of this. The House of Commons Health Committee (2005) recommended the introduction of measures to limit the influence of industry on patient groups and argued that it would be preferable for groups to be funded by companies' charitable arms rather then the companies themselves.

Different groups have their own agendas, and there are tensions between the priorities of the public, patients, consumers and research subjects. Each health consumer group lobbying for new drugs wants access to treatments regardless of cost. If all such groups were success-ful, the costs of health care would rise enormously. Such success also reinforces the dominance of pharmaceutical treatments and does nothing to enhance the availability of non-pharmaceutical methods of managing health and illness. In the rush to license a new product, the interests of research subjects may be overlooked, as their main threat is exposure to potentially harmful substances. While the tactics of the animal rights movement are for the most part undemocratic, the questions they raise about the conduct of scientific trials are worthy of serious discussion.

Kelleher (1994) claimed that medicine had lost its way, and rather than being driven by the needs of patients as defined in the lifeworld, it was driven by the demands of the system and its associated measures of instru-mental rationality. Patient groups clearly have some potential to redress the balance, and this potential is greatly enhanced by the scope of the Internet. If this potential is to be fully realized, public debate will need to address the various conflicts of interest and differing perspectives. In Chapter 9 I will consider how lifeworld and system might be brought together in a more fruitful dialogue, to achieve a more mature balance between access to new medicines and the monitoring of old ones, in a sys-tem which creates a level playing field between non-pharmaceutical and pharmaceutical treatments.

Box 8.5   Example: Herceptin

The UK National Institute for Health and Clinical Excellence, known as NICE, was set up in 1999 as an independent source of advice on new and existing technologies for the NHS in England and Wales. After certain drugs have been licensed, NICE assesses their benefits, costs and value for money. NICE appraisals have been criticised for delaying the introduction of effective new medicines. In 2005 there was pressure from various groups to extend the use of the drug Herceptin (generic name trastuzumab) to include patients with early stage breast cancer, despite the fact that the drug was not licensed for use in such patients at the time. Individual women lobbied their Primary Care Trusts (PCTs) for access to the drug and some took their cases to the high court or lobbied the Prime Minister. The lobby made good use of the media, and couched the debate in terms of individuals being deprived of an effective drug. These efforts were successful in a number of cases. Much less attention was paid to the need for evaluation of the drug's benefits and harms, or the potential impact on the availability of treatments for other patients. While the media angle focused on the distress of individuals with a life threatening disease being denied a 'wonder drug', the manufacturer's role was mostly ignored. Few questions were asked about the drug's exorbitant price (£30,000 or $52,000 a year), industry profits or its role in orchestrating the patient lobbies. However, the manufacturer Roche had approached at least one well known academic who happened to have breast cancer asking if she would contribute to its campaign to promote Herceptin.

Source: Boseley 2006.

Part V

Conclusion

9
Balance between System and Lifeworld

It's a bit like doing an operation under a local anaesthetic. If you have a patient who is having an epidural for a caesarean you find that people are polite to each other, nobody swears, no instruments are thrown on the floor and there is a general sort of feeling, well, the patient is awake and it's their operation and you've got to be reasonable. I mean the whole atmosphere is very different. (Hospital consultant talking about patient access to medical records, cited in Britten 1991)

Obviously when you know the media are interested then it makes you more careful to get it right – that's only human. It does keep you on your toes. (Former member of the Committee on the Safety of Medicines, cited in Abraham and Sheppard 1997)

Introduction

In this final chapter I will consider how the system colonization of the lifeworld might be reversed, what a more balanced relationship between the lifeworld and the system might look like, and what it might lead to. In previous chapters we have seen how people draw on a wide range of resources, and not just medicines, for managing their own health and illness. People make decisions based on their own lifeworld criteria, and they are motivated both by concerns about safety as well as the wish to have access to new and promising treatments. Throughout the book, the tensions between access and resistance to taking medicines, between benefit and harm, have been evident. Despite this, much professional discourse is dominated by the notion of adherence, and patients and citizens have little influence over the kinds of treatments that are developed or over the value judgements that are an inevitable part of drug licensing. Much of the information about medicines emphasizes the benefits rather than the harms and fails to address the questions that patients ask. Prescribing is treated as a primarily technical issue in which the views and expectations of patients are often seen as irrelevant or even problematic. There is little discussion of the lifeworld in many health care consultations, and some people value their interactions with complementary practitioners precisely because the lifeworld is included. The activities of patient groups have the potential to redress the balance, and this potential is greatly enhanced by the Internet, but their independence may be compromised by industry sponsorship. All these issues and more indicate that patients and the public are not properly represented in the development and use of medicines or in the assessment of what kinds of treatments are offered. Greater involvement of patients and the public has the potential to reduce the emphasis on pharmaceuticals in modern health care systems. In the second half of this chapter, I will consider ways in which the balance between lifeworld and system might be redressed.

Lifeworld and System

In Chapter 1, I introduced Habermas' theory about the colonization of the lifeworld and in subsequent chapters we saw many examples to support it. The consequences of this colonization are a lack of attention to patients' own perspectives and experiences to the extent that these are often perceived as a nuisance factor, which is the cause of 'inappropriate' prescribing or of 'non compliance'. Other pathologies are an overemphasis on pharmaceutical treatments and the neglect and marginalization of other ways of managing health and illness, a tendency to emphasize the benefits of pharmaceutical treatments rather than their harms, a converse tendency to pay more attention to the harms of complementary and alternative treatments than to their benefits, and treating strategic issues such as licensing or prescribing decisions as if they were purely technical. Similar conclusions have been reached by others: Busfield argues that 'an industry in the business of meeting health needs in fact creates a culture in which the use of drugs is encouraged even when this is unhelpful, counterproductive and even harmful' (Busfield 2006, p. 300).

In Giddens' terms, medicine is an example of a disembedded expert system. Decisions, such as the licensing of drugs, are taken at national or international level yet have profound implications for intimate aspects of people's lives, including the possibility of death. For many people, such trust as they have in prescribed medicines arises from ignorance of the potential dangers rather than a considered balance between trust and acceptable risk (Giddens 1990). Growing public awareness of the inherent conflicts of interest, and suspicion of commercial interests, may undermine confidence in systems of licensing and regulation. Face-to-face consultations between patients and professionals are one kind of reembedding mechanism or access point, but the risks attached to pre-scribed medicines are not fully discussed in most consultations. This omission may serve to enhance trust in the professional but equally may lead to severe disappointment when adverse events occur as well as loss of confidence in systems of drug regulation. Professionals may justify the withholding of information about side effects by pointing to the necessity for 'compliance', but this long-standing and paternalist atti-tude ignores patients' agency and is not supported by the evidence (Raynor et al. 2007). On the other hand, some professionals may over-whelm patients with information about adverse effects in order to reduce their medico-legal liability in case things go wrong. Although often unacknowledged, lay people have their own frameworks for assess-ing the harms and benefits of treatment, and their attitudes towards pre-scribed medicines are characterized by ambivalence. If, however, the potential harms of medicines were discussed and the nature of the evi-dence base explained or at least made available to those who want it, this could form the basis for more mature conversations on which people could make their own informed decisions. Beck (1992) asserted that technical risk experts are mistaken in their assumptions about what is acceptable to the population: if lay people had access to the data on which drugs are licensed, their decisions might well differ from those made by professionals. In the case of Vioxx, although early results of the VIGOR (Vioxx gastrointestinal outcomes research) study found a 79 per cent greater risk of death or serious cardiovascular event in one treatment group compared with the other, the data safety monitoring board allowed the study to continue (Krumholz et al. 2007; see Box 5.1). It is very possible that lay assessors would not have judged this risk to be outweighed by the drug's potential benefits in relieving pain associated with arthritis. At the other end of the access–harm spectrum, the with-drawal of the drug Tasmar (tolcapone) for Parkinson's disease following reports of hepatotoxicity might well have been challenged by those people with Parkinson's whose quality of life it had greatly improved (Bennion 2002).

In sociological terms, although patient groups have the potential to bring lifeworld concerns into the debate, redress the balance of power and promote a more open public debate, this potential is threatened by system interests. In a four way game (state, professionals, industry and patients), the combination of two partners (industry and patients) makes for a powerful force. The pharmaceutical industry is more likely to have its appeals against National Institute for Health and Clinical Excellence (NICE) decisions upheld if these are made in partnership with patient groups. Each of the other three parties claims to be acting in patients' interests, and derives legitimacy by doing so, but their own interests are overriding. Abraham (1995) argues for an explicit model of interests in which behaviour and interests are conceptually distinct. System interests are those of the state and the economy. The interests of the state are to promote healthy citizens and especially healthy workers while enhancing the economy within an effective regulatory framework, and the interests of the pharmaceutical industry can be presumed to be the maximization of sales, especially of new drugs, and therefore profits. Health professionals, particularly in state and social security systems of health care, support the state in managing health and illness but also contribute to the economy by creating a market for prescription drugs. Even in private systems of health care, there are common interests between the state and health professionals if only in terms of state legitimization of professionals' claims and the social management of ill health by legitimating work absence, for example. Individual professionals may be motivated by altruism or self-interest or a combination of both. They may also see their role, in part, as patient advocates and, therefore, representatives of the lifeworld in the public sphere. However, these claims to act on behalf of patients may also serve professional interests (Britten 2001). Lifeworld interests are those in the public sector, such as patient groups, and the interests of individuals. The interests of patient groups lie in advocating for their constituencies and seeking to influence decision making at levels beyond the individual as well as supporting individual members; the interests of individual patients are to manage and improve their health as well as to maintain a normal life even though these two goals are not always compatible. Recent events, such as industry sponsorship of patient groups, could perhaps be characterized as signalling a move from the ignoring of patients' interests and concerns to a harnessing of lifeworld interests to bolster those of different sectors of the system. To achieve this move, only those lifeworld concerns which are compatible with system interests, such as access to new drugs, will be recognized. Other lifeworld concerns, such as those about drug safety, are much less likely to be championed.

It may not be either possible or desirable to avoid such partnerships, but in a more open debate, the interests being served could be made transparent. The media coverage of Herceptin may be seen as an example of distorted communication in which the argument appeared to be about the rights of individual patients to have access to unlicensed and expensive drugs (see Box 8.5). Clearly the interests of the manufacturer were served by this version of events, in which health authorities were eventually forced to underwrite the costs of prescribing the drug, and few questions were asked about its cost or about industry profits. In this case, industry harnessed the 'access' agenda, and in this context of women with breast cancer, issues of harm (to do with cardiovascular risk) might have seemed irrelevant to those diagnosed with a potentially fatal illness.

Patient and Public Involvement

Throughout this book I have argued for greater involvement of patients and the public. This is not a new recommendation; the House of Commons Health Committee (2005) on the influence of the pharmaceutical industry recommended greater inclusion of the public in policy making and implementation. In fact the challenge is much wider than this, but the question arises of how involvement might be achieved.

To make patient and public involvement a reality, it is necessary to include the various constituencies and stakeholders who might be interested in participating. There are many such groups including members of self-help groups and voluntary organizations, individual patients not belonging to organized groups, families and carers of patients, citizens and taxpayers, and even members of extremist groups. Those arguing against the involvement of patients have often queried the representativeness of those wishing to become involved on the basis that they are people with a particular axe to grind or are 'professional patients' who like to join committees.

It is clear that there are conflicts of interest between some of these different groups. To take an extreme example, animal rights' campaigners wanting to prevent the testing of new drugs on animals may come into direct conflict with patient groups who desperately want new treatments. Indeed, there have been occasions when patients suffering from chronic and unpleasant diseases have been heckled at meetings. A less extreme example is to point out that in a publicly funded system, there are finite resources, and money spent on one group of patients may reduce the choices of another group. In a genuinely open public debate, even the arguments of extremists should be considered and discussed in a non-coercive environment. The issues raised, for example, the relevance of animal tests for humans, are not in themselves extreme.

However, the main point of tension discussed in this book has been that between the benefits and risks of pharmaceutical and other treatments, and between access or hope and harm. Patient groups lobbying for new pharmaceutical treatments are motivated by the hope of a cure or relief of troubling symptoms, but pay less attention to the potential harms of treatment. A more mature public debate would address the appropriate balance between benefit and harm, as well as issues of inequity across patient groups.

In the next section I will explore practical suggestions for enhancing patient and public involvement in the different stages of the life cycle of medicines.

Lay Involvement in Different Stages of the Life Cycle of Medicines

Use of Treatments in the Lifeworld

The three sectors of health care systems discussed in Chapters 2 and 3 are, for many purposes, indivisible. People who manage their own health and illness using all kinds of resources are already integrating treatments. What they need is support for their own existing methods of self-manage- ment rather than admonishments about non-compliance or dismissal of their lifeworld concerns. In this way, the distinction between use of treat- ments in the lifeworld and communication with professionals would be broken down.

This vision of integrated health care is one in which health professionals have greater knowledge and understanding of the range of treatments used by patients including complementary medicine; patients are not afraid of talking about their own methods of self-management, and there is open communication between patients, clinicians and complementary practi- tioners about the benefits and harms of all types of treatment. Although the users of complementary and alternative medicine (CAM) therapies are able to discuss their lifeworld concerns with CAM practitioners, this does not usually extend to discussing their use of CAM with their physicians. The two systems operate a kind of apartheid, which is unhelpful to patients having to manage their own conditions, but may also be unsafe in those cases where biomedical and CAM treatments interact with one another.

The current arrangements for the licensing, production and prescribing of drugs do not allow for the individualization of treatments. As we saw in Chapter 4, at the licensing stage pharmaceutical companies are mainly concerned with demonstrating the efficacy of their products compared with existing treatments or placebo. At this stage, less attention is paid to safety than to efficacy, partly because safety is irrelevant if a drug does not work and partly because safety concerns have the potential to derail the licensing application. Drugs used at higher doses are likely to be more effective, and so this means that there are incentives for companies to test drugs at higher rather than lower doses. Higher doses are also likely to pro- duce more side effects. Once licensed, the dose of the drug is fixed, and it is then manufactured in doses dictated by the license. It is easier for pre- scribers to prescribe drugs according to the dosage specified in the license than to individualize dosages without adequate supporting information. However, as we saw in Chapter 3, patients often test the medicines they are prescribed and may well experiment with different doses in order to balance benefits and side effects. Studies of patients' use of medicines show that people usually minimize their medicine taking rather than the opposite, which may be seen as a reasonable response to the bias towards higher doses, although patients are probably not aware of this bias. Most patients probably do not know that the benefit/harm ratio varies with the dosage, although their personal experiments may well be commensurate with this variation (Herxheimer 1999). As Pollock has noted, 'it may be that non-compliance and personal experimentation is an effective strategy in helping to reduce the extent of overmedication and experience of ADRs' (Pollock 2005, p. 25). These domestic experiments are carried out in the lifeworld and are not usually discussed with prescribers or monitored in any way. One of the criticisms of biomedical treatments, and a motivation for consulting CAM practitioners, is that treatments are not individualized. As we saw in Chapter 6, prescribers themselves have the problem of translating the evidence of population-based clinical trials and average effect sizes into treatments for individual patients.

A more productive way forward than blaming patients for not taking their medicines as prescribed would be to bring the system and lifeworld together by a method of monitoring, which I will refer to as supported self-management. Prescribers and other health professionals could support patients first of all by acknowledging that people are active agents: many people like to test their medicines for themselves using their own criteria. Professionals could support those patients attempting to individualize their own treatments by providing structured methods for titrating drug doses. Rather than using ad hoc methods, prescribers and patients could devise systems for recording actual medicine use, the reasons for altering doses or timings, and the effect on the patients' symptoms or disease markers. In this way, patients could be encouraged to record the details of their own experiments and the results and then discuss them with the professionals. The US publication *The Write Track* is one such tool for helping patients record their own medicine taking, their own treatment goals and effects of their medication (The Write Track 1997). This booklet also provides space for patients to write down the questions they want to ask their practitioners, formulated at home rather than in the time-pressurized context of the consultation. Wiederholt was a professor of pharmacy who had cancer, and who developed *The Write Track* as a method to help manage his own medication use. Using such a method, patients on long-term treatments could be supported in determining their own optimal drug doses and achieving an acceptable balance of symptom control and side effects. The role of health professionals in this process would be to ensure that patients' questions were answered and that patients had the information they needed to carry out their own experiments safely. Such a process would also help professionals translate the evidence of clinical trials into management strategies relevant to their own patient populations in a systematic way. If patients' drug minimization experiments were successful, patients struggling to meet the costs of their medicines could find that their new regimen was more affordable. The logical consequence of these strategies would be to set up further post-licensing clinical trials to establish the efficacy and safety of lower doses informed by the data gathered from patients' own monitored self-experimentation.

The implementation of supported self-management and the acceptance of patients' agency in relation to medicine taking will require a shift in professional attitudes. In doing so, the potential for communicative action is likely to increase. It is likely that more active involvement of patients could reduce unnecessary or inappropriate prescribing. This will probably need to be done by teams requiring more interprofessional communication than at present.

Regulation, Development and Licensing

Holme Hansen (1992) has advocated user involvement in the 'pre technology' stage when research priorities and needs assessment are considered. Such involvement might well articulate the preference for non-pharmaceutical treatments in which case the balance of research spending would need to shift away from the current emphasis on pharmaceuticals. Such a possibility has been identified by Harrison (2003) writing for the King's Fund. He advocated the setting-up of a Health Research and Development Task Force to identify all the areas poorly served by the current implicit Public Private Partnership in health care and to recommend the appropriate response on behalf of the state, the rest of the public sector and the private sector. He recommended that such a Task Force should consist of the users of research such as clinicians and decision makers, and members of the public as potential or actual users of health services. Among other tasks, Harrison suggested that the Task Force could redefine the need for clinical trials so as to create a level playing field between trials driven by commercial interests and those undertaken for socially beneficial reasons. If clinical trials were evaluating technologies that might eventually be marketed as products, commercial sponsors might be willing to invest in them. If, however, clinical trials were evaluating lifestyle interventions, other sponsors would need to be found. The generation of an evidence base to support non-pharmaceutical interventions has the potential to transform the nature of health care, and while this could threaten the interests of the pharmaceutical industry, it might serve other interests, especially the public interest.

In the more usual scenario of pharmaceutical interventions, the development stage involves clinical trials. These constitute another point at which patients and citizens come into contact with the licensing process. While volunteers are in no position to influence the design of such studies, they can at least attempt to protect their own interests. Questions for volunteers to ask when being recruited to drug trials might include the following: which phase the trial represents; whether the drug is licensed yet or not; what information is already available about it; how different it is from any other drug; whether it is a new drug and if so how much is known about it.

Once a drug is licensed, there are particular problems associated with new drugs. For many people suffering from troubling and possibly untreatable conditions, such as multiple sclerosis or cancer, the possibility of a cure is their greatest hope. In these situations, hopes are often intense while the information about potential harms is minimal. Unsurprisingly, new drugs are often portrayed in the media as long awaited miracle cures. Patients are correspondingly vulnerable, which is not to present them as dupes or to deny the powerful healing properties of hope. One could argue that new drugs have a very strong placebo effect. In this situation, it is particularly important that the information about benefit-harm ratios is available, and that patients are not given misleading information.

There are various ways in which patients (rather than citizens) might wish to influence the introduction of new drugs. They may wish to influence decisions about priorities for new treatments and the ways in which these are evaluated. Patients are much more likely to argue for genuinely new treatments than for me-too drugs with little obvious advantage over their commercial rivals. They might argue that, to be helpful to patients, medicines should be tested in real-life settings in pragmatic trials; they may argue that statistical intention-to-treat analyses hinder the identification of biological mechanisms because those not taking the drug are included as well as those who did take the drug; patients may argue for more attention to adverse reactions during clinical trials and the mandatory collection of patient reports of adverse drug reactions (ADRs) during trials; they may wish to influence the choice of patient generated outcome measures. Most of these issues would require those designing and running clinical trials to consult patients rather more than they do at present, but unless researchers think that this is in their own interests to do so, or funders require such consultation, it may not happen.

A number of suggestions have already been made about how patients and the public could make a greater contribution to the regulation, development and licensing of medicines. Abraham and Sheppard (1997) point out that while some expert science advisers in the United Kingdom are in favour of greater public participation, they acknowledge that industry's concern about protecting trade secrets is a major obstacle. Thus any moves in this direction will require a political commitment to more transparent processes. Abraham and Sheppard argue for public participation in decision making about what constitutes acceptable and non-acceptable risks and for whom and how benefit-harm assessments are made. This would involve a degree of commitment from those members of the public and patient groups wanting to participate, as they would need to read and assess a considerable amount of complex information. Abraham and Sheppard advocate the setting-up of a public interest subcommittee of the (now) Commission on Human Medicines to include representatives of consumer and patient organizations with a special interest in medicines safety as well as some direct citizen participation based on statistical representativeness. Such a committee would not include industry representatives on the grounds that industry has other avenues for pressing its interests. Abraham and Sheppard's research showed substantial divergence between expert and non-expert perspectives on medicines control deriving as much from differences in values as from information deficits. A public interest subcommittee could advise the Commission on Human Medicines (CHM) and Medicines and Healthcare products Regulatory Agency (MHRA), and it could nominate some of its members to sit on the CHM itself. It would enhance the influence of patients' interests on regulatory outcomes as well as politicizing those taking part. Abraham and Sheppard suggest that the breaking down of regulators' isolation from the public might have an invigorating effect on their deliberations, as suggested by the quotations at the beginning of this chapter. The National Institute for Health and Clinical Excellence has a Patient and Public Involvement programme which includes a Citizens' Council and a Partners' Council. The former consists of 30 people drawn from all walks of life but with no links to the health service, who are asked to give their views on the social values which should underpin NICE's work. The Partners Council consists of individuals nominated by groups representing patients and the public, health professionals, academic organizations, industry, trade unions and health service management; its role is to provide NICE with a range of views from different perspectives. In the United States, the Food and Drug Administration (FDA) has a Patient Representative Program. Patient representatives serve on advisory committees, usually in a voting capacity, when a product relating to a specific disease is being considered. Consumer representatives need to be affiliated to or actively involved in consumer or community-based organizations. Little evidence is yet available about the ways in which such representation of patients and the public have influenced decision making at national levels.

As we have seen in Chapter 4, the patent system creates perverse incentives which provide rewards for the production of me-too medicines at the expense of the genuinely innovative or socially beneficial treatments. As Harrison (2003) noted, if the system were to be redesigned from scratch, it is not at all obvious that patents would emerge as the best option. Given the existing system, Harrison argues that it should be revised to allow for experimentation and innovation in the rewards systems for both the private sector and those parts of the public sector which compete for funding in order to create new incentives. A different proposal would be to change the patent system by requiring changes to both the patenting and licensing arrangements which are inextricably linked. In such a system, the licensing of a new drug should be provisional, for say a two-year period. During that time, the pharmaceutical company would be expected to perform detailed clinical studies of any adverse effects of their product including Prescription-Event Monitoring studies (in which physicians follow up all their patients prescribed the drug for a year afterwards, recording all events reported by patients) and genuine phase IV trials aimed at providing robust epidemiological data on its safety. At the end of the two years, the company would apply for a full licence providing the MHRA with complete safety data. If the MHRA was satisfied with the quality and results of these data, it would grant a full licence as well as an extension of the patent for a fixed duration of say 10–15 years. In this way, the safety profiles of new drugs would be more robust, and companies marketing safer drugs would be rewarded with an extension of their patent.

Information about Medicines

In Chapter 5, we saw that there is a general bias towards information about the benefits of medication, and that much written and spoken information reflects a 'patient education' discourse aiming to increase adherence to medication. The provision of this kind of information provides examples of strategic action on the part of professionals pursuing an adherence agenda and, in the case of Direct to Consumer Advertising (DTCA), industry wishing to increase sales in the guise of 'patient empowerment'. Both of these strategic goals are served by information about the benefits rather than the harms of medicines. A more balanced relationship between system and lifeworld would be served by more balanced information about the benefits and harms of medicines. Patient leaflets could be improved if they addressed patients' questions more explicitly and providing a better balance of information about harms and benefits. There is a particular need to provide appropriate information about new drugs which acknowledges the limited evidence base and encourages patients to report any new symptoms or potential side effects even if they are unsure about their exact cause.

The UK government's response to the Health Committee's report on the influence of the pharmaceutical industry included the recommendation of a WHO single portal to access information about clinical trials. This would provide open access to information about clinical trials conducted worldwide with pharmaceutical companies providing summary findings of clinical trials within one year of the granting of marketing authorization in any country (Secretary of State for Health 2005). If this happens, patients will need guidance when accessing this information. Given the financial and intellectual resources needed to assess this information, patient groups would be likely to want to assess data on drugs relevant to their own situations.

In addition to adopting a more open and balanced approach to existing information, new forms of knowledge are also required. In Chapter 5 we saw that little research is carried out to enable patients to individualize their medication regimens. It is, however, accepted that minimum effective doses can vary with inter-individual differences in characteristics such as body weight and organ functioning. There are some data already available to support the safe minimization of a few selected drugs (de Smet et al. 2007), but much more research is required. In addition to such work on dose minimization, the wider possibilities of personalized health care, tailored to selected biological features of individuals such as variation in the microbiome composition, will also require new kinds of clinical trials (Nicholson 2006). Ideally, these new routes to personalized drug treatments would work hand-in-hand with, for example, drug minimization experiments supported by appropriate systems biology research and pharmaco-metabonomic research informed by patients' perspectives.

The advent of the Internet and the growth of patient cyber groups has the potential to build up another new kind of patient-based knowledge base. Discussion groups already share expertise, compare notes and arrive at their own assessments of the treatments they are offered (Saukko in press). A Wikipedia-type methodology could be created in which patient groups create, distil, edit and update their own online knowledge base to create an authoritative source of experiential information about medicines. This could be organized to reflect criteria of importance to patients using everyday language to describe patients' experiences. Such an information source may give patients more confidence in talking to professionals once they know that their experiences are not unique and that they cannot be accused of 'imagining it'. Whether such knowledge bases would provide the kind of information which could help patients in their own evaluations of medicines, or whether they are taken over by dominant or maverick interests, remains to be seen.

Prescribing

If the process of lifeworld colonization in relation to prescribing is to be reversed, then prescribing has to be seen as more than just a technical issue and should in part reflect patients' perspectives. A broad definition of prescribing, which includes consideration of what happens after the prescription is written, would have to allow for patients' agency in relation to medicine use. In Chapter 6, we saw examples of such broader definitions, but they are hard to use in practice and require further development. Barber's definition of good prescribing does acknowledge the fact that patients have their own choices and that there are competing interests; the challenge will be to turn this definition into a practical tool. This could follow on from the method of supported self-management discussed above. Thus, any judgement about the quality of a prescribing decision would be made on the basis of its benefit–harm ratio in the context of actual use in addition to considerations of cost. This requires a shift from assessing prescribing decisions as isolated events towards a consideration of their impact over time. This would require more data to be collected than is currently the case, but as I have argued above, this can be done in active collaboration with patients to achieve individualized regimens and to improve communication between patients and professionals.

Such assessments of the quality of prescribing need to include both system and lifeworld perspectives. Patients may want to make their own trade-offs which will not necessarily coincide with the priorities of professionals. Taking the example of coronary heart disease, some individuals may prefer to trade future years of life against their present enjoyment of tobacco, rich food and alcohol on the grounds that they would prefer to die while their friends are still alive than outlive them and spend lonely years in a nursing home with strangers. On the basis of the evidence I reviewed in Chapter 3, it seems likely that supported self-management and the monitoring of prescribing will reduce prescribing levels and doses rather than increase them, at least for many chronic diseases. The value of Habermas' concept of strategic action is that it draws attention to the fact that different parties have different goals and the need to understand better what patients' goals are and how they can be helped to achieve them.

Conclusion

The problem of colonization of the lifeworld was introduced in Chapter 1, and in this book I have examined the ways in which system imperatives come to dominate the lifeworld. Stevenson and Scambler (2005) point out that lifeworld decolonization requires only that the limits of expert systems are acknowledged and that doctors remain collectively and individually accountable to the populations they serve. The achievement of a better balance between the benefits and harms of medicines at all stages of medicine use would make a major contribution to decolonization. The involvement of patients, carers and the public is likely to promote greater professional accountability.

Habermas' vision of communicative action was inspired by the public debates in the café society of eighteenth-century Europe. The Internet may be regarded as a new public sphere, the modern equivalent of the eighteenth-century cafes which Habermas wrote about. If so, it shares some of the same strengths and weaknesses: the possibility of unconstrained discussion and criticism of governments and industry but also the exclusion of those groups without access to the Internet (in the same way as women and working classes were excluded from café society). It remains to be seen if patient groups can harness the potential of the Internet to constrain system colonization of the lifeworld. If they do, the health services of the future may take a wider view of the management of health and illness than the current pharmacologically dominated provision. More attention to safety and efficacy would lead to fewer but better treatments and more room for other kinds of treatment if they were properly researched and supported.

References

Abraham, J. (1995) *Science, Politics and the Pharmaceutical Industry: Controversy and Bias in Drug Regulation* (London: UCL Press).

Abraham, J. (2002) 'Making regulation responsive to commercial interests: streamlining drug industry watchdogs', *British Medical Journal*, 325, 1164–69.

Abraham, J. and J. Sheppard (1997) 'Democracy, technocracy, and the secret state of medicines control: expert and nonexpert perspectives', *Science, Technology and Human Values*, 22, 139–67.

Abramson, J. (2004) *Overdosed America: The Broken Promise of American Medicine* (New York: Harper Collins).

Adams, S., R. Pill and A. Jones (1997) 'Medication, chronic illness and identity: the perspective of people with asthma', *Social Science & Medicine*, 45, 189–201.

Almarsdóttir, A. B. and J. M. Traulsen (2005) 'Rational use of medicines – an important issue in pharmaceutical policy', *Pharmacy World and Science*, 27, 76–80.

Alzheimer's Society website, www.qrd.alzheimers.org.uk, accessed 16 April 2007.

Angell, M. (2004) *The Truth about the Drug Companies: How They Deceive Us and What to Do about It* (New York: Random House).

Arluke, A., (1980) 'Judging drugs: patients' conceptions of therapeutic efficacy in the treatment of arthritis', *Human Organization*, 39, 84–8.

Armstrong, D. (2002) 'Clinical autonomy, individual and collective: the problem of changing doctors' behaviour', *Social Science & Medicine*, 55, 1771–77.

Audit Commission (1994) *A Prescription for Improvement – Towards More Rational Prescribing in General Practice* (London: Audit Commission).

Avery, A. J. and V. James (2007) 'Developing nurse prescribing in the UK: prescribing should be integrated into education for advanced nursing practice' (editorial), *British Medical Journal*, 335, 316.

Avorn, J., M. Chen and R. Hartley (1982) 'Scientific versus commercial sources of influence on the prescribing behaviour of physicians', *The American Journal of Medicine*, 73, 4–8.

Baggott, R., J. Allsop and K. Jones (2005) *Speaking for Patients and Carers: Health Consumer Groups and the Policy Process* (Basingstoke: Palgrave Macmillan).

Bakx, K. (1991) 'The "eclipse" of folk medicine in western society', *Sociology of Health & Illness*, 13, 20–38.

Banks, M. H., S. A. A. Beresford, D. C. Morrell, J. J. Waller and C. J. Watkins (1975) 'Factors influencing demand for primary medical care in women aged 20–44 years: a preliminary report', *International Journal of Epidemiology*, 4, 189–95.

Barber, N. (1995) 'What constitutes good prescribing?', *British Medical Journal*, 310, 923–25.

Barnes, P., E. Powell-Griner, K. McFann and R. Nahin (2004) *CDC Advance Data Report #343*. (United States: Complementary and alternative medicine use among adults, 2002, 27 May).

Barry, C. A., N. Britten, N. Barber, C. Bradley and F. Stevenson (1999) 'Using reflexivity to optimize teamwork in qualitative research', *Qualitative Health Research*, 9, 26–44.

Barry, C. A., F. A. Stevenson, N. Britten, N. Barber and C. P. Bradley (2001) 'Giving voice to the lifeworld. More humane, more effective medical care? A qualitative study of doctor–patient communication in general practice', *Social Science & Medicine*, 53, 487–505.

Bateman, N. (1998) 'Approaches to rational prescribing', in F. D. R. Hobbs and C. P. Bradley (eds) *Prescribing in Primary Care* (Oxford: Oxford University Press) pp. 95–108.

Baum, M. (2004) 'An open letter to the Prince of Wales: with respect, your highness, you've got it wrong', *British Medical Journal*, 329, 118.

Beck, U. (1992) *Risk Society: Towards a New Modernity* (London: Sage publications).

191

Beecher, H. K. (1955) 'The powerful placebo', *Journal of the American Medical Association*, 159, 1602–06.

Bekelman, J. E., Y. Li and C. P. Gross (2003) 'Scope and impact of financial conflicts of interest in biomedical research: A systematic review', *Journal of the American Medical Association*, 289, 454–65.

Bennion, E. (2002) 'Commentary: The freedom of informed choice', *British Medical Journal*, 325, 1169.

Benson, J. and N. Britten (2003) 'Patients' views about taking antihypertensive drugs: questionnaire study', *British Medical Journal*, 326, 1314–15.

Bero, L. A., R. Grilli, J. M. Grimshaw, E. Harvey, A. D. Oxman and M. A. Thomson (1998) 'Closing the gap between research and practice: an overview of systematic reviews of interventions to promote the implementation of research findings', *British Medical Journal*, 317, 465–68.

Berridge, V. (1999) *Opium and the People* (London: Free Association Books).

Beyerstein, B. L. (2005) 'Alternative medicine and common errors of reasoning', chapter 5 in G. Lee-Treweek, T. Heller, S. Spurr, H. MacQueen and J. Katz (eds), *Perspectives on Complementary and Alternative Medicine: A Reader* (London: Routledge) pp. 37–51.

Bissell, P., C. R. May, P. R. Noyce (2004) 'From compliance to concordance: barriers to accomplishing a re-framed model of health care interactions', *Social Science & Medicine*, 58, 851–62.

Blaxter, M. and E. Paterson (1982) *Mothers and Daughters* (London: Heinemann).

Blenkinsopp, A. and C. Bond (2003), 'Self-care and self-medication' in R. Jones, N. Britten, L. Culpepper, D. Gass, R. Grol, D. Mant and C. Silagy (eds) *Oxford Textbook of Primary Medical Care* (Oxford: Oxford University Press) pp. 111–16.

Blenkinsopp, A., P. Wilkie, M. Wang and P. A. Routledge (2006) 'Patient reporting of suspected adverse drug reactions: a review of published literature and international experience', *British Journal of Clinical Pharmacology*, 63, 148–56.

Bobbio, M., B. Demichelis, and G. Giusetto (1994) 'Completeness of reporting trial results: Effect on physicians' willingness to prescribe', *The Lancet*, 343, 1209–11.

Bodenheimer, T. (2000) 'Uneasy alliance: Clinical investigators and the pharmaceutical industry', *New England Journal of Medicine*, 342, 1539–44.

Boon, H., J. Belle Brown, A. Gavin and K. Westlake (2003a) 'Men with prostate cancer: making decisions about complementary/alternative medicine', *Medical Decision Making*, 23, 471–79.

Boon, H., J. Belle Brown, A. Gavin, M. A. Kennard and M. Stewart (1999) 'Breast cancer survivors' perceptions of complementary/alternative medicine (CAM): making the decision to use or not to use', *Qualitative Health Research*, 9, 639–53.

Boon, H., K. Westlake, M. Stewart, R. Gray, N. Fleshner, A. Gavin, J. Belle Brown and V. Goel (2003b), 'Use of complementary/alternative medicine by men diagnosed with prostate cancer: prevalence and characteristics', *Adult Urology*, 62, 849–53.

Boon, H., M. Stewart, M. A. Kennard, R. Gray, C. Sawka, J. Belle Brown, C. McWilliam, A. Gavin, R. A. Baron, D. Aaron and T. Haines-Kamka (2000) 'Use of complementary/alternative medicine by breast cancer survivors in Ontario: prevalence and perceptions', *Journal of Clinical Oncology*, 18, 2515–21.

Boseley, S. (2006) 'Selling of a "wonder drug"', *The Guardian Weekly*, 7–13 April.

Bradley, C., (1990) A Critical Incident Study of General Practitioners' Discomfort Arising from Prescribing Decisions (University of Dublin: MD thesis).

Bradley, C. P., (1992a) 'Uncomfortable prescribing decisions: a critical incident study', *British Medical Journal*, 304, 294–96.

Bradley, C. P. (1992b) 'Factors which influence the decision whether or not to prescribe: the dilemma facing general practitioners', *British Journal of General Practice*, 42, 454–58.

Bradley, C. and A. Blenkinsopp (1998) 'Responding to changing healthcare systems: adapting prescribing in the new NHS', in F. D. R. Hobbs and C. P. Bradley (eds) *Prescribing in Primary Care* (Oxford: Oxford University Press) pp. 141–64.

British Market Research Bureau (1997) *Everyday Health Care. A Consumer Study of Self-Medication in Great Britain* (London: British Market Research Bureau).

Britten, N. (1991) 'Hospital consultants' views of their patients', *Sociology of Health & Illness*; 13, 83–97.

Britten, N. (2001) 'Prescribing and the defence of clinical autonomy', *Sociology of Health & Illness*, 23, 478–96.

Britten, N. (2003) 'Concordance and compliance' in R. Jones, N. Britten, L. Culpepper, D. Gass, R. Grol, D. Mant and C. Silagy (eds) *Oxford Textbook of Primary Medical Care* (Oxford: Oxford University Press), pp. 246–49.

Britten, N., F. Stevenson, C. A. Barry, N. Barber and C. P. Bradley (2000) 'Misunderstandings in prescribing decisions in general practice: qualitative study', *British Medical Journal*, 320, 484–88.

Britten, N., F. Stevenson, J. Gafaranga, C. Barry and C. Bradley (2004) 'The expression of aversion to medicines in general practice consultations', *Social Science & Medicine*, 59, 1495–1503.

Britten, N., L. Jenkins, N. Barber, C. Bradley and F. Stevenson (2003) 'Developing a measure for the appropriateness of prescribing in general practice', *Quality and Safety in Health Care*, 12, 246–50.

Britten, N. and O. Ukoumunne (1997) 'The influence of patients' hopes of receiving a prescription on doctors' perceptions and the decision to prescribe: a questionnaire survey', *British Medical Journal*, 315, 1506–10.

Britten, N., O. Ukoumunne and M. Boulton (2002) 'Patients' attitudes to medicines and expectations for prescriptions', *Health Expectations*, 5, 256–69.

Brown, C. M. and R. Segal (1996) 'The effects of health and treatment perceptions on the use of prescribed medication and home remedies among African American and White American hypertensives', *Social Science & Medicine*, 43, 903–17.

Bucher, H. C., M. Weinbacher and K. Gyr (1994) 'Influence of method of reporting study results on decision of physicians to prescribe drugs to lower cholesterol concentration', *British Medical Journal*, 309, 761–64.

Bugge, C. and A. Jones (2007) 'Methods for studying patient participation', chapter 2 in S. Collins, N. Britten, J. Ruusuvuori and A. Thompson (eds), *Patient Participation in Health Care Consultations: Qualitative Perspectives* (Maidenhead: Open University Press) pp. 22–40.

Busfield, J. (2006) 'Pills, power, people: sociological understandings of the pharmaceutical industry', *Sociology*, 40, 297–314.

Cassidy, C. M. (1998) 'Chinese medicine users in the United States Part II: preferred aspects of care', *The Journal of Alternative and Complementary Medicine*, 4, 189–202.

Charles, C., A. Gafni and T. Whelan (1997) 'Shared decision-making in the medical encounter: what does it mean? (Or it takes at least two to tango)', *Social Science & Medicine*, 44, 681–92.

Charmaz, K. (1983) 'Loss of self: a fundamental form of suffering in the chronically ill', *Sociology of Health & Illness*, 5, 168–95.

Chewning, B. and J. C. Schommer (1996) 'Increasing clients' knowledge of community pharmacists' roles', *Journal of Pharmaceutical Research*, 13, 1299–1304.

Cockburn, J. and S. Pit (1997) 'Prescribing behaviour in clinical practice: patients' expectations and doctors' perceptions of patients' expectations – a questionnaire study', *British Medical Journal*, 315, 520–23.

Cohen, D., M. McCubbin, J. Collin and G. Pérodeau (2001) 'Medications as social phenomena', *Health*, 5, 441–69.

Collier, J. and O. Dwight (1997) *Medicines and the NHS: A Guide for Directors*. (London: Consumers' Association).

Conrad, P. (1985) 'The meaning of medications: another look at compliance', *Social Science & Medicine*, 20, 29–37.

Conrad, P. (2005) 'The shifting engines of medicalization', *Journal of Health and Social Behavior*, 46, 3–14.

Coombes, R. (2007) 'Cancer drugs: swallowing big pharma's line?', *British Medical Journal*, 334, 1034–35.

Cooperstock, R. and H. L. Lennard (1979) 'Some social meanings of tranquilizer use', *Sociology of Health & Illness*, 1, 331–47.

Cotter, S., M. McKee and N. Barber (1993) 'Pharmacists and prescribing: an unrecorded influence' (editorial), *Quality in Health Care*, 2, 75–76.

Coward, R. (1989) *The Whole Truth: The Myth of Alternative Health* (London: Faber & Faber).

Cox, K., F. Stevenson, N. Britten and Y. Dundar (2004) *A Systematic Review of Communication between Patients and Health Care Professionals about Medicine-Taking and Prescribing* (London: Medicines Patnership).

Crawford, R. (2006) 'Health as a meaningful social practice', *Health: An Interdisciplinary Journal for the Social Study of Health, Illness and Medicine*, 10, 401–20.

Cribb, A. and N. Barber (1997) 'Prescribers, patients and policy: the limits of technique', *Health Care Analysis*, 5, 292–98.

Cunningham-Burley, S. and U. Maclean (1987) 'The role of the chemist in primary health care for children with minor complaints', *Social Science and Medicine*, 24, 371–77.

DeGrazia, D. (2002) *Animal Rights: A Very Short Introduction* (Oxford: Oxford University Press).

Dixon-Woods, M. (2001) 'Writing wrongs? An analysis of published discourses about the use of patient information leaflets', *Social Science & Medicine*, 52, 1417–32.

Donovan, J. and D. R. Blake (1992) 'Patient non-compliance: deviance or reasoned decision-making?', *Social Science & Medicine*, 34, 507–13.

Donovan, J. L. (1995) 'Patient decision-making – the missing ingredient in compliance research', *International Journal of Technology Asssessment in Health Care*, 11, 443–55.

Dowell, J. and H. Hudson (1997) 'A qualitative study of medication-taking behaviour in primary care', *Family Practice*, 14, 369–75.

Duckenfield, M. and D. Rangnekar (2004) *The Rise of Patient Groups and Drug Development* (London: University College).

Elston, M. A. (1994) The anti-vivisectionist movement and the science of medicine, chapter 9 in J. Gabe, D. Kelleher and G. Williams (eds) *Challenging Medicine* (London: Routledge) pp. 160–80.

Elwyn, G., A. Edwards, M. Wensing, K. Hood, C. Atwell and R. Grol (2003) 'Shared decision making: developing the OPTION scale for measuring patient involvement', *Quality and Safety in Health Care*, 12, 93–9.

Entwistle, V. (1995) 'Reporting research in medical journals and newspapers', *British Medical Journal*, 310, 920–23.

Ess, S. M., S. Schneeweiss and T. D. Szucs (2003) 'European healthcare policies for controlling drug expenditure', *Pharmacoeconomics*, 21, 89–103.

Etkin, N. (1992) ' "Side Effects": Cultural constructions and reinterpretations of western pharmaceuticals', *Medical Anthropology Quaterly*, 6, 99–113.

Evans, D. (2003) *Placebo: The Belief Effect* (London: HarperCollins).

Fallsberg, M. (1991) *Reflections on Medicines and Medication: A Qualitative Analysis Among People on Long-Term Drug Regimens* (Linkoping, Sweden: Linkoping University Press).

FDA DTCA website, www.fda.gov/cder, accessed 18 January 2006.

Finlayson, J. G. (2005) *Habermas: A Very Short Introduction* (Oxford: Oxford University Press).

Frank, A. W. (2006) 'Health stories as connectors and subjectifiers', *Health: An Interdisciplinary Journal for the Social Study of Health, Illness and Medicine*, 10, 421–40.

Frank, A. W. (1989) 'Habermas's interactionism: the micro-macro link to politics', *Symbolic Interaction*, 12, 333–60.

Frank, R. and G. Stollberg (2004) 'Medical acupuncture in Germany: patterns of consumerism among physicians and patients', *Sociology of Health & Illness*, 26, 351–72.

Frederikson, L. G. (1995) 'Exploring information-exchange in consultation: the patients' view of performance and outcomes', *Patient Education and Counselling*, 25, 237–46.

Fulder, S. (2005) 'The basic concepts of alternative medicine and their impact on our views of health', chapter 1 in G. Lee-Treweek, T. Heller, S. Spurr, H. MacQueen and J. Katz (eds) *Perspectives on Complementary and Alternative Medicine: A Reader* (London: Routledge), pp. 3–8.

Gabe, J., U. Gustafsson and M. Bury (1991) 'Mediating illness: newspaper coverage of tranquilizer dependence', *Sociology of Health & Illness*, 13, 332–53.

van der Geest, S. and S. R. Whyte (eds) (1988) *The Context of Medicines in Developing Countries: Studies in Pharmaceutical Anthropology* (Dordrecht: Kluwer Academic Publishers).

van der Geest, S. and S. R. Whyte (1989) 'The charm of medicines: metaphors and metonyms', *Medical Anthropology Quarterly*, 3, 345–67.

van der Geest, S., S. R. Whyte and A. Hardon (1996) 'The anthropology of pharmaceuticals: a biographical approach', *Annual Review of Anthropology*, 25, 153–78.

Giddens, A. (1990) *The Consequences of Modernity* (Cambridge: Polity Press).

Giveon, S. M., N. Liberman, S. Klang and E. Kahan (2004) 'Are people who use "natural drugs" aware of their potentially harmful side effects and reporting to family physician?', *Patient Education and Counseling*, 53, 5–11.

Government Statistical Service (2006) *Prescriptions Dispensed in the Community: Statistics for 1995 to 2005: England* (London: Information Centre).

Graham, H. and A. Oakley (1981) 'Competing ideologies of reproduction: medical and maternal perspectives on pregnancy', in H. Roberts (ed.) *Women, Health and Reproduction* (London: Routledge and Kegan Paul) pp. 62–3.

Grime, J. and K. Pollock (2003) 'Patients' ambivalence about taking antidepressants: a qualitative study', *The Pharmaceutical Journal*, 271, 516–19.

Guirguis, L. M. and B. A. Chewning (2005) 'Role theory: literature review and implications for patient-pharmacist interactions', *Research in Social and Administrative Pharmacy*, 1, 483–507.

Hall, D. (1980) 'Prescribing as social exchange', in R. Mapes (ed.), chapter 3 in *Prescribing Practice and Drug Usage* (London: Croom Helm) pp. 37–57.

Hardey, M. (1999) 'Doctor in the house: the Internet as a source of lay health knowledge and the challenge to expertise', *Sociology of Health & Illness*, 21, 820–35.

Harrison, A. (2003) Getting the right medicines? Putting public interests at the heart of health-related research (London: King's Fund discussion paper).

Hassell, K., A. Rogers, P. Noyce and G. Nicolaas (1998) *The Public's Use of Community Pharmacies as a Primary Health Care Resource* (London: The Royal Pharmaceutical Society of Great Britain).

Heisler, M., K. M. Langa, E. L. Eby, A. M. Fendrick, M. U. Kabeto and J. D. Piette (2004) 'The health effects of restricting prescription medication use because of cost', *Medical Care*, 42, 626–34.

Helman, C. G. (1990) *Culture, Health and Illness*, 2nd edn (London: Wright).

Hemminki, E. (1975) 'Review of literature on the factors affecting drug prescribing', *Social Science & Medicine*, 9, 111–15.

Herxheimer, A. (1994) 'The NHS drug budget enquiry: a note for the Commons Health Committee', *Journal of the Royal College of Physicians*, 28, 261–63.

Herxheimer, A. (1998) 'Many NSAID users who bleed don't know when to stop' (editorial), *British Medical Journal*, 316, 492.

Herxheimer, A. (1999) 'Leaflets with NSAIDs do not warn users clearly – a UK survey', *The Pharmaceutical Journal*, 262, 559–61.

Herxheimer, A., C. S. Lundborg and B. Westerholm (1993) 'Advertisements for medicines in leading medical journals in 18 countries: a 12-month survey of information content and standards', *International Journal of Health Services*, 23, 161–72.

Hirst, J. (2003) 'Charities and patient groups should declare interests' (letter), *British Medical Journal*, 326, 1211.

Holme Hansen, E. (1992) 'Technology assessment in a user perspective – experiences with drug technology', *International Journal of Technology Assessment in Health Care*, 8, 150–65.

Holmer, A. F. (1999) 'Direct-to-consumer prescription drug advertising builds bridges between patients and physicians', *Journal of the American Medical Association*, 281, 380–82.

Horne, R. and J. Weinman (1999) 'Patients' beliefs about prescribed medicines and their role in adherence to treatment in chronic physical illness', *Journal of Psychosomatic Research*, 47, 555–67.

House of Commons Health Committee (2005) *The Influence of the Pharmaceutical Industry* (London: The Stationery Office Limited).

Hunter, M. S., I. O'Dea and N. Britten (1997) 'Decision-making and hormone replacement therapy: a qualitative analysis', *Social Science & Medicine*, 45, 1541–48.

Illich, I. (1976) *Limits to Medicine. Medical Nemesis: The Expropriation of Health* (Harmondsworth, Middlesex: Penguin Books).

International Committee of Medical Journal Editors (2007) Uniform requirements for manuscripts submitted to biomedical journals, www.icmje.org, accessed 13 January 2008 (Philadelphia: ICJME).

Johnson, M. J., M. Williams and E. S. Marshall (1999) 'Adherent and nonadherent medication-taking in elderly hypertensive patients', *Clinical Nursing Research*, 8, 318–35.

Johnston Roberts, K. and T. Mann (2000) 'Barriers to antiretroviral medication adherence in HIV-infected women', *AIDS Care*, 12, 377–86.

Jones, M. I., S. M. Greenfield and C. P. Bradley (2001) 'Prescribing new drugs: qualitative study of influences on consultants and general practitioners', *British Medical Journal*, 323, 1–7.

Jørgensen, K. J. and P.C. Gøtzsche (2004) 'Presentation on websites of possible benefits and harms from screening for breast cancer: cross sectional study', *British Medical Journal*, 328, 148.

Kaptchuk, T. J. and D. M. Eisenberg (2005) 'A taxonomy of unconventional healing practices', chapter 2 in G. Lee-Treweek, T. Heller, S. Spurr, H. MacQueen and J. Katz (eds) *Perspectives on Complementary and Alternative Medicine: A Reader* (London: Routledge) pp. 9–25.

Kelleher, D. J. (1991) 'Patients learning from each other: self-help groups for people with diabetes', *Journal of the Royal Society of Medicine*, 84, 595–97.

Kelleher, D. (1994) 'Self-help groups and their relationship to medicine', chapter 6 in J. Gabe, D. Kelleher and G. Williams (eds) *Challenging Medicine* (London: Routledge) pp. 104–17.

Kelleher, D. (2001) 'New social movements in the health domain', in G. Scambler (ed.) *Habermas, Critical Theory and Health* (London: Routledge) pp. 119–42.

Kleinman, A. (1980) *Patients and Healers in the Context of Culture* (Berkeley: University of California Press).

Kooiker, S. and L. van der Wijst (2004) *Europeans and Their Medicines: A Cultural Approach to the Utilization of Pharmaceuticals* (Amsterdam: Social and Cultural Planning Office of the Netherlands).

Kripalani, S., X. Yao and R. B. Haynes (2007) 'Interventions to enhance medication adherence in chronic medical conditions: a systematic review', *Archives of Internal Medicine*, 167, 540–49.

Krumholz, H. M., J. S. Ross, A. H. Presler and D. S. Egilman (2007) 'What have we learnt from Vioxx?', *British Medical Journal*, 334, 120–23.

Langman, M. J., D. M. Jensen, D. J. Watson, et al (1999) 'Adverse upper gastrointestinal effects of Rofecoxib compared with NSAIDs', *Journal of the American Medical Association*, 282, 1929–33.

Latter, S. and M. Courtenay (2004) 'Effectiveness of nurse prescribing: a review of the literature', *Journal of Clinical Nursing*, 13, 26–32.

Latter, S., J. Maben, M. Myall and A. Young (2007) 'Perceptions and practice of concordance in nurses' prescribing consultations: Findings from a national questionnaire survey and case studies of practice in England', *International Journal of Nursing Studies*, 44, 9–18.

Lexchin, J. (1999) 'Direct-to-consumer advertising: impact on patient expectations regarding disease management', *Disease Management and Health Outcomes*, 5, 273–83.

Lexchin, J., L. A. Bero, B. Djulbegovic and O. Clark (2003) 'Pharmaceutical industry sponsorship and research outcome and quality: systematic review', *British Medical Journal*, 326, 1167–70.

Loader, B. D., S. Muncer, R. Burrows, N. Pleace and S. Nettleton (2002) 'Medicine on the line? Computer-mediated social support and advice for people with diabetes', *International Journal of Social Welfare*, 11, 53–65.

Locker, D. (1981) *Symptoms and Illness: The Cognitive Organization of Disorder* (London: Tavistock Publications).

Long-term Conditions Alliance website, www.ltca.org.uk, accessed 17 April 2007.

Loudon, I. (1986) *Medical Care and the General Practitioner 1750–1850* (Oxford: Clarendon Press).

Luff D. and K. J. Thomas (2000) ' "Getting somewhere," feeling cared for: patients' perspectives on complementary therapies in the NHS', *Complementary Therapies in Medicine*, 8, 253–59.

Macfarlane, J., W. Holmes, R. Macfarlane and N. Britten (1997) 'Influence of patients' expectations on antibiotic management of acute lower respiratory tract illness in general practice: questionnaire study', *British Medical Journal*, 315, 1211–14.

MacLennan, A. H., D. H. Wilson and A. W. Taylor (1996) 'Prevalence and cost of alternative medicine in Australia', *The Lancet*, 347, 569–73.

MacPherson, H., K. Thomas, S. Walters and M. Fitter (2001) 'The York acupuncture safety study: prospective survey of 34,000 treatments by traditional acupuncturists', *British Medical Journal*, 323, 486–87.

Makoul, G., P. Arntson and T. Schofield (1995) 'Health promotion in primary care: physician–patient communication and decision making about prescription medications', *Social Science & Medicine*, 41, 1241–54.

Mangione-Smith, R., M. N. Elliott, T. Stivers, L. L. McDonald and J. Heritage (2006) 'Ruling out the need for antibiotics: are we sending the right message?', *Archives of Pediatrics and Adolescent Medicine*, 160, 945–52.

Mansfield, P. R. (2007) 'The illusion of invulnerability' (letter), *British Medical Journal*, 334, 1020.

Mayor, S. (2006) 'In the eye of the storm', *British Medical Journal*, 333, 570.

McClean, S. (2005) '"The illness is part of the person": discourses of blame, individual responsibility and individuation at a centre for spiritual healing in the North of England', *Sociology of Health & Illness*, 27, 628–48.

McDonald, K., M. Bartos and D. Rosenthal (2000) 'Australian women living with HIV/AIDS are more sceptical than men about antiretroviral treatment', *AIDS Care*, 13, 15–26.

McKinlay, J. B. and L. D. Marceau (2002) 'The end of the golden age of doctoring', *International Journal of Health Services*, 32, 379–416.

Medawar, C., A. Herxheimer, A. Bell and S. Jofre (2002) 'Paroxetine, Panorama and user reporting of ADRs: consumer intelligence matters in clinical practice and post-marketing drug surveillance', *International Journal of Risk and Safety in Medicine*, 15, 161–69.

Medawar, C. and A. Herxheimer (2003) 'A comparison of adverse drug reaction reports from professionals and users, relating to risk of dependence and suicidal behaviour with paroxetine', *International Journal of Risk and Safety in Medicine*, 16, 5–19.

Melander, H., J. Ahlqvist-Rastad, G. Meijer and B. Beermann (2003) 'Evidence b(i)ased medicine – selective reporting from studies sponsored by pharmaceutical industry: review of studies in new drug applications', *British Medical Journal*, 326, 1171–73.

Meystre-Agustoni, G., F. Dubois-Arber, P. Cochand and A. Telenti (2000) 'Antiretroviral therapies from the patient's perspective', *AIDS Care*, 12, 717–21.

MHRA website, http://www.mhra.gov.uk, accessed 15 March 2006.

Mintzes, B. (2006) 'Disease mongering in drug promotion: do governments have a regulatory role?', *PLoS Medicine*, 3, e198.

Mintzes, B., M. L. Barer, R. L. Kravitz, A. Kazanjian, K. Bassett, J. Lexchin, R. G. Evans, R. Pan and S. A. Marion (2002) 'Influence of direct to consumer pharmaceutical advertising and patients' requests on prescribing decisions: two site cross sectional survey', *British Medical Journal*, 324, 278–79.

Mintzes, B., M. L. Barer, R. L. Kravitz, K. Bassett, J. Lexchin, A. Kazanjian, R. G. Evans, R. Pan and S. A. Marion (2003) 'How does direct-to-consumer advertising (DTCA) affect prescribing? A survey in primary care environments with and without legal DTCA', *Canadian Medical Association Journal*, 169, 405–12.

Mishler, E. G. (1984) *The Discourse of Medicine: Dialectics of Medical Interviews* (Norwood, NJ: Ablex Publishing Corporation).

Moerman, D. E. and W. B. Jonas (2002) 'Deconstructing the placebo effect and finding the meaning response', *Annals of Internal Medicine*, 136, 471–76.

Montagne, M. (1988) 'The metaphorical nature of drugs and drug taking', *Social Science & Medicine*, 26, 417–24.

Montagne, M. (1996) 'The Pharmakon phenomenon: cultural conceptions of drugs and drug use' in P. Davis (ed.) *Contested Ground: Public Purpose and Private Interest in the Regulation of Prescription Drugs* (Oxford: Oxford University Press) pp. 11–25.

Morgan, M. and C. J. Watkins (1988) 'Managing hypertension: beliefs and responses to medication among cultural groups', *Sociology of Health & Illness*, 10, 561–78.

Moynihan, R. (2003) 'Who pays for the pizza? Redefining the relationships between doctors and drug companies. 1: Entanglement', *British Medical Journal*, 326, 1189–92.

Moynihan, R., L. Bero, D. Ross-Degnan, D. Henry, K. Lee, J. Watkins, C. Mah and S. B. Soumerai (2000) 'Coverage by the news media of the benefits and risks of medications', *New England Journal of Medicine*, 342, 1645–50.

National Consumer Council (1991) *Pharmaceuticals: A Consumer Prescription* (London: National Consumer Council).

National Consumer Council (1993) *Balancing Acts: Conflicts of Interest in the Regulation of Medicine* (London: National Consumer Council).

Naylor, C. D., E. Chen and B. Strauss (1992) 'Measured enthusiasm: does the method of reporting trial results alter perceptions of therapeutic effectiveness?', *Annals of Internal Medicine*, 117, 916–21.

Nettleton, S., R. Burrows and L. O'Malley (2005) 'The mundane realities of the everyday lay use of the internet for health, and their consequences for media convergence', *Sociology of Health & Illness*, 27, 972–92.

Newman, S., L. Steed and K. Mulligan (2004) 'Self-management interventions for chronic illness', *The Lancet*, 364, 1523–37.

Nicholson, J. K. (2006) 'Global systems biology, personalized medicine and molecular epidemiology', *Molecular Systems Biology*, 3 October, doi: 10.1038/msb4100095.

Nichter M. and N. Vuckovic (1994) 'Agenda for an anthropology of pharmaceutical practice', *Social Science & Medicine*, 39, 1509–25.

Novins, D. K., J. Beals, L. A. Moore, P. Spicer and S. M. Manson (2004) 'Use of biomedical services and traditional healing options among American Indians: sociodemographic correlates, spirituality, and ethnic identity', *Medical Care*, 42, 670–79.

Noyce, P. R., C. Huttin, V. Atella, G. Brenner, F. M. Haaijer-Ruskamp, M-B. Hedvall and R. Mechtler (2000) 'The cost of prescription medicines to patients', *Health Policy*, 52, 129–45.

Outhwaite, W. (1994) *Habermas: A Critical Introduction* (Stanford: Stanford University Press).

Parish, P. A., (1974) 'Sociology of Prescribing', *British Medical Bulletin*, 30, 214–17.

Paterson, B. L. (2001) 'The shifting perspectives model of chronic illness', *Journal of Nursing Scholarship*', 33, 21–26.

Paterson, C. (2002) The Context, Experience and Effects of Acupuncture Treatment: Users' Perspectives and Outcome Questionnaire Performance, PhD Thesis, (University of London).

Paterson, C. (2007) 'Patients' experiences of Western-style acupuncture: the influence of acupuncture "dose", self-care strategies and integration', *Journal of Health Services Research & Policy*, 12, 39–45.

Paterson, C. and N. Britten (1999) '"Doctors can't help much": the search for an alternative', *British Journal of General Practice*, 49, 626–29.

Paterson, C. and N. Britten (2004) 'Acupuncture as a complex intervention: a holistic model', *The Journal of Alternative and Complementary Medicine*, 10, 791–801.

Pellegrino, E. D. (1976) 'Prescribing and drug ingestion: symbols and substances', *Drug Intelligence and Clinical Pharmacy*, 10, 624–30.

Peters, M. (ed.) (2004) *The BMA New Guide to Medicines & Drugs* (London: Dorling Kindersley) p. 286.

Peterson, G., P. Aslani and K. A. Williams (2003) 'How do consumers search for and appraise information on medicines on the Internet? A qualitative study using focus groups', *Journal of Medical Internet Research*, 5, e33.

Peterson, W. L. and B. Cryer (1999) 'COX-1-sparing NSAIDS: is the enthusiasm justified?', *Journal of the American Medical Association*, 282, 1961–3.

Piette, J. D., M. Heisler and T. H. Wagner (2004) 'Cost-related medication underuse among chronically ill adults: the treatments people forgo, how often, and who is at risk', *American Journal of Public Health*, 94, 1782–87.

Pinder, R. (1988) 'Striking balances: living with Parkinson's disease', chapter 3 in R. Anderson and M. Bury (eds) *Living with Chronic Illness: The Experience of Patients and Their Families* (London: Unwin Hyman) pp. 67–88.

Pirmohamed, M., S. James, S. Meakin, C. Green, A. K. Scott, T. J. Walley, K. Farrar, B. K. Park and A. M Breckenridge (2004) 'Adverse drug reactions as cause of admission to hospital: prospective analysis of 18,820 patients', *British Medical Journal*, 329, 15–19.

Pollock, K. (2005) *Concordance in Medical Consultations: A Critical Review* (Oxford: Radcliffe Publishing).

Pollock, K. and J. Grime (2000) 'Strategies for reducing the prescribing of proton pump inhibitors (PPIs): patient self-regulation of treatment may be an under-exploited resource', *Social Science & Medicine*, 51, 1827–39.

Porter, R. (1997) *The Greatest Benefit to Mankind: A Medical History of Humanity from Antiquity to the Present* (London: Fontana Press).

Pound, P., N. Britten, M. Morgan, L. Yardley, C. Pope, G. Daker-White and R. Campbell (2005) 'Resisting medicines: a synthesis of qualitative studies of medicine taking', *Social Science & Medicine*, 61, 133–55.

Pound, P., S. Ebrahim, P. Sandercock, M. B. Bracken and I. Roberts (2004) 'Where is the evidence that animal research benefits humans?', *British Medical Journal*, 328, 514–17.

Povar, G. J., M. Mantell and L. A. Morris (1984) 'Patients' therapeutic preferences in an ambulatory care setting', *American Journal of Public Health*, 74, 1395–97.

Prosser, H., S. Almond and T. Walley (2003) 'Influences on GPs' decision to prescribe new drugs – the importance of who says what', *Family Practice*, 20, 61–68.

Prosser, H. and T. Walley (2006) 'New drug prescribing by hospital doctors: the nature and meaning of knowledge', *Social Science & Medicine*, 62, 1565–78.

Public Citizen (2005) *Best Pills, Worst Pills* (Washington DC: Public Citizen)

Raynor, D. K., A. Blenkinsopp, P. Knapp, J. Grime, D. J. Nicolson, K. Pollock, G. Dorer, S. Gilbody, D. Dickinson, A. J. Maule and P. Spoor (2007) 'A systematic review of quantitative and qualitative research on the role and effectiveness of written information available to patients about individual medicines' *Health Technology Assessment*, 11, 1– 178.

Reibstein, J. (2002) *Staying Alive: a Family Memoir* (London: Bloomsbury).

Rogers, A., J. C. Day, B. Williams, F. Randall, P. Wood, D. Healy and R. P. Bentall (1998) 'The meaning and management of neuroleptic medication: a study of patients with a diagnosis of schizophrenia', *Social Science & Medicine*, 47, 1313–23.

Roter, D. L. and J. A. Hall (1992) *Doctors Talking with Patients/Patients Talking with Doctors* (Westport CT: Auburn House).

Royal Pharmaceutical Society of Great Britain (1997) *From Compliance to Concordance: Achieving Shared Goals in Medicine Taking* (London: The Royal Pharmaceutical Society of Great Britain).

Rudgley, R. (1993) *Essential Substances: A Cultural History of Intoxicants in Society* (New York: Kodansha International).

Rycroft-Malone, J., S. Latter, P. Yerrell and D. Shaw (2001) 'Consumerism in health care: the case of medication education', *Journal of Nursing Management*, 9, 221–30.

Salter, C., R. Holland, I. Harvey and K. Henwood (2007) ' "I haven't even phoned my doctor yet." The advice giving role of the pharmacist during consultations for medication review with patients aged 80 or more: qualitative discourse analysis', *British Medical Journal*, 334, 1101–04.

Saukko, P. 'Genetic risk online and offline: Two ways of being susceptible to blood clots', submitted.

Scambler, G. (1987) 'Habermas and the power of medical expertise', chapter 7 in G. Scambler (ed.) *Sociological Theory and Medical Sociology* (London: Tavistock Publications) pp. 165–93.

Scambler, G. and N. Britten (2001) 'System, lifeworld and doctor-patient interaction', chapter 3 in G. Scambler (ed.) *Habermas, Critical Theory and Health* (London: Routledge) pp. 45–67.

Schafheutle, E. I., K. Hassell, P. R. Noyce and M. C. Weiss (2002) 'Access to medicines: cost as an influence on the views and behaviour of patients', *Health and Social Care in the Community*, 10, 187–95.

Schulman, K. A., D. M. Seils, J. W. Timbie, J. Sugarman, L. A. Dame, K. P. Weinfurt, D. B. Mark and R. M. Califf (2002) 'A national survey of provisions in clinical-trial agreements between medical schools and industry sponsors', *New England Journal of Medicine*, 347, 1335–41.

Schutz, A. (1962) *Collected Papers, 1. The Problem of Social Reality.* (The Hague: Martinus Nijhoff).

Schwartz, R. K., S. B. Soumerai and J. Avorn (1989) 'Physician motivations for non scientific drug prescribing', *Social Science & Medicine*, 28, 577–82.

Seale, C. (2005) 'New directions for critical Internet health studies: representing cancer experience on the web', *Sociology of Health & Illness*, 27, 515–40.

Secretary of State for Health (2005) *Government Response to the Health Committee's Report on the Influence of the Pharmaceutical Industry* (London: The Stationery Office).

Sharma, U. (1992) *Complementary Medicine Today: Practitioners and Patients* (London: Routledge).

Siegel, K. and E. Gorey (1997) 'HIV-infected women: barriers to AZT use', *Social Science & Medicine*, 45, 15–22.

Siegel, K., E. W. Schrimshaw and L. Dean (1999) 'Symptom interpretation and medication adherence among late middle-age and older HIV-infected adults', *Journal of Health Psychology*, 4, 247–57.

Skidmore, D. (2002) 'Will you walk a little faster ... ?', chapter 9 in J. L. Humphries and J. Green (eds) *Nurse Prescribing* (2nd edn) (Basingstoke: Palgrave Macmillan) pp. 129–39.

Sleath, B., B. Chewning, B. Svarstad and D. Roter (2000) 'Patient expression of complaints and adherence problems with medications during chronic disease medical visits', *Journal of Social and Administrative Pharmacy*, 17, 71–80.

Sleath, B., D. Roter, B. Chewning and B. Svarstad (1999) 'Asking questions about medication: analysis of physician-patient interactions and physician perceptions', *Medical Care*, 37, 1169–73.

de Smet, P. A. G. M., C. Kramers and N. Britten (2007) 'Can drug regimens be adapted to patients, or vice versa?', *The Lancet*, 370, 813–14.

Smith, M. C. (1980) 'The relationship between pharmacy and medicine', chapter 10 in R. Mapes (ed.) *Prescribing Practice and Drug Usage* (London: Croom Helm) pp. 157–200.

Soumerai, S. B., T. J. McLaughlin and J. Avorn (1989) 'Improving drug prescribing in primary care: a critical analysis of the experimental literature', *The Milbank Quarterly*, 67, 268–317.

Stevenson, F. A., C. A. Barry, N. Britten, N. Barber and C. P. Bradley (2000) 'Doctor-patient communication about drugs: the evidence for shared decision making', *Social Science & Medicine*, 50, 829–40.

Stevenson F. and G. Scambler (2005) 'The relationship between medicine and the public: the challenge of concordance', *Health: An Interdisciplinary Journal for the Social Study of Health, Illness and Medicine*, 9, 5–21.

Stevenson, F., K. Cox, N. Britten and Y. Dundar (2004) 'A systematic review of the research on communication between patients and health care professionals about medicines: the consequences for concordance', *Health Expectations*, 7, 235–45.

Stevenson, F., N. Britten, C. Barry, C. P. Bradley and N. Barber (2003) 'Self-treatment and its discussion in medical consultations: how is medical pluralism managed in practice?', *Social Science & Medicine*, 57, 513–27.

Stimson, G. V. (1974) 'Obeying doctor's orders: a view from the other side', *Social Science & Medicine*, 8, 97–104.

Stivers, T. (2002) 'Participating in decisions about treatment: overt parent pressure for antibiotic medication in pediatric encounters', *Social Science & Medicine*, 54, 1111–30.

Stivers, T. (2005) 'Parent resistance to physicians' treatment recommendations: one resource for initiating a negotiation of the treatment decision', *Health Communication*, 18, 41–74.

Stivers, T, (2007) *Prescribing under Pressure: Parent–Physician Conversations and Antibiotics* (New York: Oxford University Press).

Stivers, T. and J. Heritage (2001) 'Breaking the sequential mould: answering "more than the question" during comprehensive history taking', *Text*, 21, 151–85.

Stivers, T., R. Mangione-Smith, M. N. Elliott, L. McDonald and J. Heritage (2003) 'Why do physicians think parents expect antibiotics? What parents report vs what physicians believe', *The Journal of Family Practice*, 52, 140–48.

Stone, V. E., J. Clarke, J. Lovell, K. A. Steger, L. R. Hirschhorn, S. Boswell, A. D. Monroe, M. D. Stein, T. J. Tyree and K. H. Mayer (1998) 'HIV/AIDS patients' perspectives on adhering to regimens containing protease inhibitors', *Journal of General Internal Medicine*, 13, 586–93.

Sullivan, C. (2003) 'Gendered cybersupport: a thematic analysis of two online cancer support groups', *Journal of Health Psychology*, 8, 83–103.

Svarstad, B. L., D. C. Bultman, J. K. Mount and E. R. Tabak (2003) 'Evaluation of written pre-scription information provided in community pharmacies: a study in eight states', *Journal of the American Pharmacists Association*, 43, 383–93.

Thomas, K. (2003) 'Alternative sources of advice: traditional and complementary medicine' in R. Jones, N. Britten, L. Culpepper, D. Gass, R. Grol, D. Mant and C. Silagy (eds) *Oxford Textbook of Primary Medical Care* (Oxford: Oxford University Press) pp. 116–21.

Toop, L. (2003) 'Principles of drug prescribing', in R. Jones, N. Britten, L. Culpepper, D. Gass, R. Grol, D. Mant and C. Silagy (eds) *Oxford Textbook of Primary Medical Care* (Oxford: Oxford University Press) pp. 242–5.

Townsend, A., K. Hunt and S. Wyke (2003) 'Managing multiple morbidity in mid-life: a qual-itative study of attitudes to drug use', *British Medical Journal*, 327, 837–42.

Traulsen, J. M., A. B. Almarsdóttir and I. Bjornsdóttir (2002) 'The lay user perspective on the quality of pharmaceuticals, drug therapy and pharmacy services – results of focus group discussions', *Pharmacy World and Science*, 24, 196–200.

van Trigt, A. M., L. T. W. de Jong-van den Berg, F. M. Haaijer-Ruskamp, J. Willems and T. F. J. Tromp (1994) 'Journalists and their sources of ideas and information on medicines', *Social Science & Medicine*, 38, 637–43.

van Trigt, A. M., L. T. W. de Jong-van den Berg, L. M. Voogt, J. Willems, T. F. J. Tromp and F.M. Haaijer-Ruskamp (1995) 'Setting the agenda: does the medical literature set the agenda for articles about medicines in the newspapers?', *Social Science & Medicine*, 41, 893–99.

Trostle, J. (1988) 'Medical compliance as an ideology', *Social Science & Medicine*, 27, 1299–1308.

Verhoef, M. J., L. G. Balneaves, H. S. Boon and A. Vroegindewey (2005) 'Reasons for and characteristics associated with complementary and alternative medicine use among adult cancer patients: a systematic review', *Integrative Cancer Therapies*, 4, 274–86.

Vermeire, E., H. Hearnshaw, P. Van Royen and J. Denekens (2001) 'Patient adherence to treatment: three decades of research: a comprehensive review', *Journal of Clinical Pharmacy and Therapeutics*, 26, 331–42.

Vincent, J. (1992) 'Self-help groups and health care in contemporary Britain' in M. Saks (ed.) *Alternative Medicine in Britain* (Oxford: Clarendon Press) pp. 137–53.

Waitzkin, H. (1991) *The Politics of Medical Encounters: How Patients and Doctors Deal with Social Problems* (New Haven, CT: Yale University Press).

Watkins, C., L. Moore, I. Harvey, P. Carthy, E. Robinson and R. Brawn (2003) 'Characteristics of general practitioners who frequently see drug industry representatives: national cross sectional study', *British Medical Journal*, 326, 1178–79.

Weatherall, D. (2006) *The Use of Non-human Primates in Research – The Weatherall Report* (London: Medical Research Council).

Wensing, M. (2003) 'Patients' expectations of treatment' in R. Jones, N. Britten, L. Culpepper, D. A. Gass, R. Grol, D. Mant and C. Silagy (eds) *Oxford Textbook of Primary Medical Care* (Oxford: Oxford University Press) pp. 122–6.

White, A., S. Hayhoe, A. Hart and E. Ernst (2001) 'Adverse events following acupuncture: prospective survey of 32,000 consultations with doctors and physiotherapists', *British Medical Journal*, 323, 485–86.

Williams, G. (1984) 'The genesis of chronic illness: narrative re-construction', *Sociology of Health & Illness*, 6, 175–200.

Wood, M., E. Ferlie and L. Fitzgerald (1998) 'Achieving clinical behaviour change: a case of becoming indeterminate', *Social Science & Medicine*, 47, 1729–38.

Worthen, D. B. (1973) 'Prescribing influences: an overview', *British Journal of Medical Education*, 7, 109–17.

www.worstpills.org (accessed 14 April 2007).

Wright, K. B. and S. B. Bell (2003) 'Health-related support groups on the Internet: linking empirical findings to social support and computer-mediated communication theory', *Journal of Health Psychology*, 8, 39–54.

The Write Track: Personal Health Tracker (1997). Princeton, NJ: Doctors and Designers.

Wynne, B. (1996) 'May the sheep safely graze? A reflexive view of the expert-lay knowledge divide' in S. Lash, B. Szerszynski and B. Wynne (eds) *Risk, Environment and Modernity: Towards a New Ecology* (London: Sage Publications), pp. 44–83.

Wynne, H. A. and A. Long (1996) 'Patient awareness of the adverse effects of non-steroidal anti-inflammatory drugs (NSAIDs), *British Journal of Clinical Pharmacology*, 42, 253–56.

van der Zee, J., W. G. W. Boerma and M. W. Kroneman (2003) 'Health care systems: understanding the stages of development' in R. Jones, N. Britten, L. Culpepper, D. Gass, R. Grol, D. Mant and C. Silagy, *Oxford Textbook of Primary Medical Care* (Oxford: Oxford University Press), pp. 51–55.

Ziebland, S., A. Chapple, C. Dumelow, J. Evans, S. Prinjha and L. Rozmovits (2004) 'How the Internet affects patients' experience of cancer: a qualitative study', *British Medical Journal*, 328, 564–68.

Index